Born in 1932, Robert Philippi spent his early childhood in Hampshire with his parents, his father British and mother Chilean. He left school and went to Sandhurst to join the cavalry, spending three years in service, finishing with a tour in Egypt. He came back to Hampshire where he continued his love of country pursuits.

Robert's mother inherited a family *estancia* in Argentina called Guer-Aike, primarily a sheep farm for wool, which he ran for the family from around 1959 to 1964, when it was sold. Robert spent many years thereafter living in Buenos Aires. He made many friends in South America and these experiences, combined with a fascination for history, were the inspiration to embark on this book in the 1990s.

He lived in Scotland until his wife passed, and then with his sister in Hampshire close to where he had grown up. He left a draft manuscript on his death, and his son, having watched him for many years labour on first a typewriter and then a computer, resolved to publish these papers as a book, albeit that Robert would have doubtless continued to work on the text. His love of history, storytelling and adventure is all here, including untold moments from a unique and fascinating moment of history.

A volume of his collected short stories and non-fiction, *Tales From a Stalking Life*, was produced for his funeral in 2021.

Argentina

The British Invasion of Buenos Aires, 1806

Robert Philippi

First published in Great Britain in 2024 by Coco Publishing.

Copyright © the estate of Robert Philippi 2024.

The right of Robert Philippi to be identified as the author of this work under the Copyright, Designs and Patents Act 1988 has been asserted.

All rights reserved. No part of this publication may be reproduced, stored in a retrieval system or transmitted, in any form or by any means, without the publisher's prior permission in writing.

This book is sold subject to the condition that it shall not, by way of trade or otherwise, be lent, resold, hired out or otherwise circulated without the publisher's prior consent in any form of binding or cover other than that in which it is published and without a similar condition, including this condition, being imposed on the subsequent purchaser.

Every reasonable effort has been made to trace copyright holders of material reproduced in this book, but if any have been inadvertently overlooked the publishers would be glad to hear from them.

Edited, designed and produced by Tandem Publishing
http://tandempublishing.yolasite.com

ISBN: 979-8-3344-5901-4

A CIP catalogue record for this book is available from the British Library.

Contents

FOREWORD	vii
PROLOGUE	1
INTRODUCTION	3
'THE PRECEPTOR OF FREEDOM'	5
THE DISCOVERY OF THE RIO DE LA PLATA	22
RIO DE LA PLATA IN THE SEVENTEENTH CENTURY	33
POTOSI AND POPHAM	38
GENERAL SIR DAVID BAIRD: 'A KIND BUT ROUGH DIAMOND'	53
WILLIAM CARR, 1ST VISCOUNT BERESFORD: 'EL TUERTO, THE ONE-EYED ONE'	66
THE CAPE OF GOOD HOPE	75
FULL SAIL FOR SOUTH AMERICA	83
ST HELENA AND THE RIVER PLATE	89
BUENOS AIRES AUTUMN 1806	94
THE INVASION	101
BUENOS AIRES UNDER BRITISH RULE	109
SANTIAGO LINARES	123
LA RECONQUISTA	133
A SUCCESSFUL ENTERPRISE	141

MALDONADO	151
THE SIEGE OF MONTEVIDEO	155
MONTEVIDEO UNDER BRITISH RULE	168
GENERAL JOHN WHITELOCKE	172
THE VOYAGE OF THE LIGHT BRIGADE	178
CAPE TOWN AND ST HELENA	190
WHITELOCKE'S INVASION PLANS	197
LA DEFENSA	205
BANISHMENT TO THE PROVINCES	214
THE BATTLE FOR SAN PEDRO	223
ENSENADA DE BARRAGAN	235
THE ADVANCE ON BUENOS AIRES	245
THE RIACHUELO AND PUNTA GALVEZ	253
CROSSING THE RIACHUELO	258
THE CORRAL DE LA MISERERE	262
THE STORMING OF THE CITY: PART 1: THE RIGHT FLANK	270
THE STORMING OF THE CITY: PART 2	283
THE STORMING OF THE CITY: PART 3	293
A DEFEATED ARMY	297
PEACE AT LAST	307
THE ENGLISH AFTERMATH	314
THE ARGENTINE AFTERMATH	350
BUENOS AIRES TODAY	376

FOREWORD

My father started writing *Argentina: The British Invasion of Buenos Aires, 1806* when we lived in Scotland, tapping away on an electric typewriter. At the time he smoked a pipe, and I remember smoke filling the room and drifting slowly down the corridor. We then moved to a smaller house, and he was instructed to remove himself to an outhouse when working. Finally, after my mother passed away, he moved to England with his sister. Here, finally, the book was almost completed, in the greenhouse at the end of the garden. He had moved on from the electric typewriter and pipe to a laptop and cigars; this transition would see him out. My father's fascination with history, combined with his relationship with South America, led him to this particular subject, but sadly the book remained unpublished by the time of his death in July 2021. The text was almost complete and so, in memory of him, I thought it appropriate to edit lightly and publish.

To get an understanding of what my father was like in 1957, while he was living in South America, I turned to a good friend, Meme Lariviere, to compose some words about him at that time.

> Robert became a close friend of ours, and though I can't place exactly how long he stayed in Argentina, I am sure that everything happened before 1974. He was very popular in certain social circles. He had a true passion for horses and he and Maurice (my husband) often went to the races. At that time we used to have a thoroughbred stud at our *estancia*, and Robert came to visit us quite frequently. They got along well and

shared a great interest in world history, above all British history and the Second World War. Both of them were very learned and intelligent. Maurice introduced him to quite a lot of historical writers and politicians and spent quite a long time at his *estancia* in Santa Cruz. While Robert was in Buenos Aires he lived in a nice apartment, beautifully furnished and with a valet. He lived a very social life and entertained often. I remember him as a very lively, handsome man with a great sense of humour, and I can still hear his laugh. On the one hand he was a true and typical British gentleman: sociable, funny and well mannered, loved by quite a number of very good friends; on the other hand he would spend quite long periods at his *estancia*, leading a hard life away from everyone, which I think he also liked.

He used to come to our *estancia*, "Arroyo Verde" in Patagonia, as well as Micky Ortiz Basualdo's *estancia* "Las Estacas". She and her cousin Teresita Ortiz Basualdo were close friends. What amazes me is he was always interested in Argentine politics. He read *La Nacion*, our main newspaper, online, and he always kept up his Spanish. He never lost touch with this part of the world.

Lastly, before you begin, I would like to thank my family, brother and friends who have helped, particularly Robert's sister and nieces, who looked after him so well in later life. I hope you all enjoy this more than the endless smell of cigar smoke!

—Jeremy Philippi, 2024

PROLOGUE

The sun shone, the dice rattled, and the bubbles on top of my *clarito* seductively whispered, 'Drink Me.' Spring 1957 and tension ran high as I sat on the shady terrace of the 'Argentino Golf Club, Buenos Aires' concentrating on winning an intricate dice game called 'La Generala'. The result of this game was important as the losers paid both for the drinks and the winner's lunch before tackling the course's intricate fairways. Every Saturday and Sunday, a group of eight or more friends would meet to play this game, lunch together, and then divide into partners to play a competitive round of golf. Master of Ceremonies and doyen of this little *tertulia* (group of friends) was Don Alberto, a patrician of an old and eminent Argentine family. Fluent in many languages and a scratch golfer in his day, Don Alberto was without doubt one of the most charming people I have ever had the privilege of meeting.

As a nation Argentines love nicknames that many countries would certainly consider politically non-correct, and our little group at times would consist of '*El gordo*' (fat one), '*El flaco*' (thin one), '*La Ongara*' (the Hungarian), '*El Danes*' (the Dane) and so on. I of course was called '*El Ingles*' until miraculously I holed a long putt to win a match or swept the board at La Generala, when I instantly became '*La Pirata Ingles*' or '*El Imperialista Britanico*'.

The first I could understand as, to this day, mothers and nannies warn any naughty child that *El Paco Drago* (Sir Francis Drake) will get them 'if they continue to misbehave'. The '*Imperialista Britanico*', however, bewildered me, as at no time in my history studies at school and Sandhurst had I encountered any mention of the British Government being interested in colonising Argentina. I therefore challenged my Argentine friends, who were delighted to relieve me of my ignorance, and gave me a vivid description of how the gallant Argentine ladies had put the British invaders to flight by pouring scalding oil down the redcoats' pants. This picturesque description aroused my interest and I set out to discover the truth, which took longer than I expected.

As far as Argentina is concerned the British Invasion of the River Plate in 1806 is probably one of the most important events in its history, and second only to the arrival of the Spanish Conquistadors three centuries earlier. Libraries, museums, and bookshelves abound with accounts of this event which, only three years later, would lead to '*La Revolution de Mayo*' and the creation of the first '*Junta de Gobierno*'.

British historians in contrast scarcely mention the event and, if they do, they wrongly call it General Whitelocke's or Craufurd's invasion of South America, when in fact it was entirely due to an ambitious middle-ranking British naval officer who launched the attack without any authority from the Admiralty or knowledge of his Government, purely to satisfy an insatiable appetite for prize-money.

— Robert Philippi

INTRODUCTION

Night was falling, the dying rays of a wintry sun fought a desperate battle to penetrate the clouds of cannon smoke lingering low above the city, and eerie shadows flitted nervously across the rooftops. The unpaved streets were dangerously slippy: not from the torrential rain which had fallen non-stop the previous week, but from the rivulets of blood that trickled into the narrow trenches hastily dug across them. Crimson sludge filled the potholes, and the gutters overflowed with an evil smelling effluence pervading the nostrils with the stench of death.

As night fell on 5 July 1807, Buenos Aires was a city of ruined houses, rotting corpses, despondent prisoners, and jubilant citizens. Over seven thousand British soldiers were prisoners of war; hundreds lay wounded, and more than a thousand dead; their lives sacrificed by an incompetent General, himself the victim of an inept Government ironically called 'The Ministry of all the Talents.'

Squeezed between Trafalgar and the Peninsular War, the Invasion of the Rio de la Plata began a year earlier in 1806 when a tiny squadron of British ships unexpectedly appeared at the mouth of the River Plate and without any warning attacked Buenos Aires. Under Commodore Sir Home Riggs Popham's orders, Major-General William Beresford launched this unwarranted attack on 27 June with a force of only 70 officers; 72 sergeants; 1,466 rank and file, and 27 drummer boys, and, for the loss of one man killed, thirteen wounded, and a soldier missing, Spain's second largest city in South America became part of the British Empire when her reluctant citizens were forced to swear allegiance to George III, King of England, Ireland and Scotland. In less than ten days, the city's treasure was on board a British ship sailing for England where it was triumphantly paraded through the streets of London, and safely deposited in the Bank of England.

Shakespeare in his play *As You Like It* declares, 'All the world's a stage and men and women are merely players.' If this is true then destiny brought together a strange collection of players to perform this human tragedy, as a Venezuelan devised the plot; a British naval officer chose the venue; a Scottish General authorised the performance, and the one-eyed bastard son of an Irish Earl played the leading role.

Don Francisco Miranda, Commodore Sir Home Riggs Popham, Major General Sir David Baird, and Brigadier Sir William Beresford, can truthfully claim to have transformed South America into the continent that we know today. As the defeat of a 10,000-strong British Army sent a year later to rescue Popham's imprisoned raiding party gave Argentina the confidence to shake off four hundred years of Spanish domination, and heralded a move for independence that spread like wildfire across the continent to create new countries each with their own borders, laws, and Constitutions.

ONE

'THE PRECEPTOR OF FREEDOM'

On a hot summer's morning in July 1784, the streets of London stank. Rotting excrement filled the unswept gutters, and the rank odour of gin, porter, and vomit overwhelmed the early morning tradesmen as they picked their way through the bottle-strewn alleyways to their place of work.

Bravely ignoring this distasteful atmosphere, the line of petitioners standing patiently outside 10 Downing Street hastily shielded their faces as, in a cloud of dust, a hired carriage drew abruptly to a halt outside its famous portals, and out stepped a tall well-dressed gentleman with aquiline features and a fair complexion. William Brummell, the Prime Minister's Private Secretary who greeted him, could see by the cut of his coat and style of neck cloth that this was a foreigner, and as such welcomed him with caution.

Brummell was right on both counts, for the gentleman in question, Don Sebastian Francisco Miranda, was Venezuelan and the bulging portmanteau clutched firmly between his hands contained not only a mountain of maps and statistics, but also an extensive portfolio of dangerous dreams.

Born in Caracas in 1750, Sebastian Miranda was the son of a first-generation immigrant from Spain who by hard work and good fortune had become a successful merchant, and as such could afford to send his son to a good school. The boy worked hard at his studies but from his childhood days Francisco Miranda had only one deep-rooted and determined ambition: not only to free Venezuela from the domination of the King of Spain but more optimistically liberate the whole of South America from Spanish rule.

Named by modern historians as 'The Preceptor of Freedom', Miranda planned, dreamed, and dedicated his entire life to this dangerous ideal which would ultimately lead to his death in a Spanish jail and the slaughter of three thousand British soldiers in the faraway streets of Buenos Aires.

On leaving school, Miranda joined the Army and on reaching twenty set sail for Spain to enter the Spanish Military Academy in Seville and, successfully gaining his commission, was sent to fight with the Spanish Army in Morocco where he quickly showed himself to be a brave and efficient officer. However, during the campaign he fell out with his Commanding Officer, who he rashly accused of incompetence. Not surprisingly, this inappropriate behaviour upset his military superiors who from then on sought any excuse to put this young colonial upstart in his place.

Their chance came in 1780 when, as aide-de-camp to General Juan Manuel de Cajigal in Cuba, he was sent to negotiate an exchange of prisoners with the English in Jamaica. On his return, the authorities unjustly accused him of betraying the plans of Havana's fortifications to the English and, despite Miranda vehemently protesting his innocence, they placed him under house arrest to await trial for treason.

This was not the only charge brought against him, for while away in Jamaica, the Inquisition discovered a large collection of banned books among his belongings and likewise demanded his arrest. Church doctrine at the time strictly prohibited the reading or possession of any work containing an expression contrary to its teaching, and with his interest in modern thinking, Miranda had avidly acquired the works of Thomas Paine, Rousseau and other revolutionary writers. Seizing this dangerous collection, the Inquisition threatened to put him on trial for heresy, and realising that in this climate of suspicion he would inevitably be found guilty Miranda bribed a local fisherman before his trial came up and fled to Florida.

The year was 1783; America was in the throes of celebrating her freedom from British rule and on his journey north from Charleston to Washington, the ambitious young soldier made a point of visiting all the major battlefields of the war. Carefully studying the adversaries' positions, he made detailed diagrams of the contours of the land, and meticulously noted down the opposing Generals' tactics. His time was not wasted, as eight years later they would be of great assistance when, during their war against Austria, a French Revolutionary Government placed him in command of an army of brave but untrained 'sans culottes'.

Miranda found Washington bristling with activity as politicians, soldiers, and businessmen fought to have their ideas accepted in the creation of a new Constitution. Arguments and squabbles incessantly broke out over the ways and means of running their new-born country but, despite arriving in the middle of all this controversy, Miranda received a hospitable welcome from the Americans, who introduced him to all their leaders including Jefferson, Hamilton, and General Washington, who surprisingly failed to impress him.

The welcome was flattering but the young Venezuelan quickly realised that any hope of the Americans aiding his cause was wishful-thinking as they were far too occupied in establishing the future of their own country to have any interest in anyone else's, and it soon became obvious that he was wasting his time. So, armed with letters of introduction from his American friends to the most important figures in

English society, he set sail for London, and it was these that brought him to 10 Downing Street on that sultry summer's day in 1784, and an interview with Lord North, Prime Minister of England.

Reputed to be the ugliest man in Great Britain and described by Horace Walpole, 'As having two large prominent eyes that rolled about for no purpose for he was short-sighted, a wide mouth, thick lips, and inflated visage, which gave him the air of a blind trumpeter,' Lord North was not unaware of his appearance. Asked one night at Covent Garden by a distant acquaintance to 'identify that plain looking lady in the box opposite', His Lordship replied in an amiable tone that she was in fact his wife. Horrified by his *faux pas*, the questioner quickly said, 'No! No! I meant the monster sitting next to her.' Unruffled, His Lordship declared 'That Sir, is my daughter. I believe we are considered to be three of the ugliest people in London.'

The Prime Minister already had some acquaintance with South American politics, as thirteen years earlier, in 1771, he had signed an agreement with Spain over the Falkland Islands. This allowed a British garrison that had surrendered there the previous year to return to the Islands without any prejudice to the right of its sovereignty. Although of little significance at the time, two hundred years later British and Argentine politicians would resurrect this long-forgotten treaty and fiercely discuss its validity.

The Venezuelan had chosen a bad time to ask the Prime Minister to promote his revolutionary scheme for, still smarting from the loss of the American colonies, His Lordship showed little interest in liberating the country from Spanish rule and even less in embarking the British Government on some wild South American venture.

Disappointed but undeterred by North's obvious lack

of interest, Miranda now embarked on a lengthy tour of Europe in search of more sympathetic ears into which to pour his revolutionary ideas. Visiting almost every court in Europe, he met most of the reigning monarchs of the day, including Fredrick the Great of Prussia, who was courteous but unhelpful, and the Empress Catherine of Russia, who was both helpful and courteous. Attracted by his personality, she offered to help him with his revolutionary plans.

Their meeting took place in the Crimea where, having crossed the Bosphorus from Turkey, Miranda grandly introduced himself to Prince Potemkin as 'Count Miranda'. The bogus title proved unnecessary, as the Prince quickly fell under the South American's spell and invited him to stay in his vast palace at Kherson, then suggested he should accompany him on a tour of his newly created towns and settlements that the Empress was on her way to inspect.

Although ruling her own country with a rod of iron, Catherine was liberally minded as far as others were concerned and for many years had enjoyed an exchange of letters with Voltaire, Diderot, and most of the other new-age philosophers of the time, to many of whom she gave liberal financial support. This kindred interest in modern thinking quickly established a close bond of friendship between the two and, seduced by the young man's charm, the Empress generously presented Miranda with a Russian passport, authorising him to use all her European Embassies. In return for this generosity, he satisfied her well known libido with customary Latin vigour, so much so that her favourites Potemkin and the Orlov brothers began to worry over his rising favour. After watching this affair flourish for several months, they strongly suggested the time had come for him to leave Russia and resume his noble plan of liberating South America.

Aware that his position was rapidly becoming precarious, the Liberator took the hint and, bidding a reluctant farewell to the Empress and to two other tearful ladies, Madame Tarnowski and the Princess Lubomirska, he wisely left Moscow to continue his search for someone equally important to sponsor his revolutionary plans.

During his long journey across Europe, Miranda kept a diary in which he carefully recorded a wide spectrum of daily life. This covered a multitude of interests, ranging from diagrams of military fortresses, hospitals, prison systems, and mining to lucid descriptions of the local whorehouses and their comely or otherwise inmates.

Aware of his revolutionary schemes, the Spanish Government at all times kept him under close observation, and gave their Embassies strict instructions to keep a watchful eye on all his movements and if possible arrest him.

Scandinavia came next on his itinerary, which proved unfruitful for the future of South America, but gratifyingly rewarding for his amatory skills and, during his stay in Sweden, he embarked on a passionate affair with the beautiful Cristina Suarez. While Count Rantzau, on his arrival in Norway, generously placed a seventeen-year-old girl at his disposal, and thoughtfully gave him a long list of available women.

But despite of all these hospitable gestures, the ambitious Revolutionary could find no Government or ruler prepared to assist him in his great project, and he returned to England in 1790 to find William Pitt, the new Prime Minister in power.

Miranda had arrived at a propitious moment, as Pitt was heavily engaged in dealing with the Nootka Sound problem. This controversy had started two years earlier when, intent on opening up a market with China, the British East

India Company established a trading post in this sheltered Canadian anchorage off the west coast of Vancouver Island.

Quickly hearing of the encroachment by British traders on territory they considered their own, the Spaniards immediately dispatched two warships from Mexico who, easily seizing the three unarmed British merchant ships at anchor in the Bay, carried them and their crews in chains off to Mexico. News of this dastardly act reached England on 4 May 1790, to coincide with Miranda's arrival, and the British Government was now heavily engaged in demanding redress from Spain for its outrageous behaviour.

The international situation was definitely dangerous, as both countries and their allies prepared for war and Pitt, being a shrewd tactician, quickly realised that Miranda could be a useful pawn in his diplomatic struggle with Spain and her ally France. He therefore ostentatiously showed an interest in the Venezuelan's revolutionary plans and, to put further pressure on the Spaniards to accept his terms, threatened to send an Army to invade South America.

At the last moment, Spain's ally France's National Assembly voted against a confrontation; war was averted, and now that the Spaniards had surrendered all claim to Nootka Sound, Pitt no longer had any interest in the matter, and diplomatically shelved his South American plans.

The sudden lack of interest by the British Government in his noble scheme briefly cast a shadow over Miranda's life, but this quickly vanished when from across the Channel came wafting the stirring cry of '*Liberté, Egalité, et Fraternité.*' A revolution had broken out in France and, attracted by this seductive call, the disappointed patriot hurriedly left for Paris convinced that the new-born Republic would help him with his revolutionary ideas of ending the King of Spain's tyrannical rule in South America.

Argentina: The British Invasion of Buenos Aires, 1806

Arriving in Paris ten days later, he disappointingly discovered that the French, like the Americans before them, were far too heavily engaged in defending their own borders from the advancing Austrian Army to have either the time or means to assist him with his noble cause. They were, however, desperately in need of experienced officers, as most of their own had either joined the Royalist Army gathering on the Austrian frontier, or lost their heads on the guillotine. Instead of offering to aid him with his plans, they invited him to join their Army and, with the backing of the Girondins, and Monsieur Petion, the Mayor of Paris, gave him the rank of General and sent him to join General Dumouriez and his Army stationed on the Belgium frontier.

It proved a shrewd choice as, thanks to his military experience in Morocco and the lessons learnt from the American battlefields, after seven hours fighting on the borders of Belgium and Holland he successfully defeated Graf von Kelkreuf and his Army of 6,000 Prussians with a force of only 2,000 men, and delighted by this success, his superiors promptly promoted him to Commander-in-Chief and placed him in command of the French Army in Flanders.

Despite his remarkable achievement, the war soon took a turn for the worse and, following the Prussians' successful siege of Maastricht, Miranda and his little Army were forced to beat a hasty retreat back to the French border. Seriously displeased by this setback, the Revolutionary Government immediately recalled him to Paris and, on 19 April 1793, the Chief Prosecutor Fouquier-Tinville ordered his arrest and charged him with not only conspiring against the Republic and aiding Pitt and the British Government, but also for good measure the Americans and Russians as well.

Miranda ably defended himself and, with the aid of the Girondins and Mayor Pétion, he was acquitted and released from prison. The trial, in reality, had been little more than a political flexing of muscles between the Jacobins and Girondins rather than about any fault of Miranda's military competence, but on the Girondins falling from power his life was once again in danger when, after being soundly defeated at Neerwinden, General Dumouriez, his former Commanding Officer, changed sides and deserted to the Austrians.

Furious at Dumouriez's desertion, the vengeful Jacobins reopened Miranda's case, and finding him guilty of treason incarcerated him in the gruesome prison of *La Force* where he languished for a year under the shadow of the guillotine, and only the fall of Robespierre on 27 July 1794 saved him from a terminal trip in the tumbrels.

Freedom came as a relief; Paris was *en fete*, and South America for the time forgotten as, determined to make up for his year of deprivation in prison, Miranda rented a luxurious apartment in the Rue St Florentin and embarked on a round of elegant parties, theatres, and an orgy of beautiful women. Prominent among the latter was 'Delfina', the beautiful Marquise de Custine, who he had met with her husband imprisoned in *La Force*.

Pretty, voluptuous and undoubtedly a nymphomaniac, 'Delfina' was reputed to be the illegitimate daughter of Louis XV, and famous for being one of the most accomplished courtesans of her time who, according to one contemporary wit, 'Loved everyone including even her husband.' Considering himself her equal in the gymnastics of the bedchamber, Miranda happily kept Madame la Marquise's sexual appetite satisfied for several months but their heated affair abruptly ended when he discovered that the beautiful Delfina was sharing her favours not just with him, but was also satisfying the lusts of many other gentlemen including

Chateaubriand, Fouché, Alexandre Beauharnais, Monsieur de Grouchy, and Comte Louis de Ségur.

The discovery was a severe blow to his Latin pride and Delfina's attractions quickly began to wane. Angry at her behaviour, and with France for forming an alliance with Spain, he returned to England in 1798 to once again present his plans to Pitt and the British Cabinet.

The outlook looked brighter as Britain was again at war with Spain, but the Government's enthusiasm for his enterprise steadily began to dwindle and vanished completely three years later in 1801, when Pitt resigned over the King's refusal to consent to any measure of Catholic emancipation.

Thoroughly disheartened by the British Government's behaviour, the Venezuelan returned to France with two aims in view: firstly to gain the support of Napoleon, the new First Consul, and secondly to present the French Government with a valid request for the pension owed to him as a former General in the French Army.

Failing on the first count he succeeded on the second, as in recognition of his military success in Flanders the future Emperor granted him a pension and ordered his name to be inscribed on the Arc de Triomphe where it can be seen today. Napoleon spoke kindly of the Venezuelan and referred to him, 'As a soul filled with sacred fire' but apart from this flattering eulogy, showed little interest in invading South America.

With his funds now replenished, he returned to London in 1803 where he met the financier Nicholas Vansittart, Secretary to the Treasury, and future Lord Bexley who introduced him to an ambitious and rising young naval officer, Captain Sir Home Riggs Popham. This enterprising young sailor had already had a varied career that ranged from diplomatic missions to the Tsar of Russia to operating a freebooting enterprise in the Indian Ocean. The latter, a shady but lucrative business, had brought him into close contact with the most important businessmen in the City of London, and realising the potential benefit a new market in South America could bring to the hard-pressed merchants now suffering under Napoleon's blockade, Popham instantly showed a keen interest in Miranda's plan, rightly speculating that free trade with South America would not only increase the merchants' fortunes but in the process hopefully his own. He therefore enthusiastically offered Miranda every assistance possible, and throughout the following months he and Miranda fought a non-stop and aggressive battle to get the Government to accept the Liberator's plans.

These, to say the least, were inventive, and suggested that an army of sepoys from India should invade the western coast of South America at the same time as General Sir Arthur Wellesley launched an attack on the east. Attracted by the idea, the Government in 1804 sought Sir Arthur's opinion of the scheme and invited him to submit plans for an invasion of the Orinoco. When doing so, he was to take into consideration that once his Army had landed, the liberated citizens would rise to assist him. Fresh from his successes in India, the future Duke of Wellington was unimpressed by the scheme, declaring that any hope of a popular uprising was highly unlikely, and wisely observed, 'That from my own personal knowledge as an Irishman, the Catholic Church would not be won over, and without it the citizens will never assist an army of mainly heretics.'

From this comment it was obvious that Sir Arthur had neither the inclination, nor intention, of leading an army up the Orinoco on such a hare-brained enterprise, and had little faith in a South American regicide who had established a friendship with England's archenemy, Napoleon

Bonaparte. As for regime change, he would later wisely remark, 'I always had a horror of revolutionising any country for political object. If they rise themselves well and good, but to stir them up is a fearful responsibility.'

Events began to change rapidly, as having secretly agreed to send the Spaniards arms to help them in their fight against Napoleon, the British Government now realised they could hardly surreptitiously embark on a plan to invade their colonies and, much to his unease, gave Sir Arthur the unhappy task of informing Miranda of their decision. The Venezuelan's volatile temper was well known and, for one of the few moments in his illustrious life, the Iron Duke was nervous. Describing their encounter in his memoirs, Wellington writes,

'I think I never had a more difficult business than when the Government bade me tell Miranda that we would have nothing to do with his plan. I thought it best to walk out in the streets with him and tell him there to prevent his bursting out. However, even there he was so loud and angry that I told him to walk on a little so that we might not attract the notice of everybody passing by. When I joined him again, he was cooler and said, "You are going over into Spain... You will be lost, nothing can save you, that however is your affair but what grieves me is that there was never such an opportunity thrown away."'

With the return of his ally Pitt to power in 1804, Miranda's outlook began to improve but the threat of a French invasion of England came first on the Prime Minister's agenda. This luckily came to nothing, due more to Napoleon's stubbornness than to any effort of the British Navy.

Visiting Boulogne in the spring of 1804, the Emperor decided to inspect his invasion force, and despite a severe gale being forecast ordered Vice Admiral Bruix in command of the flotilla to take the ships out to sea and anchor them under the cliffs where he took his daily morning ride.

A strong south-westerly wind had been blowing since the previous day, making it obvious to any experienced seaman that a gale was in the offing, and Bruix wisely postponed the review for another day. Arriving at the appointed place to inspect the fleet, Napoleon was furious to find the Admiral had disobeyed his orders. A stormy scene erupted between the Emperor and Bruix during which they nearly came to blows and, peremptorily dismissing Bruix, Napoleon replaced him with Rear-Admiral Morgan and ordered him to take the fleet out to sea and anchor the boats in the same bay as originally planned.

In the afternoon, the weather turned worse, thunder rumbled overhead; fork lightning lit up the sky, and the wind swinging round to the northeast reached gale force, turning the sea into a cauldron of crashing waves. Seeing the fleet in serious danger, Morgan hastily ordered the ships to weigh anchor and seek safety where they could, and the universal cry went up of 'Sauf qui peut' that was quickly muffled by the howling wind.

The fifty-foot waves breaking at the entrance of Boulogne Harbour made it too dangerous to enter, so most of the ships headed for Étaples. Forty-two managed to reach their destination but four gunboats, two shallots, and two *caucus* were driven ashore at Boulogne and came to grief on the rocks. Over two hundred men died, and Napoleon nearly drowned in the towering waves when he insisted on getting into a small boat to lead the rescue efforts.

Spin is not a new invention, as two days later Marshal Soult sent a report to the War Ministry in Paris that would be the envy of any modern day politician. Carefully playing down the disaster, the Marshal made much of Napoleon's rescue attempts and casually describes the whole affair, 'As an extremely unfortunate event took place at Boulogne which caused the loss of a few soldiers, and damaged several of the ships... His Imperial Majesty himself passed the night on the shore and in the surf directing the salvage operations, and his august presence was of the greatest comfort to the unfortunate men on the rocks.'

After this debacle, Napoleon abandoned his plans for the invasion of England and turned his thoughts to Ireland and the West Indies. French naval activity in the Caribbean began to increase and General Myers, the Governor of Barbados, hearing that a French fleet of twenty-nine sail was approaching *Fort de France*, pessimistically wrote to the British Government, 'Of course none of the Islands are safe, for along with the enemy so strong here, a more deplorable force than our Militia in Barbados was never seen.'

Now thoroughly alarmed, the Government in May 1805 ordered a British fleet to assemble off Cork to deter any such action and seven thousand soldiers began embarking onto the transport ships, where they were firmly held as the men detested serving in the West Indies, and if allowed on land they would certainly have deserted.

Life aboard a transport ship in Cork Bay was not a pleasant experience and, writing in his book *Gleanings and Remarks* Major Gillespie declares, 'Imprisoned on a transport ship throughout the following months in Cork Bay was a tedious existence but some diversion or other at times would occasionally arise to entertain the troops, and this boring sojourn had moments of relief. I should not forget to mention that among other "Varieties of the Season," we had a female convict ship from Cork, and these ladies enlivened us now and then with choice specimens of their conversational powers whenever we came within hail.'

The Major prudently fails to recount the subject of these conversations, which would undoubtedly have shocked the delicate feelings of his female readers.

Throughout the following months, the Cork convoy remained on constant alert as Admiral Villeneuve and Lord Nelson played out their game of cat and mouse prior to their engagement at Trafalgar. Twice, General Sir Eyre Coote in command of the expedition received orders to prepare to sail, only to have them rescinded at the last moment. However, on hearing of Nelson's arrival in the West Indies, the War Office ordered Sir Eyre to stand down and ordered Major General Sir David Baird to take his place.

All the fleet now lacked was its naval commander, the newly promoted Commodore Popham who was still aboard his ship the *Diadem*, being fitted out for foreign travel in Portsmouth harbour. Classified as top secret, her future destination remained unknown and, to throw any enemy spy off the scent, every day a great many packages and letters were delivered to the ship addressed to Constantinople, which convinced the officers on board that they were about to embark on a diplomatic mission to the East. However, the unexpected arrival of a number of horses with the letters D.B. written on their saddlecloths 'let the cat out of the bag', as these were Sir David Baird's initials. As it was common knowledge that he was at present in command of an invasion force anchored off Cork, those on board now knew they were bound on a mission that needed gunpowder, shot, and shell, as opposed to paper, pen, and ink.

Once his ship had been refitted, the War Office presented Sir Home Riggs with his final orders and upping anchor he sailed to Cork to deliver them to Sir David Baird who on reading them immediately ordered the convoy to sail. Secrecy was still the highest priority and their destination remained unknown. Only at the last moment was Popham handed sealed orders with strict instructions not to open them until he and the fleet were safely out to sea.

The fleet, with flags flying and to the sound of marine bands playing martial music, sailed out of Cork harbour on 31 August 1805 and, as the enthusiastic cheers of the excited spectators became whispers in the distance, Popham with trembling hands opened up the envelope containing his orders. Convinced that Miranda's plans and his own hard work had at last come to fruition, his expectations were dashed when on reading them he discovered they were bound not for South America as he hoped, but for South Africa and the Cape of Good Hope.

When Miranda learnt of the Army's destination, it was a severe blow to his revolutionary dreams and he abandoned all hope of obtaining any help from the perfidious British Government. Disgusted by the way that Pitt and his ministers had treated him, he obtained permission from the Government and set sail for America to further his cause in the Land of the Free.

During his years in Europe, Sebastian Miranda had worked hard in establishing a large network of revolutionary cells throughout South America. These were mostly composed of disgruntled colonists, freethinkers and a large number of Jesuit priests. Still resenting the closing of their missions, these were free to roam from country to country under the auspices of the Pope and made excellent spies and efficient couriers. All these groups were now a serious worry to the Spanish Government but, despite their constant threat, the first blow to Spanish rule in South America came from an unexpected quarter. The avaricious eyes of Commodore Sir Home Riggs Popham had been opened to the wealth of

South America and nothing was going to stop him from grabbing his fair share of the riches of the Rio de la Plata.

TWO

THE DISCOVERY OF THE RIO DE LA PLATA

Buenos Aires, the city that had caught Popham's attention, lies on the southern bank of a 180-mile long estuary that stretches from the mouth of the Paraná and Uruguay rivers to the Atlantic Ocean. Comprising Argentina and Uruguay, in the sixteenth century the Spaniards called this area 'La Provincia del Rio de la Plata' (The Province of the River of Silver), which was a serious misnomer as no silver mines existed at the time in Argentina and furthermore the waters of the Paraná are permanently muddy. However, when Columbus discovered the New World in 1492 he was searching not for silver, gold, or land, but for something infinitely more valuable: spice, then the most sought-after product in the world.

The master chefs of the day used spice not just to enhance or disguise the taste of their dishes, but more importantly to preserve their contents from rotting. Owing to the lack of fodder, a vast amount of cattle had to be slaughtered in autumn to save the animals from dying of starvation in the winter, and spice prevented the meat from decomposing. In fact, the two greatest luxuries in Europe in medieval times were silk and spice, and a pound of cloves at this time in England was worth at least the price of two cows.

These pungent herbs also offered people a break from the monotonous winter diet of coarse bread and imperfectly preserved meat. Some favourite flavour or other was invariably used to touch up the food of the rich so that the phrase, 'It has no spice' not only became indicative of lowly living but also denoted the class of household a gentleman kept, and more importantly his status in society.

The great bales of cinnamon, cloves, mace, nutmeg, and pepper came from the Molucca Islands in the East Indies and from there were shipped by sea to the Mediterranean, or transported in long camel trains across the Arabian Desert. Both routes were dangerous and abounded with robbers, pirates, and greedy potentates, all eager to claim their share of the merchants' precious cargo, so that by the time a bale of pepper reached the European market its price had often increased a thousand-fold.

As the expense began to escalate so a hectic search began to find a new route to the Islands and due to the papal bull giving Portugal control of the eastern sea routes, the early Spanish sailors began to explore the coasts of South America hoping to find an easier passage to the Indies. It was for this reason that Juan Diaz de Solis in 1515 established a small settlement in the wide mouth of the River Plate, believing it to be the start of a new route to the fabled isles.

The tiny settlement survived for only a year before the Indians massacred De Solis and his men who they resented occupying their land, and had little interest in being converted to their strange religion. No further interest was shown in the River Plate until St Ursula's day, 21 October 1520, when Fernando Magellan passed through the straits later to be named after him and sailed into the Pacific.

His discovery not only changed the map of the world but also heralded the dawn of a new era, and his ship the *Victoria* sailed into history as the first vessel ever to circumnavigate the globe. Despite his remarkable achievement, Magellan would never live to reap the rewards of his great venture, as a few months later he was murdered by the natives of the Philippines.

With the discovery of gold and silver in Mexico and Peru, spice was quickly forgotten as, having successfully ousted the Moors from Spain, the veterans of the *Reconquista* rushed to the Caribbean to recuperate their fortunes. These tough Spanish adventurers had one steadfast ambition: to replenish their pockets with the gold and silver reported to exist throughout the whole of South America and return to Spain as quickly as possible. Once back in Seville they safely deposited the treasure in the Torre del Oro and, having carefully removed a fifth, a grateful sovereign showered them with honours and raised them to the highest ranks of the nobility.

With their coffers now overflowing with the riches of the Americas, these celebrated Conquistadors, nicknamed '*Los Indios*', returned to their birthplaces where, eager to show off their newly acquired wealth, they built the magnificent houses and palaces still seen today in Cáceres, Trujillo, and throughout most of Extremadura.

To present an acceptable face to the world, the Spaniards declared that these predatory raids were to convert the natives to Christianity; a pious aim that not only gained them the support of the Catholic Church and the blessing of the Holy Father in Rome but also the financial aid of 'Isabella la Católica,' the intensely religious Queen of Spain.

There can be little doubt that the Spaniard's religious fervour was genuine, but his lust for gold was greater and gave rise to the systematic and well organised rape of the New World, now sanctimoniously perpetrated in the name of God, and the Crown.

Gold was the dream but the reality was different for, even had Juan de Solis and the early settlers survived the Indian attacks, they would have been disappointed as the Paraná River was neither a route to the Indies nor did any precious metal exist in this particular area of South America.

Another ten years would elapse before Sebastian Cabot, under the patronage of the Emperor Charles V, arrived in 1526 at the mouth of the River Plate in search of a safer passage to the Pacific, avoiding the dangerous seas and treacherous winds of the Straits of Magellan.

Up to now, his voyage had been long and hazardous, but worse was to follow as, rounding a bend in the Paraná River, he and his men came face to face with three hundred canoes full of hostile Indians determinedly blocking his way and, unable to turn back, the Spaniards drove their ship into the screaming mass of Indians. Although heavily outnumbered, they somehow managed to fight their way to the other side of this floating barricade. The battle was fierce and the river literally became a bloodbath, as in seconds the hungry piranha fish tore the flesh off the bones of all those falling into the water, turning the river into an ocean of crimson waves.

Once through this ambush, the adventurers continued their journey unmolested and reached the land of the peaceful Guarani who, dressed in colourful clothing, came down the riverbank to greet them. Brightly coloured feathers adorned their hair; strange discs of silver hung around their necks and ears, and from these ornaments Argentina and the Rio de la Plata are wrongly said to have taken their name, as the silver came from Chile, Bolivia, or Peru.

In 1528, Cabot returned to Spain to report his findings to Charles V who in recognition of his services appointed him Captain General of this new-found territory and confirmed that from now on, this area should be called La Provincia del Rio de la Plata. A few months later, after receiving this gratifying appointment, Cabot was on the verge of returning to take up his position in his new-found Province, when three noblemen unexpectedly appeared at Court and accused him of leaving them behind to die on a desert island.

It was a serious accusation and the Emperor promptly annulled his position. Disgusted by Charles's behaviour, Cabot sailed to London where Henry VIII greeted him with open arms and commissioned him to discover a Northwest Passage to Asia.

Realising he had made a serious error in losing Cabot, some years later the Emperor re-instated him as his Master Navigator and the explorer returned to his Spanish patron. Their reconciliation lasted for only a short time, as in the reign of Edward VI he returned to London to form the successful Muscovy Company and create his famous map of the world, today on display in the Louvre.

Now reaping the riches of Peru and Mexico, the Emperor Charles became ever more eager to increase his wealth by enlarging his South American dominions, so summoning his advisers to a Grand Council ordered them to organise an expedition to avenge the dastardly murder of Juan de Solis and his founding settlers. Numbering over fifteen hundred men and a hundred horses, this would be by far the largest expedition ever mounted by the Spanish Crown to the Americas, but the animals in the end would play a more important role in the history of Argentina than the men. As these were the ancestors of the herds of wild horses and cattle that, two hundred years later, would freely roam across the rolling pampas, bringing the country enormous wealth and prosperity.

The Emperor placed Don Pedro de Mendoza in charge of this great expedition, a Spanish nobleman of impeccable lineage who chose its members carefully. Many of these came from the most aristocratic families in Spain and were experienced officers who had distinguished themselves in the bloody campaigns in Italy. Seduced by the wildly exaggerated tales of the River of Silver and the mystical legend of El Dorado, they flocked from far and wide to join this daring expedition to conquer a remote and unknown part of the Western hemisphere and in the process hopefully make their fortunes.

By the summer of 1535, the expedition was complete and this great convoy of ships and men, three times larger than that led by Hernando Cortés to conquer Mexico, sailed majestically down the Guadalquivir and passing through the Pillars of Hercules entered the stormy and perilous waters of the Atlantic. Expectations were high and every man from grandee to cabin boy was determined to carry out the Emperor's wishes to subjugate this new and exciting land, and return to Spain with their pockets bursting with the silver and gold rumoured to exist throughout South America.

After a long and arduous journey the fleet finally reached the Rio de la Plata a year later, only to find the water too shallow to approach the shore, forcing the great galleons to anchor a mile out to sea. Disembarking into little boats, Don Pedro and these great hidalgos of Spain, accompanied by their wives, were rowed ashore to land with suitable pomp and ceremony at La Boca, today a picturesque suburb of Buenos Aires much admired for its colourful streets and brightly painted houses.

It was then a far from salubrious spot. The temperature was high; the air hot and humid, but just as the little party stepped onto land, a gentle breeze sprang up and the first man to land optimistically declared, 'Que buenos aires' ('What good air this land has') and from this casual comment the city is said to have taken its name.

Despite the Emperor's meticulous planning, this invincible expedition was doomed to suffer the same fate as Juan de Solis and his men. Mendoza was not a great leader, and happened to be suffering at the time from a severe attack of syphilis. Owing to this unhappy affliction, he spent most of his time in bed but, despite this painful handicap, he bravely threw his heart, if not his body, into the coming enterprise.

To begin with, the Indians were friendly and for the next two weeks supplied the strangers with all the provisions they needed, but when the Spaniards began taking this for granted and stopped paying them, they saw little point in remaining on the coast as winter was approaching; food was scarce. With gifts no longer forthcoming from the foreigners, they no longer had any incentive to remain and, striking camp, began to journey inland.

Hearing of their departure, a worried Don Pedro hastily sent an officer and two bodyguards after them to discover what was wrong. However, his malady must have seriously affected his judgement as his choice of ambassadors proved disastrous. After a lengthy search, this inept delegation eventually found the Indian camp, and striding arrogantly into its centre demanded in a high-handed manner to know why the Indians had ceased delivering them food.

Probably not understanding a word the Spaniards were saying, the Indians at first showed no sign of cooperating, but when Mendoza's men began to threaten them, they quickly recognised the change in tone and promptly gave the Spaniards a sound thrashing. Taking to their heels, the terrified little party fled back to the safety of Mendoza's camp.

Outraged by the natives' insolent behaviour, Don Pedro immediately dispatched his brother with thirty horsemen and three hundred soldiers to teach the impudent savages a lesson. It proved a major error, as the soldiers had practically no knowledge of the terrain and their horses were still desperately weak from their long sea voyage.

The Indians quickly laid an ambush in the rushes of a stream. Hiding among the reeds until half the Spanish troops had crossed the river, they suddenly attacked the divided party and with a hail of missiles drove the intruders back into the water. Somehow, the Spaniards managed to scramble out of the creek and began massacring the Indians but it was a hollow victory as during the battle Mendoza's brother was killed, and worse thirty valuable horses were slaughtered.

It was a serious setback and taught the Spaniards to respect the Indians as dangerous adversaries, and also their first encounter with the dreaded bolas. This lethal weapon, constructed of three rounded stones strung together by a rope, when thrown accurately could bring down a horse and rider, and in the capable hands of the Indians almost put them on a par in combat with the Spaniards.

A relentless war began and over the following months, the little settlement came under constant attack and the eagle-eyed Indians slaughtered any settler found foraging outside the stockade. Fire tipped arrows burnt their huts to the ground and the mud wall defences soon began to disintegrate in the heavy rain as, being constructed without straw, the bricks had not yet hardened due to the lack of sunshine.

Despite this ordeal, the colonists survived the attacks but in the end, famine proved to be their greatest enemy and they were forced to eat rats, mice, snakes, lizards, and even their boots. To make matters worse, Don Pedro's malady had by now become too painful to bear, so, appointing Captain Juan de Ayolas to take over his command, he set sail for Spain and died at sea on the journey home.

The situation looked grim and, realising the colonists had little hope of surviving in their present location, Ayolas ordered his men to build eight shallow boats and, embarking the major part of the remaining two hundred settlers into them, set off up the Paraná River in search of food and safety. The countryside slowly became more benign as they progressed and the unbroken pampas on either side of the river supplied them with all the game and food they needed. The Indian attacks began to cease and now, for the first time since arriving in the New World, the outlook began to look rosy.

After travelling up the river for several weeks, the settlers finally reached the territory of the Guarani, who hearing of the Spaniards' barbaric behaviour on the coast, were now openly hostile. A fierce battle ensued but, after a hard fought struggle, Spanish armour proved too strong. A truce was made and, now with the help of the vanquished Indians, the settlers began to build Asunción, the future capital of Paraguay.

Work progressed rapidly, for unlike the flat and treeless countryside around Buenos Aires, they had plenty of wood to construct their houses. First, a great wooden stockade was quickly erected to guard the settlement from marauders, and matters further improved when, as a show of friendship and to cement the peace treaty, the Guarani thoughtfully presented Ayolas with seven young Indian maidens. He generously gave two to each of his men. This ritual soon became a habit as, over the following years, other revolts took place, all of which the Spaniards successfully put down and after each peace treaty Ayolas and his men received further gifts of attractive young Indian girls. Ulrich Schmidt, a humble German soldier in Mendoza's Army, later to become the chronicler of the expedition on his return to Germany in 1553, writes, 'Thus we became friends.' It was a serious understatement, as these gifts of nubile young girls rapidly increased the birth rate, and helped found the present day Paraguayan nation.

The settlers left behind by Ayolas at the mouth of the river finally gave up the struggle to defend Buenos Aires in 1541. Abandoning what little remained of the settlement, they collected up their few belongings and joined the Spaniards in Asunción. All they left behind were a few escaped horses, which the Indians quickly caught and over the following years became expert horsemen and the forefathers of the gauchos.

Asunción quickly began to flourish but after thirty years, the settlers began to get home sick. Life at the settlement was lonely and remote, and they yearned for a port on the coast to make contact once again with the mother country. Those who found the loneliness unbearable crossed the Chaco (sub-tropical forest) through Portuguese territory to reach Sao Vicente (today's Sao Paulo). It was a long and dangerous route, as Spain and Portugal were frequently at war and there was no way of knowing what state of relationship existed between the two countries before embarking on the journey.

Finally, in 1573, Juan de Garay with nine Spaniards and seventy young men left Asunción and set off to establish a colony at Santa Fé. His plan was to reconstruct Buenos Aires in stages, and by first establishing a settlement at Santa Fé, halfway between Asunción and the sea, he hoped to ensure that communications could be kept up by the river to eliminate the threat of famine. After seven years of hard work, Santa Fé was eventually completed and Garay moved on to the coast, taking with him, 'More than sixty men along with the necessary farm implements, a thousand horses, and five hundred cows.' Buenos Aires was rebuilt in 1580, but this time there were no blue-blooded hidalgos among its sixty-three inhabitants as all but ten were *mestizos* (half-breeds), showing that in the forty-four years since Mendoza's arrival not just the horses and cattle had been prodigiously breeding.

THREE

RIO DE LA PLATA IN THE SEVENTEENTH CENTURY

Spain would never recognise that Argentina's 250,000 or more square miles of unbroken pampas constituted her greatest potential source of wealth in the New World. Gold and precious metals were all the Spaniards were interested in and the emerging Argentine nation was neglected in favour of Bolivia and Peru. Although the most fertile region of all Spanish America, Argentina for the next 100 years was deliberately dismissed so that the immediate wealth from those countries with gold and silver mines should fill the coffers of the mother country.

Rules were made, and carefully adhered to. Direct trade with Buenos Aires was strictly forbidden and all imports for Argentina were brought in great trading fleets from Spain to Portobello on the coast of Panama, where they were loaded onto mules and carried across the Isthmus to be shipped to Lima. Once safely in the city, the merchandise was loaded onto mules again and carried over the Andes to Bolivia where high-wheeled wagons waited to transport it across the pampas to Buenos Aires. It was a long 3,000-mile dangerous journey over towering mountains, dusty roads, and dense forests teeming with wild animals, ruthless robbers, and hostile Indians.

Trade between the settlers was strictly forbidden and only Spaniards were allowed to trade with the colonies and only Spanish ships permitted to carry the merchandise. Goods sent from one colony to another first had to go to Lima before being shipped back to another part of the continent, a draconian law that not only increased the price of every article the colonists bought but more importantly ensured every ounce of colonial gold safely reached the mother country. Spain in return was expected to provide her colonies with the imports they so badly needed but, owing to wars and the steady collapse of her economy, this she was incapable of doing.

During the seventeenth and first half of the eighteenth century, Buenos Aires, as far as Spain was concerned, remained a minor military outpost; populated by poorly paid soldiers, situated in an unimportant backwater of the Empire. The Spanish Crown and her explorers took little interest in either the settlement or its surrounding regions and the only importance to the Empire was its strategic position near the rival Portuguese settlements along the Brazilian coast.

This changed in the middle of the eighteenth century when interest in South America began to mount, as the European nations struggled to hold or gain new land. The French and Dutch by now had begun an unending battle to establish a colony and fortress at Rio de Janeiro, and at some time or other the latter would occupy most of the principal cities along the central and north-eastern coasts of Brazil. The British were also firmly ensconced at the mouth of the River Amazon and, adding further to the increasing international turmoil, Spain and Portugal were permanently at each other's throats.

During these turbulent times, trade was the little colony's only hope of survival but this, as already explained, was severely restricted by the Crown. Buenos Aires stood isolated from all the major cities of Spain's South American dominions and unlike the others had no resident Indian workforce, or native industry to produce any marketable goods. All it could rely on was a small trade in leather hides but as these had to pass through Lima, any hope of making a profit was out of the question as transporting the merchandise across the Andes was a risky business and once there the greedy Peruvian merchants dominated the market, manipulating the price of every commodity to their advantage.

Due to this unfair handicap, Argentina began to depend almost exclusively on a rapidly burgeoning contraband trade. Relatively small to begin with this, it was left largely unharassed by the authorities, except for the occasional crackdown, and smuggling soon became recognised as a natural part of the country's economy. Still under Portuguese control, Colonia del Sacramento, on the northern side of the River Plate, swarmed with smugglers from every nation heavily intent on thwarting the King of Spain's selfish monopoly. Every night, small ships crossed the estuary to land their wares in hidden coves along the Argentine coastline, while the more prosperous smugglers, having first negotiated a suitable agreement with the greedy customs officers, brazenly sailed their larger vessels into port under the protection of a neutral flag.

Ships from Holland, France, and the United States filled the harbour, and when the news reached Buenos Aires in 1805 that a British Fleet had anchored in the Brazilian port of Bahia, the authorities became extremely anxious. In fact, the Viceroy, the Marquis of Sobremonte, was so worried that he immediately ordered a list to be drawn up of all suspicious foreigners residing in Buenos Aires along with their religion. This revealed that there were nine Protestants; one converted Christian; one Lutheran; one Anglican, and two agnostics living in the city.

Argentina: The British Invasion of Buenos Aires, 1806

Little changed until the middle of the eighteenth century for, although having a Governor, Buenos Aires was still overshadowed both politically and economically by the Viceroy's capital in Lima. But with the new alliance between England and Portugal in their war against France, Spain woke up to the fact that her distant colonies were in danger and to keep these faraway territories intact she radically needed to modernise her colonial system.

Charles the Third's new colonial policy in 1776 changed the whole structure of the Empire, and the creation of new Viceroyalties ended the detested power of Lima. Local governments became increasingly more important and the founding of the Viceroyalty of the Rio de la Plata, with its capital at Buenos Aires, brought new life and prosperity to the Province. The city rapidly began to flourish and soon changed from a forgotten military garrison with a few underpaid soldiers into a major commercial centre and, recognising the area now needed stronger leadership, the King hurriedly sent important administrators and competent officers to deal with the situation.

As the war steadily surged its way across Europe, the city's finances further improved, as the growing number of armies urgently needed the Rio de la Plata's major export: leather. The demand rapidly began to increase; faster sailing ships could now transport the heavy cattle hides directly to Spain, and by 1750 the indiscriminate killing of the cattle by the gauchos and Indians had almost ended. Up to now this had been a free-for-all, but with the introduction of branding to show the ownership of the animals, the haphazard slaughter of the herds had almost ended and with this escalation in trade the fortune and wealth of both Buenos Aires and her population spectacularly began to increase.

The new Viceroyalty brought with it many other

advantages, but by far the greatest bonus of all was the richly populated mineral producing area of Alto Peru. This not only opened up a new market for her goods, but more importantly gave Argentina access to the great wealth of the Potosi gold and silver mines. From now on, the entire traffic in gold and silver bullion shipped to Spain would pass through the welcoming hands of the *Porteños* (citizens of Buenos Aires) and in the process make them very rich.

FOUR

POTOSI AND POPHAM

POTOSI

Once the most populous community in the Western Hemisphere, the great silver mining area of Alto Peru and its centre the city of Potosi (today a World Natural Heritage site in Bolivia), resembled a cross between a Wild West frontier town and the modern day city of Las Vegas. When the news leaked out in 1545 of that fortuitous gust of wind, which blew Don Diego Gualpa to his knees onto a shining strip of silver on the mountain above Potosi, a horde of adventurers descended on this cold and desolate mountainside, bringing with them 6,000 negro and mulatto slaves, and over 65,000 Indians. This was just the beginning, as within a few years 40,000 Spaniards from all over the continent arrived at this remote spot, thirteen thousand feet above sea level and by 1580, the population had risen to around 160,000 inhabitants.

The Indians did all the labour and lived in 139 native villages scattered around the outskirts of the city. Mining was dangerous work so large numbers of labourers were needed as four out of every five Indians died in their first year of employment, unselfishly making their employers very rich.

Wealth in fact dominated the society and money was spent as ostentatiously as possible. General Pereira for instance gave his daughter Placida a vast dowry of $2,000,000 on her wedding day while General Mejias, perhaps more economically minded or less affluent, gave his a mere $1,000,000 on such a joyous occasion.

Fortunes were built not only by mining but also by trade, and the popular Señora Catalina Argandona was reputed to make a profit of $800,000 a year from her vineyards; a beneficial enterprise much appreciated by a thirsty populace. Dress was in keeping with the prosperity of this 'nouveau riche' society, and the women of Potosi wore different jewels and dresses for every fiesta. Each ensemble was said to be worth twelve to fourteen thousand dollars and one woman of fashion was rumoured to have spent over a hundred dollars on pearls just to adorn her overshoes. Even the *mestizos* (Spanish and Indian half-breeds) wore sandals, and silken belts adorned with gold, pearls, rubies, and other rich jewels, while their skirts and jackets were made of only the finest cloth. To suitably display this exotic apparel, the town boasted fourteen dancing schools, thirty-six gambling houses and a theatre, 'to which the price of admission ranged from forty to fifty dollars'.

Popular celebrations were carried out on a similarly magnificent scale and on Philip II's accession to the throne in 1556, the city spent eight million dollars on a twenty-four-day extravaganza of bullfights, carnivals, masked balls, and banquets, during which free liquor of every description was liberally served. These, combined with jousts, tourneys, and dramatic representations in extravagant dress, provided a saturnalia never before witnessed in the New World.

Chattering crowds of jostling people filled Potosi's narrow streets, 'On foot, on horseback, in carriages and litters, as if going on a pilgrimage' reported a chronicler of the time. Every class and colour brushed shoulders together, as the finely dressed whores displayed their attractive assets and the street vendors shouted out their wares in a cacophony of unintelligible sounds. The shops and market stalls displayed luxuries that could be found nowhere else in the Americas and wealthy merchants flocked from all over the world to purchase the expensive items on display.

Nevertheless, despite this outward show of splendour, Potosi society was far from refined and armed soldiers, miners, and government officials came to blows at the slightest provocation. Duels were a daily occurrence, and the contestants wore scarlet robes to hide any sign of spilt blood that might unsettle their concentration or, worse, encourage their adversary. Whenever the *Cabildo* (administrative council) met, its members attended fully armed in coats of mail as the meetings inevitably ended in a duel or brawl.

Due to the wealth from the Potosi mines, Buenos Aires in June 1806 at the time of the British invasion was a vibrant and prosperous city. Although not architecturally as grand as Lima, it still had a theatre and a bullring where performances and *corridas* were regularly held to entertain the rapidly growing population. Food was cheap as more cattle were killed for their hides than could be consumed, and meat so plentiful that nearly every day the slaughterhouse gave away free carcasses.

This gave future generations of Argentines their love of beef, which in the middle of the twentieth century reached the staggering figure of half a kilo of beef per head per day, a statistic that included children and babies. Four large stores containing an enormous amount of diversified stock supplied most of the interior, and the traveller Concolorcorvo writes,

'The people here hardly think about anything else but their business. Everybody wants a good house and a house in the country for recreation. Meat is so abundant that when it is carted in quarters across the plaza should a quarter happen to slip off, the driver never stops to pick it up if someone tells him and even a poor beggar on the street doesn't bother to carry it home with him.'

Occupation, race, and money, rather than breeding or family tree decided a citizen's position in society. Family name, although a factor, was not important and social position rested more on wealth than on any claim to blue blood, as few permanent residents of Buenos Aires could claim relationship to the aristocratic or noble families of Spain.

Cattle abounded; horses were numerous and cheap but surprisingly the city had only two blacksmiths. In a British officer's opinion, writing at the time of the British invasion, these were,

'... very slow in their work but solid in their finish. All sorts of iron and steel were in great demand and a set of horseshoes cost five dollars, while the animal itself might be purchased for only two.'

Colonel Fletcher Wilkie interestingly notes, 'Chilean horses were greatly prized, and could fetch a hundred dollars. Some of these were brought down to our races at Montevideo and are jet black, and very beautiful animals.'

Life in the Rio de la Plata at the time of the British invasion was relatively peaceful, and the Spanish Army stationed in Buenos Aires had only two enemies to concern them: the Indians and the Portuguese. Neither were serious threats, as after Napoleon's kidnapping and the execution of the Duke d'Enghien, Dom Joao the Regent of Portugal was far too frightened of the French to embark on a territorial war in South America and the Indians by now had been pushed back deep into the interior.

This meant that the Spanish officers had little to do and were infinitely more interested in furthering their careers in the Viceroy's Court or obtaining lucrative Governmental positions in the Provinces, than in training their men. In fact, at the time of Popham's invasion in 1806 *El Fijo* (the regular Army) in Buenos Aires numbered only 720 regular soldiers and 94 officers instead of the 5,000 men there should have been, with only 2,000 men throughout the rest of the country.

This was principally due to the Spanish Government insisting that all the Potosi treasure should be shipped to Spain, leaving the Authorities with little money to pay the soldiers their wages. Few soldiers had uniforms and many lived at home. Describing the state of the Army when a prisoner of war in the Province of Cordoba in 1807, Major Gillespie declares, 'Widely scattered over the Pampas frontiers in small bodies and never regimented for exercise or combined evolution, the Spanish soldiers were strangers to obedience and on the day of trial they could be expected to act only as a rabble without either object or motive. The officers had no control over their men who being ill paid and clothed cared little for them or their Government. Their duties were irregularly performed and their sentries might be daily seen asleep basking in the sun. The main object of the Commandants of these *Guardias* was to traffic and smuggle where they could, either with their own itinerant countrymen or with the neighbouring Indians.'

As South America entered the nineteenth century, all appeared calm on the surface but an undercurrent of resentment was swiftly growing. Unhappy with the stifling controls, taxes, and domination of the mother country, the well-established founding families begrudged the Crown giving all the major positions of Government to the King's favourites whose interests lay less in the welfare of the colony, and more in their own. This fostered much bitterness and jealousy, and attracted by Miranda's openly declared plans to remove the Spanish yoke from off their shoulders, groups of citizens began to join his secret network of independence seekers. Dissatisfied Argentines and those from other South American countries travelled to Europe to meet Miranda, now living in London striving to win over the British Government, and assist him in ending Spain's domination of their continent.

This was the rich and prosperous land that had caught Captain Sir Home Riggs Popham's avaricious eyes, and he firmly believed it only right and proper that he should obtain his share of the expanding wealth of the Provincia del Rio de la Plata.

SIR HOME RIGGS POPHAM
'A VERY SLIPPERY CHARACTER'

At the beginning of the nineteenth century, Britannia ruled the waves and, depending on the interpreter's view, her sailors were famous or notorious throughout the world. At the drop of a hat, an admiring British populace raucously sang 'Rule Britannia' along with other patriotic songs, and enthusiastically followed the deeds of Rodney, St Vincent, Nelson, and other famous Admirals in the same way that soccer fans pursue their favourite players' careers today. Following in this tradition, Commodore Sir Home Riggs Popham after his capture of Buenos Aires became a household name. However, there was one major difference: these renowned Admirals fought for fame, glory, and their country, whereas Sir Home regarded the Navy as a commercial enterprise and fought for his and the City of London's financial benefit.

Born in Gibraltar on 12 October 1762, Sir Home Riggs

was the son of Joseph Popham, His Majesty's Consul General to Tetuan. Mary, his mother, tragically died giving birth to him and, referring to this sad event in a biography of Sir Home's life, printed after his capture of Buenos Aires, *The Naval Chronicle* reports, 'If we are accurately informed her death was occasioned by the circumstances of Admiral Gells firing a salute at a period when the enemy were expected.' A family weakness Sir Home fortunately failed to inherit.

Riggs was his mother's maiden name but why he was christened Home remains a mystery as it was not a name from either side of his family. However, it may be no coincidence that only eighteen months prior to his birth, the eighth Earl of Home had been the Governor of Gibraltar.

Popham's childhood days were very unsettled as within only nine months of his mother's death, Joseph married Catherine Lamb and Home and his new stepmother were constantly being shuttled between Gibraltar and Tetuan, where his father rented rooms for £150 a year in the Palace of the Sultan, Prince Sidi Mahomet Ben Abdulla, to carry out his diplomatic duties.

The Barbary Coast was then a dangerous place to live in, as its whole existence centred on kidnapping and piracy. Joseph spent most of his time negotiating ransoms for the captured English subjects, which the scheming Emperor used as diplomatic pawns to aid him in his nefarious schemes. This made their relationship difficult. Unpleasant incidents frequently arose, as happened when the Sultan sent his coach to be repaired in Gibraltar where owing to a lack of the requisite materials to mend it, it remained for rather a long time. Furious at the delay, the impatient Prince blamed Joseph and threatened to dismiss him unless the coach was not instantly repaired, and returned in proper working order.

Joseph survived the threat, but there was another serious drawback to being His Majesty's Consul in Tetuan. Every time he visited the Emperor he was expected to bring him lavish gifts, for which the penny-pinching British Government were reluctant to reimburse him, leaving him constantly in debt. Fortunately, after an acrimonious dispute with Sidi Mahomet over a hijacked ship from Alexandria, the Foreign Office recalled him in 1769 and he thankfully returned to England.

Three years later aged ten, Home was sent to be educated at Westminster School and on his father's death in 1788 when barely sixteen he entered the Navy, and joined the crew of the *Hyena* under the command of Captain Edward Thompson, technically as an able seaman but in practice as a probationary midshipman.

The Naval Chronicle in the article already mentioned suggests that Ned Thompson, 'Acted the part of father and protector to his boyish years' and 'Poet Thompson', as he was nicknamed in the Navy, was certainly a kind and talented man. As well as being a competent naval officer, Ned also wrote poetry, satire, and plays, and due to their success became a close friend of the famous actor David Garrick and that political firebrand, 'The Friend of Freedom' John Wilkes.

Over the next five years, the young midshipman's life was one of constant warfare: first against America, then France, and shortly afterwards Spain. The *Hyena* was kept busily employed escorting convoys to the Caribbean; sinking privateers; capturing Spanish treasure ships, and in January 1780 took part in the second battle of Cape St Vincent.

This famous engagement involved a British squadron of twenty-two ships of the line and a number of frigates in a fight against a fleet of eleven Spanish battleships. Six of them they captured, and the English crews watched in awe as the Spanish Admiral's flagship exploded into a shower of smoking debris. The action continued throughout the night and is known in naval history as the 'Moonlight Battle.'

Life was full of exciting moments and Admiral Rodney, hearing that 900 French troops were about to invade Tobago in 1781, hurriedly dispatched Popham aboard the *Sheilanagig* (a small sloop of 14 guns) with *The Fly*, and *Munster Lass* to inform the islanders that a British squadron was on its way to protect them. Their orders were to search for a likely enemy landing place and if possible find the exact location of the French fleet. To ensure they were not discovered together, they should anchor in different bays along the coast, which turned out to be a wise precaution. On 30 May, a French battleship overhauled the *Sheilanagig* and carried Popham and his crew off in chains to Martinique. Here they remained for the next four months, and released on parole returned to the *Hyena*, which immediately upped anchor and sailed for England.

Having completed the necessary arrangements for an exchange of prisoners as agreed on by the Kings of England and France, the Admiralty appointed Popham to the frigate *Alarm* on the Jamaica station where he remained until 1783, when the Admiralty recalled him to England. After promoting him to First Lieutenant, they dispatched him to the more peaceful but disease ridden waters off the coast of Guinea where he spent the next three years surveying the trading forts along the coast aboard the *Grampus* under the command of his old mentor Ned Thompson.

It was now that Popham showed his skill as a cartographer by completing a 'Marine Survey' of Anna de Chavas Bay on the island of St Thomas off Gabon, which was much acclaimed and five years later published in Alexander

Dalrymple's famous book of nautical charts.

The British had built the forts along the Guinea coast to protect the profitable gold and slave trade, and the station chief at Cape Coast Castle proudly reported that both were doing well,

'In the last twelve months, thirteen ships with 5,852 slaves on board have sailed from *Annamaboe*; another from *Winnebah* with 250 more for Charleston, and an American ship with another 250 slaves was presently on its way to Boston. Slaves were fetching £4 a head and the price of gold was good, but the ivory trade indifferent.'

Ned Thompson was also involved in his own venture, which was to find a suitable spot between Namibia and the Cape of Good Hope where the Government could start a convict colony. Owing to Lord Cornwallis's disastrous defeat at Yorktown, transportation to the colonies had now ended and the Government badly needed a new destination to banish the criminals. Ned's motives, although sound, were not entirely altruistic as should the scheme be successful, he not unnaturally expected a grateful Government to appoint him the Governor of the Colony.

Popham spent the next three years making valuable surveys of the coast that the Admiralty would later compliment him on and all seemed well but tragedy struck in January 1786, when Ned Thompson suddenly died from a fever. His death was a sad loss to Popham, and at the end of the year the Admiralty recalled him to England to find that peace had been declared with France and his services were no longer needed.

It was a severe blow, especially as the Admiralty disappointingly refused his request to retire on half pay. Now unemployed with his income gone, the ambitious young naval officer was left with no alternative but to remedy this uncomfortable state of affairs himself and, obtaining leave of absence from the Admiralty, he set off to go freebooting in the Indian and China seas to recuperate his rapidly dwindling finances.

The India Act of 1784 had given the Honourable East India Company the right to seize and confiscate the assets of any British subject found trading independently with India but it had no authority to curb the legitimate commerce of genuine foreign companies like the Dutch, Swedes, and Danes from trading with their settlements along the coast. It did, however, give the Company the right to fine any British subject found trading to India under the authority of a foreign Prince of State the sum of £500. This clause gave the freebooters room to manoeuvre, as the fine was a mere bagatelle compared to the profit they could make from the sale of the cargo.

Taking advantage of this loophole, Popham in 1790 commandeered an Italian ship, the *Etrusco* out of Leghorn, which was nominally under the command of a Genoese, Captain Francisco Coppi. Then to increase the illusion, he acquired a passport from Prince Leopold, the Austrian Emperor and Grand Duke of Tuscany, permitting him to sail to the East Indies under the protection of the Tuscan flag; having obtained this valuable document, he set off to make his fortune in India.

The risks were high, for should the East India Company prove he was sailing under false colours they could not only confiscate the ship and cargo but also arrest and deport him. It was not the only danger facing the erstwhile Italian trader, as should he be hauled to by the Royal Navy, they could impress any British seaman found on board, leaving him almost crewless.

Although dubious, the enterprise was well worth taking as

it proved a huge success. Not only were the financial results spectacular but it also brought him into contact with all the most important merchants in London and Europe, who from now on would remain his friends for life.

In 1793 war broke out again, with France bringing this profitable enterprise to a disastrous end, for while peacefully at anchor in Ostend harbour the *Etrusco* was suddenly seized, not by the French but by His Majesty's frigate *Brilliant* whose Captain, Lt Robinson, claimed the ship and her cargo as a Prize of War.

It proved a costly setback, as the following case in the High Court of the Admiralty and subsequently the Court of Appeal dragged on for the next fifteen years, and although his lawyer De Rebeque managed to establish the now Admiral's claim to a third of the cargo's value of just over £12,000, Popham lost £27,000 on freight charges, and on top of that the legal expenses and his lawyer's exorbitant fees.

Once again with no form of income or employment, Popham spent the following months persistently badgering the Admiralty to re-instate him in the Royal Navy, and eventually they gave him the rank of Lieutenant. However, instead of posting him to a ship, they sent him on detachment to the Grand Old Duke of York's ill-fated Army currently campaigning in the Netherlands and, although at first unhappy with the appointment, Popham soon gained the reputation of being a brilliant liaison officer and the nickname of 'The Duke of York's Admiral.'

He returned to England in 1795 as a Post-Captain, an appointment his fellow officers greatly resented. Firstly, because the Army had requested it and secondly, up to now his only command had been a small sloop, and certainly not a ship of the line as normally required to obtain this rank. Ignoring this petty jealousy, Popham spent the next

Argentina: The British Invasion of Buenos Aires, 1806

four years on land organising Britain's defences against Napoleon's threatened invasion until 1799, when probably due to his father's profession the Government dispatched him on a diplomatic mission to Russia.

His mission proved a huge success, as Tsar Paul in a moment of good humour made him a Knight of Malta, and presented him with a snuff box set with diamonds and to show her appreciation, the Tsarina gave him a valuable ring.

Flushed with success he returned to London where George III surprisingly granted him permission 'to receive and bear' his newly granted title. This was most unusual, as by now the King had become extremely nonplussed with the Tsar, who as Grand Commander of the Order had been liberally awarding the honour to all and sundry and especially to visiting British officers. Out of pique and to show his disapproval of the Tsar's behaviour, His Majesty refused to allow many of the recipients the right to use the title in England and Popham was one of the few exceptions granted the Royal favour.

A second visit to Russia the following year proved less successful, as in the intervening nine months Russian policy towards Great Britain had changed, and the manic-depressive Tsar stubbornly refused to grant the now Sir Home an audience. After a frustrating month waiting for Paul to change his mind, Popham finally received a verbal message from His Imperial Majesty delivered to him by Count Panin declaring, 'That if he Sir Home Popham wishes to leave, His Imperial Majesty would not dream of detaining him, and therefore wishes him a good journey home.' This abrupt dismissal ended his mission, and after suffering an uncomfortable journey over eleven hundred miles on rough icy roads, snow-swept plains, and wolf-infested woods in temperatures well below zero, he returned to London having achieved absolutely nothing.

The next unfortunate incident occurred in 1803, when after a two-year tour in the Red Sea and India as Captain of the *Romney*, 'the crankiest ship I ever was in,' he was arraigned before the Navy Board and charged with excessive and fraudulent expense. Under his command, the ship had been refitted in Calcutta and the cost of repairs forwarded to the Admiralty claimed to be £70,000, but on investigation the true figure was judged to be just over £7,000.

This type of fraud at the time was common practice in the Navy, and the ensuing enquiry found Sir Home not responsible and exonerated him from all charges of malpractice. Despite the verdict, the mud stuck and only increased the suspicion among his contemporaries that he was indeed 'a very slippery character.'

Over and above his naval activities, Popham's interests were far ranging, for in the summer of 1804, he was made a Fellow of the Royal Society, and the rotten borough of Yarmouth elected him as their Member of Parliament. The latter was rumoured to have been an expensive affair that cost him the immense sum of £4,000, but once in Parliament he became a keen supporter and personal friend of William Pitt, the Prime Minister.

As well as an expert surveyor, Sir Home was also a renowned inventor and had developed an efficient signalling code that the Admiralty adopted and would later be used by Lord Nelson at the battle of Trafalgar. Nevertheless, there had been other less successful enterprises along the way, including a submarine and torpedo designed by the eccentric American inventor Robert Fulton, which after successful trials in the Thames and much touting by Popham and the inventor, the British Government disappointingly refused to purchase.

Now aged forty-four, Sir Home's life in 1805 had already been an adventurous affair, and he had watched his fortunes seesaw from the heights of glory to the verge of disgrace. His reputation among his contemporaries was that of being a highly able and experienced officer but very ambitious and not averse to skulduggery should the financial gain look sufficiently rewarding. Prize money was undoubtedly the most important factor in the majority of his actions, which made him popular with his crews who knew that serving under his command the rewards would be far greater than under any other Captain in the Royal Navy. His brother officers mistrusted him, and he had already made many enemies in the Admiralty. In contrast, the Army greatly admired him after his successful campaign in the Low Countries but by far his greatest admirers of all were the London merchants who knew that wherever Popham went, trade and profit would follow. This lust for financial gain, rather than any noble vision of liberating South America, was undoubtedly the reason that attracted Sir Home to Miranda's cause.

In 1806, the Admiralty promoted him to the rank of Commodore and placed him in command of a squadron of ships carrying soldiers to retake the Cape of Good Hope. The rank gave him no authority to command a military force, let alone embark on the invasion of a foreign country, such an action needing the consent of a senior officer; the responsibility for this decision descended on the broad but reluctant shoulders of General Sir David Baird.

FIVE

GENERAL SIR DAVID BAIRD

'A KIND BUT ROUGH DIAMOND'

Without Sir David Baird's authorisation, Popham's disastrous expedition to South America could never have taken place. It was a decision he would never regret for, although never actually setting foot in South America, as the official commander of the expedition, Baird received in 1808 the handsome sum of £24,000 as his share of the captured Spanish Treasure. It was enormous sum of money and the equivalent of well over £1,400,000 today.

Born in December 1757 at Newbyth, East Lothian, David Baird was a tall bluff Scot whose life would be one of non-stop warfare. Theodore Hook, his enthusiastic biographer, describes him 'As having countenance that was cheerful and animated,' while Lt Colonel Fletcher Wilkie who accompanied him to the Cape of Good Hope declares, 'He was a kind but rough diamond.' Not everyone was quite so complimentary, as an officer stationed in India refers to him, 'As a bloody bad tempered old Scotsman.'

There was undoubtedly some degree of truth in the last remark for, on being told that her son had been chained to another person when a prisoner of war in India, his mother replied in her pure Scots accent, 'Lord help the mon who is chained to ma son Davie!'

Baird's father died when he was only eight and, at the age of fifteen, his mother bought him a second lieutenancy in the 2nd Regiment (The Queen's Royal Regiment), which he joined the following year in Gibraltar. The posting was short-lived for, after only three years stationed on the Rock, the regiment was recalled to England in 1776, luckily missing the horrors of the Great Siege.

Promoted two years later to Lieutenant, Lord McLeod, a friend and neighbour of his mother, offered him the command of a company of grenadiers in his newly raised regiment the 73rd, soon to become the famous 71st or Highland Light Infantry. This he gratefully accepted and in 1780, sailed with his regiment to India.

They were the first Highland Regiment to arrive in Madras and the men with their kilts and bagpipes caused a major sensation among the natives who to begin with, but not for long, were uncertain of their sex.

The Regiment had arrived in India at a dangerous moment, as the Madras Government was now at war with Haidar Ali, the Regent of Mysore, and had stupidly allowed his 100,000-strong Army to pour through the narrow mountain passes onto the Carnatic Plain without attempting to stop them.

They were now bitterly regretting their decision, as this ferocious horde was rapidly advancing on the city and, terrified by the news of their approach, the Governor hastily offered command of the Army to Lord MacLeod, which he politely declined, as he was far too experienced to accept command under such dangerous circumstances, especially not of his own making. Instead, he assured the Governor of his full co-operation in every other way and, now thoroughly alarmed, the Governor hastily dispatched Sir Hector Monroe with a force of less than 6,000 men to confront Haidar's Army at Arcot, and at the same time sent a message to Colonel Bailey stationed in Northern Circar to join Sir

Hector with his 3,000 men as soon as possible.

Bailey set off immediately, and arriving at Conjeveram found his little force surrounded by Haidar's Army. Short of provisions and ammunition he sent an urgent message to Monroe begging him for help, and on receiving his request Sir Hector immediately dispatched Colonel Fletcher with eleven companies of sepoys and the flank company of the 73rd under the command of David Baird to join him.

The relief party set off at night and by constantly changing direction avoided an ambush and met up the following evening with the besieged Colonel and his men. After a good night's rest, the whole force set off at first light the next morning for Arcot. They had covered less than four miles when they came under heavy attack from Haidar's Army. They resisted during daylight hours, but with his soldiers exhausted and the day coming to an end, Bailey ordered his men to halt for the night. It proved a serious error, as this gave Haidar Ali time to bring up his whole Army during the night and surround his position. Explaining his reasons for halting that evening to Baird, Bailey declared, 'I am determined to halt till daylight, so that I may have an opportunity to see about me.' His wish was swiftly granted, for as dawn broke the following morning the Colonel woke to see, surrounding his little force: 30,000 cavalry; 50,000 infantry; 70 cannons, and the Mysore elephants magnificently adorned in their full regalia.

The odds of survival were slim, but Bailey and his men bravely held the enemy at bay for several hours, until two ammunition tumbrels suddenly exploded; seeing his enemy in turmoil, Haidar immediately gave the order for his Army to advance and, with their uniforms shining brightly in the morning sunshine, the Mysore Cavalry slowly lowered their lances. As the pennons circled in an arc of red and white, the trumpets sounded the charge and, breaking into a gallop, they spurred their plunging animals into the British lines. The points of their lances ripped viciously through the redcoats' ranks and, under the impact of the charge, the British line began to wilt; in the panic that followed, Colonel Fletcher rushed to support the rear-guard with the 73rd's grenadier company and was never seen again. Many of the sepoys took to their heels and ran for their lives but, despite being badly wounded, Colonel Bailey shouted at his men to form a square and, with no ammunition left, his men bravely held off thirteen charges with only their bayonets.

It was a desperate stand, and realising his position was hopeless the Colonel ordered Baird and his men to stop firing and, tying a white handkerchief to the end of his sword, bravely stepped forward. Waving it above his head, he signalled he wished to surrender but Haidar Ali refused to accept his offer as many of the sepoys were still haphazardly blazing away, fully aware of what fate awaited once they stopped. Their fears proved justified as, the moment Baird and his soldiers laid down their arms, Tippoo Ali's cavalry charged again and cut the defenceless men to pieces. Severely wounded with blood streaming from two sabre wounds to the head, a ball in the thigh and a pike wound in his right arm, Baird fell to the ground unconscious.

Haidar's soldiers showed no mercy. Roaming across the battlefield, they slaughtered every living soul they could find and, to ensure there were no survivors, the Mysore elephants in line abreast stomped over the ground trampling to death the wounded. It was a miracle Baird survived, for an Indian trooper in search of booty was about to deliver him the coup de grace when the soldier lying next to him inadvertently groaned. Startled by the sound, the Indian decapitated the man instead of Baird.

Fearing Sir Hector's Army might appear while his men were still engaged in looting, Haidar Ali hurriedly left the battlefield and, retreating six miles away to Derma, began re-grouping his widely dispersed Army. Next morning, he generously offered to pay two rupees to any man bringing him an Englishman's head and ten for those alive or wounded.

It was this offer that undoubtedly saved David Baird's life, as an Indian trooper scouring the previous day's battlefield in search of bounty, hearing Baird's groans attempted to revive him. Giving the wounded Scotsman some water, he roughly bandaged his wounds and managed to coax him a few hundred yards. Soon realising he would never get his prize back to Haidar's camp alive, he cursed his bad luck and set off in pursuit of more rewarding prey.

That night two wounded British sergeants stumbled across Baird lying among the carnage of the battlefield and, bandaging his wounds, managed to revive him. Setting off together, they somehow found their way to the French camp where the French officers treated them kindly and helped them to convalesce. In the end, they were forced to hand them over to their Indian allies, and once in Haidar's grasp Baird and his companions were escorted to Seringapatam and thrown into the Maharajah's gruesome dungeon.

Baird's wounds had not yet healed, and realising he would never survive the weight of the heavy chains, his fellow prisoners begged the jailer to spare him the ordeal. But the man stubbornly refused to do so, declaring that he had been issued with a set of irons for each of the prisoners, and would himself be severely punished should he return with a set unused. Realising Baird would certainly die if forced to wear these heavy solid links of metal, Captain Lucas bravely volunteered to wear two sets of irons, and his heroic action undoubtedly saved David Baird's life.

Kept in appalling conditions and savagely tortured for the next three and a half years, Baird daily watched his fellow inmates go mad or die, knowing that those taken from the prison were either poisoned or tortured to death. The Indians even went so far as to force the British Regimental drummer boys to wear transparent female dresses and entertain the court as dancing girls.

Instead of food, the prisoners were given a few annas a week to buy their provisions from the Bazaar, but despite the flies, heat, and dreadful conditions, they kept their spirits up and for the next three years 'gaily drank the King's health on his birthday on 4 June with sherbet as alcohol was strictly forbidden'.

After a year in captivity, the news reached them of Haidar Ali's death, raising their hopes that they might be better treated. It proved wishful thinking as Haidar's successor Tippoo Ali, the 'Tiger of Mysore', was if anything even crueller than his predecessor, but in March 1784 a treaty was finally signed and Baird and the surviving officers were at last released from their dreadful dungeon.

Three years of torture had ended, and re-joining his regiment, the bullet still lodged in his thigh from the battle of Conjeveram was painfully extracted. Promoted to Major in 1787, Baird returned to England the following year to receive a hero's welcome.

After all the horrors he had been through, Baird took some well-earned leave in Scotland. While there he purchased the Colonelcy of his Regiment (now the 71st Highlanders) from a brother officer, who hearing he was about to be posted to India was only too happy to accept his offer. Unfortunately, Baird's agent was slow in completing the purchase and he was not gazetted until 1791; a delay that twice cost him the chance of becoming Commander-in-Chief of the British Army. This, combined with what he considered the unfair favouritism of Lord Richard Wellesley, the Governor General of India, for his younger brother Arthur, future Duke of Wellington, would rankle for the rest of his life.

War broke out again with Tippoo in 1792 and, returning to India, he was given command of a brigade of sepoys. The brigade went from success to success: first reducing the hill forts of Mysore, and successfully taking the important city of Pondicherry hardly firing a shot. By a strange coincidence, living among the residents of the city was a certain Monsieur Esteban Perichon, a French gentleman of noble birth who, fourteen years later, when living peacefully with his family in Buenos Aires, would suffer the misfortune of facing another British Army again under Sir David's command.

After these successes, Baird was sent to command the garrison at Tanjore where he promptly fell out with the Resident who on Lord Hobart, the Governor of Madras's instructions, was doing his best to swindle the Indians. Strongly disapproving of what he considered to be a sleazy affair, Baird refused to co-operate. Lord Hobart was furious but Baird was suddenly recalled with what remained of the 71st to England, and a clash between the two was luckily avoided.

Baird never reached England for, as the convoy sailed into Table Bay at the Cape of Good Hope, it was confronted by a mass of yellow flags flying from the masts of the ships at anchor in the harbour to signal a mutiny was in progress and, as the ships drew slowly closer, they could see the bodies of the dead mutineers hanging from the yardarms swinging to and fro in rhythm to the ocean swell.

Although Admiral Pringle had successfully suppressed the mutiny, Baird soon discovered it was not just the Navy that was up in arms; the whole colony was at breaking point due to the ineptitude of its Commander-in-Chief, General Sir David Dundas.

Called 'Old Pivot' by the young officers, Dundas was a soldier of the old school and had earned his nickname by insisting that his soldiers should use the Prussian system of defence when confronting the enemy in battle. This consisted of companies turning on fixed points called 'pivots.' In 1788, when still a Colonel, he had published a book called *The Principles of Military Movement*, advocating this rigid style of warfare which strongly criticised the Army's modern system of loose formations adopted from the tactics of the American colonists. These he insisted would be useless against a well-disciplined opponent and due to his military ideas and strict Prussian discipline, the Army's morale, already low, was now rapidly deteriorating. Fearing a serious revolt, Lord Macartney implored Baird to stay and calm the situation down, and as a bribe offered to promote him to the rank of Major General.

The offer was tempting, but Baird hesitated to accept it as Dundas was a friend from his Scottish days, and he felt it only correct to obtain his consent before accepting Macartney's offer. As the General was at present on an expedition up country, he realised the matter was of the utmost urgency and agreed to assist the Governor as best he could.

It was now that David Baird showed his ability as a leader, and quickly brought the situation under control. First by making himself President of the waiting courts-martial, which enabled him to deal diplomatically and fairly with the officers, and then by ordering a parade ground to be built on which he soon had his soldiers drilling. This not only had the advantage of keeping the men occupied and distracting them from any thought of mutiny, but also of keeping 'Old Pivot' happy on his return from the outback watching the soldiers practice his complicated manoeuvres.

Time passed quickly at the Cape, and after three successful years the War Office confirmed his rank of Major General and ordered him to return to India. However, on arriving in Madras he was furious to find that he had been given command only of the first European Brigade, instead of a division as his rank demanded.

It was the age-old problem. Too many Generals and not enough soldiers, but what galled him most was that the Governor General had given his brother, Colonel Arthur Wellesley and Baird's junior, the important command of the Nizam's Army, which by right and seniority should have been his.

In 1799, the siege of Seringapatam began, which was planned and executed in the traditional manner. Parallels were dug; batteries mounted; mines laid, and the walls continually bombarded until a breach was finally made. Then, as soon as it was dark, Baird and the storming party slipped silently into the forward trenches where they lay hidden until one o'clock in the afternoon – the hottest hour of the day, when hopefully the Indians would be asleep. They leapt from their trenches; sprinted a hundred yards under intense fire across open ground; forded the River Cauvery; scaled a wall, and traversing a ditch reached the breach. In less than seven minutes, British colours were flying over the ramparts of Seringapatam, and Tippoo Ali was dead.

The spoils of war were magnificent. A thousand guns taken and over £1,000,000 in cash, which still left plenty of loot to keep the victorious soldiers happy. Writing to her brother in England, Henrietta Clive declares, 'The plunder of Seringapatam is immense. General Harris will get £150,000. Two of the privates of the 74th have got £10,000 in jewels and money. The riches are extraordinary. Lord Clive has got a very beautiful blunderbuss that was Tipu's, and much else at Seringapatam. Some soldiers have got 20,000 pagodas; some have 10,000 pagodas, and one a large box of pearls…There was a throne of gold, which I am sorry to say they are breaking into pieces and selling by parts. Lord Mornington has presented me with one of the jewelled tigers from the throne.'

After suffering three and a half years at the sadistic hands of the Tiger of Mysore, revenge must have felt sweet and was probably the reason why Baird had volunteered to lead the storming party, as it was most unusual for so senior an officer to take on such a dangerous command.

After his success, Baird took some well-deserved leave but on his return was furious to find that Wellesley, who had temporarily taken over his command while he was away, had been given the Governorship of Seringapatam. After leading his successful attack, Baird not unnaturally felt the position should have been his, as not only was he senior to Wellesley (who was only a Lt Colonel), but the future Duke of Wellington had been in command of the reserve and therefore had taken little part in the engagement. Baird indignantly complained to General Harris that the appointment was grossly unfair but the General remained unmoved. He was probably right as he needed someone to win the support of the defeated Indians and show them some sympathy, which after suffering three years of torture and imprisonment at their hands, Baird was unlikely to do.

Lord Richard Wellesley, the Viceroy and Wellington's elder brother, who a contemporary once described as, 'A cross between an Irish potato, and a Spanish Hidalgo' recalled Baird to Calcutta and despite his angry remonstrance gave him a subsidiary command at Dinapore. It was here that the disgruntled Scot heard the news of Sir Arthur's appointment to the lucrative command of an important expedition to Mauritius without even being asked to relinquish his Governorship of Seringapatam. Baird, incensed, vehemently complained to the Viceroy that this was grossly unfair and a heated correspondence began, which ended by Lord Wellesley reluctantly placing Baird in command of the expedition, whose destination had by now been changed to the Red Sea.

Way back in October 1800, the British Cabinet had given Admiral Keith instructions to prepare an expeditionary Army of 17,000 men to drive Napoleon out of Egypt. This force under the command of General Sir Ralph Abercromby had now arrived there and, anxious for the operation to be a success, the strategists at Horse Guards decided that a two-pronged attack should be launched on Cairo. Hurriedly sending dispatches to India they ordered Baird to embark with 3,000 men, and land them on the Red Sea coast of Egypt and from there cross the desert, sail up the Nile, and attack Cairo from the south.

Here in the Red Sea, the three officers responsible for the capture of Buenos Aires came together for the first time. Baird and Beresford were already waiting in Jeddah when Popham arrived from India with orders from Lord Wellesley to transport the expedition up the Gulf to Kosseir. These unfortunately were contrary to those of his superior, Admiral Blankett on station, who ordered Popham to land the Army at Suez. An angry dispute began between the two naval officers as to whose orders should be followed and only Blankett's death at sea a few months later saved Sir Home from severe repercussions from the Admiralty.

Furious at being placed in such a difficult position, he wrote a long report to Lord Wellesley complaining bitterly about the confusion, and strongly suggesting that in future it should be defined as to the precedence in which orders should be obeyed, a point later to feature prominently at his court martial after the disaster in Buenos Aires.

Popham and Baird got on well together and the General was greatly impressed by Popham's ship-to-shore signalling system. He was likewise grateful when the Captain generously offered a complement of seamen to accompany his soldiers across the desert and ferry them up the Nile to Cairo.

Once the men and supplies were safely landed, Baird ordered Beresford and his Brigade to lead the Army on the long march across the desert, and the nightmare began.

It was the middle of summer: no maps, supplies nonexistent, the water containers began to leak, and the Commissariat continually broke down. Only Beresford's determination, Adjutant General Auchmuty's ingenuity, and Baird's leadership enabled the Army to reach Cairo, only to find that the city had fallen into British hands on the same day that they had left Kosseir. Their dreadful ordeal had been for nothing, but the magnificence of the Indian Army's uniforms greatly impressed the Egyptians and the march across the desert caught the romantic fancy of the English public. Catchpenny lives of Baird with bad pictures and harrowing accounts of his imprisonment by Tippoo Sahib circulated in the British press, and he, Auchmuty, and Beresford were hailed as national heroes.

The fall of Alexandria three months later brought the campaign to a close, and with the French no longer a threat in Egypt Baird was ordered back to India and given command of a division. His stay was short, as his patience finally ran out at the start of the Mahratta war when Arthur Wellesley yet again was placed over him. Realising he would never leapfrog the Governor General's brother, he resigned his command and in 1804 departed for England.

His journey home was not uneventful, as crossing the Bay of Biscay a French privateer captured his ship, but luckily a British frigate retook her before they reached France. Nevertheless, Baird had given his word of parole to the French Captain and was honour bound to wait until an exchange had been arranged with an enemy officer of equal rank before returning to active service.

Fortunately, at the time the French General Morgan was in British hands; an agreement was quickly negotiated, and, promoted to Lieutenant General in 1805, he was given command of an Army stationed off Cork where he, Popham, and Beresford came together again, bound on an expedition that would change the future of South America.

SIX

WILLIAM CARR, 1st VISCOUNT BERESFORD

'EL TUERTO, THE ONE-EYED ONE'

William Carr Beresford, future Marshal of the Portuguese Army, and last of the triumvirate involved in the capture of Buenos Aires, was the son of George de la Poer Earl of Tyrone, soon to become the first Marquis of Waterford. Born on the wrong side of the blanket in 1767, his mother's name is unknown but it was probably Carr, as this was the name added to Beresford. Writing to his friend Miss Orde on 24 August 1817, referring to William and his brother John de la Poo's (presumably Poer) antecedents, that well-known gossip Thomas Creevey declares,

'They are still ignorant of who their mother was, or whether they had the same. But from the secrecy upon this head and from their being sent from Ireland, and above all from Lady Waterford having seemed always to show more affection to them than to her own children, there is a notion that they were hers before her marriage!'

Only a few years after William's birth, the Earl made a brilliant marriage to Elizabeth, only surviving child of Henry Monk of County Wicklow and Lady Isabella Bentinck, daughter of the first Duke of Portland and reputed to be one of the richest heiresses in London. Mrs Delaney, a great friend of the Dowager Duchess of Portland, shrewdly notes in her diary,

'Weddings are going forward some wise, some otherwise. Miss Monk Lady Bell's daughter is to be married to the Earl of Tyrone… She is much commended for good nature, and not wanting in sense. No beauty between them but very good fortune, and as it will fix them in this country I think it will be agreeable to all parties.'

The marriage proved fruitful for, as well as being a popular man about town, the Earl was also a prolific breeder who would not only have four daughters and four sons by her Ladyship (one of whom became a bishop) but also for good measure sire another illegitimate offspring.

Owing to the example set by the Royal Dukes and their numerous bastards, Georgian society was tolerant of the by-blows of the aristocracy and the Earl behaved correctly by accepting William as his son, along with keeping an eye on his future career. Even so, William's childhood must have been hard, with a father who, having achieved such a successful marriage to so young a bride, saw little of his son, preferring the glittering life of London society to that of his faraway Irish estates.

William and his brother were sent at an early age to be educated at two unfashionable schools in Catterick Bridge and York, and on reaching seventeen the Earl enrolled William in the French Military Academy at Strasbourg to prepare for a military career. While still away in France, he bought him an Ensign's commission in the 6th (The First Warwickshire Regiment), which William joined on his return from Strasbourg, and the following year in 1785 sailed with them to Nova Scotia.

The American War of Independence had ended only two

years earlier, and Canada was now populated with a large number of American exiles who remained staunchly loyal to the Crown in the optimistic hope that the Treaty of Versailles would founder and the King would send an Army to regain their possessions.

Raised on an Irish estate, Beresford was a keen sportsman and an unfortunate incident occurred on his arrival in Canada, when a brother officer accidentally peppered him out shooting. This cost him the sight of his left eye and would later lead to the Argentines nicknaming him '*El Tuerto*' (the one-eyed one), when the Governor of Buenos Aires.

Shooting accidents at the time were not uncommon and although undoubtedly an expert in the handling of artillery, the Emperor Napoleon was equally renowned as being a dangerous shot. Swinging wildly through the line one day at a '*grand battu*' at Fontainebleau, the Emperor shot Marshal Massena in the eye, and in the words of A.G. MacDonnell,

'Napoleon with characteristic readiness blamed the accident on his next door neighbour, Marshal Berthier, who with characteristic subservience accepted the blame, while Massena who lost his eye with characteristic tact accepted the transference of the blame.'

English shoots were not much safer and, writing to her mother, Georgiana the Duchess of Devonshire in 1809, Lady Harriet Leveson-Gower reported that her husband, Lord Granville Leveson-Gower (uncle of the Major General who two years earlier had attacked Buenos Aires), 'Out shooting was a menace to his neighbours!'

Although a handicap, the loss of sight in one eye in no way hindered Beresford's military career, for returning to England four years later in 1790, he was promoted to the rank of Lieutenant in the 16th (The Royal Anglian Regiment)

and the following year to Captain (unattached). He did not have long to wait for a regiment, as in the spring of 1793 he was gazetted to a company of the 69th (The South Lincolnshire Regiment) who were about to sail to the West Indies.

This posting was very unpopular, as soldiering in the Caribbean was extremely unhealthy and many died from fever or tropical diseases. The annual mortality rate of the Army in the West Indies at the time was fifteen per cent and after three and a half years in Jamaica, the British Army had lost over 3,500 troops without any of them firing a shot. Out of the thousand and eight men of the 79th (Royal Liverpool Volunteers) stationed in Kingston, only eighteen survived to return to Liverpool, Major Thomas Stanley, brother of the Earl of Derby, among them. He died exclaiming against the Ministry in the bitterest of terms, 'For sacrificing him to the inclemency of an infernal clime, and was vexed at not dying by a ball in the field, rather than by a putrid fever on his bed'.

Luckily for Beresford the posting never took place, for just as the regiment was about to board their ship, war was declared with France and, instead of sailing for Jamaica, William and his company were sent to act as marines on board the *Britannia*, the hundred-gun flagship of Vice Admiral Hotham, second in command of the Mediterranean fleet, which immediately upped anchor and sailed for Toulon.

On 2 June 1793, France was in turmoil for having expelled the Girondins from the Convention, the Jacobins and Robespierre and Les Montagnards (the Mountain) now held the reins of power and, hurriedly leaving Paris, the majority of the defeated Girondins fled south to Lyons, Marseilles, and Toulon where they threatened to raise an army against the Capital. Hearing this, the Committee of

Public Safety immediately sprang into action and the well-named 'Terror' began in earnest.

Toulon, to begin with, escaped the mass executions taking place in Lyons, where the guillotine was working so efficiently that thirty-two heads were severed every twenty-five minutes. This rate lasted for only a short time, as thanks to perseverance and a hard week's practice, the executioner satisfactorily increased the number to twelve heads every five minutes. 'Le rasoir national' was working so rapidly that the citizens living in the streets around the *Place Terreaux* angrily complained to the authorities that the blood overflowing from the drainage ditch beneath the scaffold was flooding their cellars and ruining the contents.

Not just the guillotine was working overtime. Mass shootings were taking place on the *Plaine de Botteaux*, where as many as sixty prisoners were roped together in single file and economically blown to pieces by a single cannon ball. Those unlucky enough to survive, the soldiers carefully polished off with their sabres and bayonets, and the rabid Jacobin Joseph Chalier ranted, 'Nine hundred victims are needed as *La Patrie* is in peril.' Chalier was right, but not just *La Patrie* was in danger, every citizen and citizeness now feared for their lives.

Therefore, it was not surprising that the Governor Baron d'Imbert and the citizens of Toulon gave Admiral Hood and the British fleet a rapturous welcome on their arrival at the end of May. Disembarking from their ship, Beresford and his marines, with drums beating and colours flying, marched off to strengthen the town's garrison and man strategic points along the city's wall to the enthusiastic cheers of the watching crowd.

Despite the timely arrival of the British troops, the defence of Toulon was doomed to failure, for six months later a large

Republican Army arrived at its gates and seizing the surrounding forts began bombarding the city into submission.

This fierce and lengthy barrage was planned and executed by a yet unknown young artillery officer whose name was about to become famous, as it was Napoleon Bonaparte's first battle and it was purely by chance that he happened to be there.

Civil war had broken out a year earlier on the island of Corsica and, after ransacking the Bonaparte properties, the rebels declared the family outlaws. Hurriedly gathering up her numerous children *Madame Mere* fled to the mainland and Napoleon was in the process of settling them in Marseilles when he heard the news of the British fleet's arrival at Toulon. Eager to show off his prowess in battle he immediately offered his services to General Jean Carteau, the commander of the advancing Army, who gave him a free hand to organise the artillery.

On 17 December 1793, in pouring rain, Napoleon at the head of 2,000 men attacked the Toulon fort. The fighting was fierce, and the future Emperor was lucky to escape having his left leg amputated when his horse was shot from under him and a British sergeant bayoneted him in the thigh.

After a desperate rear-guard action, the French finally drove the British back onto their waiting ships and began to sack the city. Soaring high above the city, the towering flames quickly turned Toulon into a roaring inferno and panic-stricken soldiers, civilians, and screaming children scrambled for the safety of the boats. Hundreds drowned in the fight for survival, and running from quay to quay the British sailors desperately tried to destroy the twenty-two French ships of the line anchored in the harbour.

Over fifteen thousand royalist refugees crammed the

holds of the overloaded ships, fully aware of what fate awaited those that remained behind. Despite their frantic endeavours, thousands of men, women, and children were left behind to face the avenging Revolutionary Government and be shot or guillotined in the glorious name of 'Liberté, Egalité, and Fraternité'.

Once he had re-embarked as many men as possible, Lord Hood and the fleet headed for Corsica where he was joined by Sir John Moore with reinforcements from Gibraltar. Now with all the supplies he needed, His Lordship disembarked the Army and proceeded to conquer the island. Beresford and his marines led the main advance and after successfully storming the tower of Martello for which he would later receive his Brevet Majority, he successfully captured Bastia with the aid of Captain Horatio Nelson, who lost an eye spying out the forward batteries. Calvi was quickly taken and in August 1794 San Fiorenzo fell, bringing the campaign to a successful conclusion.

Beresford returned to England where he was mentioned in dispatches by Lord Musgrave, promoted to Lieutenant Colonel, and given command of the 126th the Royal Waterford Regiment raised by his father on his Irish estates. Consisting of 500 privates, 32 sergeants, 30 corporals, and 22 drummer boys, this Regiment survived for only a short time before the War Office broke it up, but he had not long to wait for another, as the following year he was given command of the 88th (The Connaught Rangers). Unfortunately, this too was broken up, but this time by the forces of nature and not the Generals at Horse Guards.

Crossing the Atlantic to join up with Sir Ralph Abercromby and his expeditionary force struggling to re-conquer the West Indies, the transport ships of the 88th were struck by a ferocious typhoon called 'Christian's storm' after the Admiral, which scattered them to every point of the compass. Blowing one company straight through the Straits of Gibraltar into the Mediterranean, it dispersed the others into little groups across the Atlantic Ocean to limp back over the coming months into different ports along the English coast. Only two companies actually reached Jamaica, and not until three years later in 1797 did the regiment finally come together again in Jersey, where they remained in St Ouen's Barracks until 1800, when the War Office ordered them to sail to India.

After a brief stay in Madras, the men of the 88th re-embarked onto the transport ships *Panther* and *Fancy* at Bombay and sailed up the Persian Gulf to join Sir David Baird and his expedition waiting for them at Kosseir. After their long journey, the men were in poor shape and suffering from a strange infection called 'worm in the leg' but overcoming this debilitating disease and the rough passage they crossed the desert, and fourteen days later as already recounted sailed up the Nile to attack Cairo.

His achievement in successfully leading the Army across the Arabian desert brought Beresford well-deserved fame. Promoted to Brevet Colonel, he remained in Egypt for the next two years as Commandant of Alexandria and returned to England with the evacuated Army and a great military reputation. This was about to increase as after successfully putting down an insurrection in Ireland, he set sail with Sir David Baird's expedition to capture the Cape of Good Hope, which would lead to his most famous action of all, the capture of Buenos Aires.

One-eyed and ginger-haired, William Carr Beresford was a stocky determined officer who exuded energy. The Duke of Wellington would openly maintain 'He was the ablest man in the Army' and in later years attempting to describe

Marshal Soult, His Lordship declared, 'Soult is a big man, very tall, and large like Marshal Beresford.' The Right Honourable Wilson Croker, founder of the Athenaeum and *Quarterly Review*, refers to him, 'As a good fellow and honest soldier,' while Mrs Delaney thought him, 'A man of more intrinsic worth than he appears to be.' Not everyone felt the same, as Thomas Creevey who obviously disliked him, scathingly remarks in his journal, 'He is a low looking ruffian with damned bad manners.' The truth lay somewhere in between.

SEVEN

THE CAPE OF GOOD HOPE

In August 1805, Baird's expedition set off on its long voyage to the Cape and reached Madeira a month later. The journey had been far from pleasant, and Lt Colonel Fletcher Wilkie declares in his recollections, 'We approached its lofty shores under the influence of extreme thirst, as aware that we should visit the island we had not laid in any white wine. Our beer and porter had all been wasted or burst and latterly as we got into warmer weather, we had no beverage but strong port wine and water that had been seven months in the transports. This we were obliged to punish with whisks to flog the offending hydrogen out of it, and to hold the nose when in the act of deglutition. It may be easily imagined with what avidity we gazed on the clear running streams when we got ashore and drank Madeira and water by the bucket and devoured grapes by the bushel.'

After replenishing his ship with fresh victuals and water, Popham sent Captain Donnelly and the *Narcissus* on to the Cape of Good Hope to spy out the enemy's strength and find a suitable landing place where the Army could safely disembark. Secrecy was still of the utmost importance, and in the event of encountering any foreign ships on the way, the Commodore gave Donnelly special permission to fly false colours to disguise his intentions.

This was a popular deception at the time as, due to continually changing hands, most ships were difficult to identify. Shape and construction gave little clue to their actual nationality, or of those on board, a problem that equally applied to forts and ports. News of their fall was often slow to be received, as happened after the fall of Toulon when, despite the Royal Navy leaving a screen of ships around Toulon bay to warn friendly vessels that the French were in control of the city, the transport ship of the 52nd, with all Colonel John Moore's baggage on board, missed them. Seeing the British flag flying over the ramparts of Toulon, it sailed into the harbour straight into the hands of the waiting French. The future General was most upset by this disaster, as he not only lost all his uniforms but, more annoyingly, an irreplaceable pair of boots, newly made for him by his expensive London shoemaker.

It soon became apparent that Madeira was incapable of producing sufficient stores to revictual the convoy so, in October, the Commodore ordered the convoy to weigh anchor and head for San Salvador (today's Bahia) on the coast of Brazil where provisions ought to be more abundant.

The weather was stormy, the sea rough, and the voyage began badly, when the transport ships *King George* and *Britannia* ran aground on the San Rocas reef. Two men were lost overboard but a woman who had given birth that morning was fortunately saved. Brigadier Yorke in command of the Artillery was not so lucky, as unwilling to lose a box of guineas carefully hidden in his cabin, he attempted to go below to save them. In the process of being lowered down he missed his footing, and falling into the sea was instantly devoured by the swarm of voracious sharks that perpetually circled around the ships waiting to feed on such unexpected delicacies.

Apart from this unfortunate incident, the fleet safely reached Bahia and began replenishing the stores. Including, much to Colonel Fletcher Wilkie's relief, 'sixty six pipes of sound port at only £24 a pipe.'

The Portuguese inhabitants of Bahia were delighted to see the convoy and, giving it a rapturous welcome, quickly doubled the price of everything on offer in their shops. Even the port's pilot got carried away by the potential gains to be made from its providential appearance and, plunging headlong into the commercial affray, opened up a grog shop. His shrewd alcoholic venture proved a sound investment, as by the time the fleet left Bahia he had made well over £5,000 profit.

Due to the success of his popular product, or perhaps because of it, the sailors encountered a certain amount of friction from the local boatmen and a serious brawl looked in the offing. To avoid a dangerous confrontation, the Brazilian soldiers were hurriedly sent for, but the mood quickly changed when on their arrival it was discovered that their cartridge pouches were crammed full of maize instead of powder and shot and, apart from a few black eyes and a number of sore heads, little damage was done to Anglo-Brazilian relations.

These boatmen were dangerous characters who needed careful watching. Major Gillespie warns future visitors to Bahia to avoid mingling with them after sunset, 'As they were consummate robbers'. He sinisterly declares,

'Beware of the boatmen who may carry you afloat after dark. Always be armed with small pistols and show these fellows that you are so, which will induce their fidelity from fear. Otherwise they may shape their course in the opposite direction and if superior will unrelentingly murder you for your imagined property, as happened to some cadets from India who being defenceless they assassinated in the most barbarous manner.'

To establish friendly relations with the town's populace, Dr Emerson, an excellent musician and a member of the medical staff, offered to play the organ in one of the city's many churches. After some hesitation, the authorities accepted his offer and a day and location was duly arranged. To everyone's relief, his recital passed off smoothly until the end, when carried away by his performance the patriotic doctor raised the roof by closing with a magnificent rendering of 'Britons, Strike Home!'; 'Rule Britannia' and 'God save the King' to the delight of the British visitors and astonishment of the Brazilian congregation.

When the news reached Buenos Aires of the sudden appearance of a British battle fleet's arrival in San Salvador, panic seized the people. The alarm was raised and rumours quickly spread through the cafes and bars that a British invasion force was on its way to sack the city. Relative calm was only restored with the arrival in port on 2 January of the Portuguese ship *Espiritu Santo*, whose Captain, Francisco de Paula, assured the nervous citizens that he had left Bahia a month earlier, and had seen no sign during his voyage of any enemy fleet. The alarm was over; life returned to normal, and the relieved citizens rightly concluded that the enemy convoy was on its way to India or the Cape of Good Hope.

Having replenished their ships with water and victuals, General Baird and the British convoy left San Salvador on 4 January 1806, and after an uneventful journey reached the Cape of Good Hope and anchored off Robben Island. Robert Fernyhough, a Captain of Marines, describing their arrival in a letter to his brother declares,

'We now made preparations for our embarkation, fired guns, and hoisted the English colours in a broad hint to the enemy of our errand. This was quickly taken as the town appeared in great confusion and we saw parties of cavalry riding in every direction.'

Next morning as soon as it was light, General Baird set

off in a small boat to reconnoitre the mainland and, despite a strong breeze blowing, the Highland Brigade, the 71st, 72nd, and 93rd Regiments began disembarking into lightweight boats ready to make a landing. However, the wind grew stronger as the day progressed and they were forced to return to the safety of their ships.

The blustery weather continued all the following morning but in the afternoon conditions began to improve, and Baird decided to make a landing at Leopards Bay. This he successfully achieved as there was little opposition, and the only casualties were thirty-six Highlanders of the 93rd who, weighed down by their heavy knapsacks and weapons, drowned when their landing craft capsized in the roaring surf. Captain Fernyhough also had difficulty landing, and plaintively writes,

'It is astonishing to me how we did land through such a tremendous surf … the nearest point we could get to the shore was forty or fifty yards so we were obliged to wade that distance up to the middle before we could reach it. I was completely ducked for in getting out of the boat, a sea came and dashed me over the head. To my great astonishment, I found an excellent pistol spoiled and all the ammunition useless.'

Over the following days, Baird's soldiers easily overcame General Janssens's 2,000 mixed contingent of French, Dutch, and native soldiers, who despite fighting bravely, were no match for Baird's professional Army. Mr Thomas Tennant, a settler in the colony and a close friend of General Janssens, helped to negotiate the terms of surrender and on 18 January 1806, the capitulation of Cape Town was duly signed. This agreed that the Dutch and French troops should be allowed to return to Europe but the Waldeckers (a troop of mercenaries from Arolsen) were imprisoned in the Fort, and given the option of changing sides and joining Baird's Army. Commenting on this agreement, Lt Colonel Fletcher Wilkie cynically writes,

'With the pleasing prospect of remaining incarcerated there for all the war, unless they volunteered into British regiments. Of the two evils, they chose the least and entered into the British regiments. They were promised a bounty of twenty dollars on enlisting but at the time, there was a scarcity of money at the Cape and this condition could not be fulfilled. Some thinking they were deceived, while others disliking the way they had been obtained began to desert but were immediately taken and tried by a court martial, which sentenced the bunch to corporal punishment.

'This was not thought severe enough and it was pointed out that, when the next delinquents were caught, a severe example was requisite to check the growing disorder. The Court therefore sentenced six men to death, little expecting I believe that it would be enforced but to their surprise and that of the others, the whole six were shot that day, three at Cape Town, three at Simon's Bay and in this way desertion was certainly stopped!'

Thirty-six Chinese artillerymen and their six light guns also opted to join Baird's Army, and the General was delighted to enlist them, 'as they handled their weapons admirably.' The whole enterprise had been a huge success and the arrival of a ship from England bringing the splendid news of Lord Nelson's great victory at Trafalgar capped the new colony's victory celebrations.

Unfortunately, the ship arrived at an unpropitious moment, as the band happened to be playing at the time in the Dutch gardens in front of the Fort and, carried away by this exciting news, they picked up their instruments and rushed to the Governor's house and began playing patriotic tunes under the General's window. Their uninvited show of patriotism had an unexpected outcome, as Sir David happened to be dining with the Dutch General Janssens. Furious at this interruption, which he declared an insult to his guest, he immediately placed the bandmaster and his band under arrest, and to their mortification they were bundled off to the guardroom.

The good luck continued as a few days later, the French 48-gun frigate *La Volontaire*, hotly pursued by the *Raisonable* and *Narcissus*, came flying into Table Bay believing it to be still in the hands of the Dutch. Seeing her approach, the garrison and the ships at anchor in the harbour immediately ran up the Dutch flag, and Robert Fernyhough triumphantly writes,

'As soon as she came into range, we opened our ports; hauled down the Dutch colours; hoisted the English ensign; showed our broadside, and ordered her to strike her colours.'

Confronted by this threatening fire-power, *La Volontaire* offered no resistance, and immediately surrendered. Her crew were in poor shape as over half of them were suffering from scurvy, including a number of British officers and men of the 2nd (The Queen's) and the 54th foot (The Norfolk Regiment) that the French had captured on their way to India. Not surprisingly, they were greatly relieved to be back in British hands, and after a few weeks' convalescence were sent back to England along with the French crew and badly wounded.

The capture of *La Volontaire* was to prove a controversial affair that would later lead to a vitriolic legal battle between Captain Donnelly and Popham over the question of prize-money. Donnelly claimed the major part should be his as he had driven her into port, but Popham insisted the whole fleet had been involved in the capture. Being the senior officer in command, he should therefore receive the major share. In the end, the court gave judgment in Donnelly's favour and Popham was forced to return £2,000.

On board *La Volontaire* was a naval lieutenant from Hamburg called Steitz who claimed to be an old acquaintance of Sir Home Riggs Popham and was delighted to see him again. He also gave him a free and candid report on the state of affairs in Europe, along with vital information on the escape of the French squadrons from their ports and their current position. The German generously lent the British sailors his uniforms to wear when boarding any enemy ship entering the bay, and confided to their astonishment that at one time he had been a spy in Scotland, where he had married a lady of good family and fortune with whom he still held an uninterrupted correspondence.

The whole expedition had been a great success and, with the Cape now safely back in British hands, Baird sent a dispatch to the War Office declaring that he had accomplished his mission, and the route to India once again lay open to British shipping.

EIGHT

FULL SAIL FOR SOUTH AMERICA

It was April, winter had arrived and Sir Home Riggs Popham was bored. Although a relatively easy affair, the capture of the Cape had not been nearly as lucrative in prize-money as the Commodore would have liked and, furthermore, all was quiet and there appeared little hope of this changing. Admiral Villemauriez and his fleet, rumoured to be carrying Jérôme Bonaparte on board, failed to materialise, and a newly arrived trading ship confirmed that Admiral Ganteaume and most of the French ships had either fled to the West Indies or returned to their home port of Brest.

The outlook looked decidedly bleak and, adding further to his despondent mood, the Commodore had been forced to move the fleet to False Bay as at this time of year the storms in Table Bay were so notorious that Lloyd's of London refused to insure any ship anchored there after 14 April.

With no sign or threat from the enemy, the prospect of spending winter in this desolate place filled Sir Home with gloom and he saw little point in remaining in this wretched bay, just to watch over Baird's Army comfortably ensconced in Cape Town's fort.

It was now that his thoughts returned to his discussions with Pitt, Miranda and Melville over the situation in South America, and the arrival of an American slave ship, *The Elisabeth*, gave further impetus to these wistful reflections. Especially when its Captain, Mr Wayne, assured the Commodore that he knew Buenos Aires well and gave him the following important information:

'Buenos Aires,' he emphatically announced 'was relatively undefended (true); Montevideo was lightly fortified (untrue); and the inhabitants of both cities were seething with discontent and longed to be free of their Spanish rulers (half true).' The garrulous Captain then went on to assure Popham that the citizens of Buenos Aires would welcome him with open arms and a force of no more than 500 trained soldiers would easily overcome any resistance, and to show he was 'not trying to mislead the British,' Wayne convincingly added, 'I would gladly be one of the 500, though I hope that you would not use my name improperly, as it may injure me greatly.' By this last remark, it was obvious that the Captain in no way wished to run the risk of losing his passport of neutrality.

It was the news Popham had been waiting for and his enthusiasm knew no bounds when Wayne further informed him that all the treasure from the Philippines and Potosi mines was at present lying in Buenos Aires's port, waiting to be shipped to Spain. As an afterthought, he also added, 'The surrounding countryside abounded with beef and corn.'

This put the icing on the cake, as Cape Town was running short of food and this last remark could help the Commodore obtain permission from Baird to embark on his long-desired enterprise to South America. Writing to William Marsden, Secretary of the Admiralty on 13 March 1807, explaining his reason for his future actions Sir Home declared,

'Mr Wilson, an eminent merchant in the City of London informed me before leaving town that Montevideo was defenceless and a thousand men could easily obtain possession of that place, which communication I made to Mr Pitt. Buenos Aires is an open town but after the Spanish troops were sent from the country, the natives would easily keep possession of it under an amelioration of their export and import duties, and some other heavy and oppressive taxes.' He continues; 'Under every kind of cross examination, a ship's carpenter who had just arrived in a Spanish vessel and had been eleven years in Montevideo adhered without variation to this account and further declared that there are not above two hundred and fifty cavalry and militia in the town. Moreover, its walls are in a ruinous state, and he believes the inhabitants would force a surrender without firing a shot. Another Englishman who had resided eight years in Buenos Aires, two of them spent as an interpreter in the Customs House confirmed all that had been said.'

Fuelled by his own report, and encouraged by Wayne's information, Popham decided the time had come to depart for South America, but first he needed General Baird's assent, who was now not only his senior officer but also the Governor General of the Colony.

Vexingly, Sir David showed little enthusiasm for the enterprise as by nature he was a straightforward soldier, who obeyed his orders which had been to capture and hold the Cape. Once this had been achieved and the town sufficiently garrisoned he was to send any surplus troops on to India and no mention had been made of invading the River Plate. Although a friend and admirer of Popham, the General had no inclination or intention of allowing his men to set off on some wild South American goose-chase, and firmly refused to give the Commodore his assent.

Undeterred, and using all his charm and every wile in his extensive repertoire, Sir Home attempted to convince the stubborn soldier to release the troops. He strongly warned him that his ships would certainly become unseaworthy if forced to winter in False Bay and pointed out that the River Plate could produce all the food that Cape Town so badly needed. But in spite these valid reasons, Baird remained stubbornly uncooperative and, in desperation, Sir Home fired his Parthian shot and announced that, if the General failed to give him any troops, he would set off and free the country with his own marines.

The arrow struck home and was tantamount to blackmail, as it placed the General in an awkward position: for should Popham's expedition fail he would be blamed for allowing it to leave, and if successful not only miss out on all the glory but be severely criticised for refusing to give the Commodore the support he had so strongly requested.

Faced with this nasty dilemma, Baird capitulated and reluctantly gave Popham 800 men of his own regiment the 71st to take with him, placing Beresford in command, whose judgement he trusted after the Egyptian campaign. As a further precaution he promoted Beresford to Major General, to hold equal rank with Popham, in the optimistic hope that this would allow him to have some brake on the Commodore's volatile actions. Then, according to *The Times* of 21 July 1807, being a canny Scot he made a secret agreement with Popham that should his venture be successful he and Popham would each receive two-fifths of the prize money, and the other fifth could go to Beresford and the Army.

Once his ships were stocked with sufficient victuals and supplies for their lengthy voyage, Popham and the convoy were about to leave when, at the last moment, six field pieces and some Light Dragoons of the 20th Regiment were loaded on board the ships. Commenting on their late arrival, Major Gillespie sarcastically writes, 'To this reinforcement, a regular staff was annexed changing its title into an expedition, instead of a predatory enterprise.'

Captain Fernyhough also had little doubt of what was at the

back of the Commodore's mind and, writing to his brother on 12 April, optimistically declares, 'Our destination is the Rio de la Plata. We calculate on making considerable prize money if we succeed in our attempt.' He was not the only one to believe the financial returns would be sensational; as, convinced he would make more money with Popham than from his previous business of slave trading, Captain Wayne sold his ship and joined the expedition.

A French prisoner of war was taken on board who alleged he was well acquainted with the layout of Buenos Aires, and knew precisely where the treasure would be stored. Although his veracity was open to doubt, the Commodore was not a man to leave even the smallest detail to chance, especially if it involved the whereabouts of gold and silver.

Finally, to give uniformity and a more imposing appearance to the expedition, Popham issued his disciplined seamen with red jackets, and combining them with their ship's marines announced that from now on this newly formed regiment should be called 'The Royal Blues.'

Baird's faith in Popham was definitely tentative as, before leaving, he gave Beresford strict instructions that if the mission failed he must immediately return to the Cape. The Commodore was quite capable of following in Sir Francis Drake's footsteps and embarking on a raiding expedition up and down the coasts of South America, and under no circumstances did Baird wish Beresford to be inveigled into such a venture or any other of the Commodore's wilder schemes.

On 14 April 1806, the men-of-war *Diadem*, *Raisonable*, *Diomede*, *Narcissus* and the gun brig *Encounter*, with four transport ships, sailed out of Table Bay, carrying on board: 36 officers, 922 men, 60 women (six to each company) and

40 children. With this force of less than a thousand men, Sir Home Riggs Popham confidently set off to conquer a country a third of the size of Europe.

NINE

ST HELENA AND THE RIVER PLATE

Once the convoy was out to sea a gale blew up and the troopship *Ocean*, with Major Tolley and 200 men on board, disappeared in the raging storm. They would later reappear off the coast of Rio, but at the time it was thought that the ship had sunk, depleting the force to little more than eight hundred men. Worse was to follow, for arriving at St Helena, Popham was greeted with the devastating news of Pitt's death and the consequent fall of Melville and the Tory administration.

It was a severe blow to his confidence, as Pitt had been both his friend and ally. Hurriedly putting pen to paper, he wrote a long letter to the new Government explaining the reason for his current action and strongly emphasising Cape Town's need for provisions. He then repeated his discussions with Pitt, Melville and Miranda over the situation in South America, and pointed out how beneficial the capture of the Philippine and Potosi treasure would be to the Exchequer. He then strongly stressed the advantage of opening up a new market in South America for the hard-pressed London merchants now suffering under Napoleon's blockade. Success, he declared, would greatly improve Miranda's scheme to free the continent from Spanish rule, but a distinct note of worry now enters the letter as he ends by assuring them,

'That if it should now be thought expedient to carry it into execution, I trust therefore the measure will be a popular one even if it should not exactly meet the policy of the present

Minister ... I trust I have judged worthy of the confidence of any Government.'

Despite the setback of Pitt's death and the change of Government, nothing was going to deter the Commodore from his venture and, to make up for the loss of the *Ocean*, the ever-plausible Sir Home successfully managed to cadge a further 276 troops out of Governor Patten, who would later be admonished for this generous deed.

The St Helena militia were not the best-trained body of men. Nevertheless, volunteers were easy to find as the soldiers had one aim in common: a strong desire to leave the island at the earliest opportunity. A disapproving Colonel Fletcher Wilkie wryly remarks, 'Sir Home wheedled the Governor out of some men. This was of little use, for it only served to get that good and kind hearted gentleman into a scrape and the vagabonds were of little value afterwards, as most of them deserted.'

Not everyone agreed with his amiable description of the Governor, for Sir Samuel Whittingham, arriving on the island six months later with Craufurd and the Light Brigade, scathingly calls him, 'A clever crotchety man who started a long and tedious discussion in the vain endeavour to prove to me the value of some very doubtful improvements in gunnery.'

Now victualled and reinforced, the convoy left St Helena on 21 May and, after a long, boring five-week journey arrived off Cape St Mary at the mouth of the River Plate. It was now the middle of winter and persistent rain pounded the decks. Hours were spent becalmed in swirling fog; food was running short and, by now, there was sufficient bread only for four more days. Moreover, supplies were difficult to obtain as the shoals and mud banks made it impossible for any ship drawing more than fifteen feet of water to approach within eight miles of the shore.

Lost one day in the middle of one these impenetrable white blankets, the lookout swaying in the crow's nest of the leading ship was startled to hear the approaching sound of raucous singing, and suddenly out the mist shot a small schooner flying a Portuguese flag. Seeing the *Diadem* looming up in front of her, she swerved violently to starboard and disappeared under the prow, nearly snapping her mast off on the warship's bowsprit.

A desperate chase ensued, and despite her frenzied attempts at evasion she was quickly captured, and all the members of this floating choir were discovered to be totally drunk. This included the pilot, who despite desperately trying to hide his nationality turned out to be a Scotsman called Russell.

When sufficiently sober, he was carefully questioned and, through a cloud of alcoholic fumes, they managed to decipher the exciting news that Buenos Aires was undefended, and better still the Philippine treasure train was lying in port waiting to be shipped to Spain. With obvious personal knowledge, Russell further declared that with the coming Feast of Corpus Christi, 'there would be a general scene of drunkenness in the city,' and disclosed that the Viceroy had just dispatched a detachment of troops to bolster the defences of Montevideo.

This was an important piece of information and Popham and Beresford immediately held a Council of War. Scrapping their original plan of first capturing Montevideo, they decided Buenos Aires should be the target, which proved a fortunate decision; Montevideo was well protected, as Sir Samuel Auchmuty would discover the following year.

In a long letter to the Admiralty explaining the reason for changing his plan, Popham writes, 'Montevideo has just been reinforced, whereas Buenos Aires lacks any defences, and furthermore its countryside is richer in provisions.'

He makes no mention in the letter of the Spanish treasure, but undoubtedly the drunken Scotsman's information concerning this was the reason why Sir Home overruled Beresford and changed the original plan of taking Montevideo first and Buenos Aires afterwards.

Slowly the fleet edged its way up the hundred-and-thirty-miles mouth of the River Plate, but the unremitting fog made navigation difficult and, under Russell's guidance, the *Narcissus* became marooned for twenty-four hours on the Chico Bank before she could be re-floated. The Scot was probably drunk at the time, as his consumption of alcohol was becoming a serious problem. But his knowledge of the river was greatly needed and from then on he was guarded night and day from the bottle. Keeping him sober proved a difficult task. Major Gillespie despondently writes,

'The acquisition of such a man at this time seemed to augur well, but his intellects were non-effective whenever he could have access to the bottle. An allowance was permitted him beyond common, and by a watch through the day over his motions as well as over his pillow throughout the night, he was debarred from excess after his propensity was known.'

The painstaking journey took over a fortnight to achieve and, when still twelve miles away from Buenos Aires, the food ran out. Faced with this dilemma, Beresford decided to land his Army at Point Quilmes, and as dawn broke on 25 June 1806 his troops transferred into lighter draught boats and braving the choppy water set off towards the shore. High waves made the landing hazardous, but no life was lost and, stranger still, no opposition was offered by a large group of Spaniards they could see standing on the top of a little hill about a mile away carefully watching their disembarkation. By counting the number of burning fires, it could be seen that this was a large body of men, but the Spaniards did not attempt to attack the beachhead, which was just as well as the heavy barges in the turbulent water were difficult to control, and to have attempted a landing under gunfire would have been little short of suicide.

By midnight, all the troops had landed and, marching his little Army inland, General Beresford bivouacked for the night at the foot of a small hill. The Spanish campfires could still be seen glowing in the distance, keeping the British outposts on the alert throughout the night, but the enemy showed no sign of taking any action and the only excitement came at dawn the next morning. Hearing the approach of galloping hooves, the sentries raised the alarm but to their relief this turned out to be a stampede of wild horses and not, as originally feared, a squadron of enemy cavalry. Apart from this unwelcome disturbance, the invasion was progressing surprisingly smoothly.

TEN

BUENOS AIRES AUTUMN 1806

The panic that had greeted the appearance of a British fleet in San Salvador slowly began to diminish, and life in Buenos Aires returned to normal. The bullfight season was in full swing; the theatre played to applauding audiences, and a happy crowd of thirsty customers crammed the brightly lit cafes and bars cheerfully imbibing Mendoza's heady wine.

Rumours still abounded of a coming invasion but these were little heeded, and seemingly unaware of any approaching danger the citizens continued with their daily activities in their customary peaceful fashion. The Royal Courts persisted in their investigations into contraband, and the Church and Administration continued their unrelenting battle over their powers of jurisdiction.

Overshadowing this return to normality, a perpetual thorn in the *Cabildo*'s side was the large number of alien ships lying at anchor in the harbour. Nevertheless, their existence was necessary, as due to its superiority at sea the British Navy instantly seized any merchandise travelling in a Spanish vessel. Without these foreign ships to transport their wares, it would be impossible to carry on trading and many merchants would inevitably go bankrupt, and the economy of both Buenos Aires and Montevideo severely suffer.

Ships from every nation crammed the port, and the brightly coloured flags of Portugal, Denmark, America and Holland fluttering gaily in the breeze gave the harbour a cheerful air of festivity. The docks were a constant scene of activity, as teams of coloured slaves precariously balancing heavy sacks of sugar on their backs weaved their way along the crowded wharfs to deposit them alongside the great chests of English and French cloth, and other contraband goods in the merchants' overflowing warehouses.

Crowds of foreign heretics swarmed the streets, whom the *Cabildo* strongly suspected of spreading revolutionary ideas such as freethinking, free trade, freedom of speech and that most pernicious demand of all – *independence*. The authorities considered the Anglo-Americans to be the most dangerous of these, and firmly believed they were British agents sent in disguise to spy out the city's defences.

Also attracting the *Cabildo*'s suspicion were the number of English residents already living in the city who had mostly been passengers on the *Lady Shore*. This ship had left London in 1792 with a contingent of five officers, seventy-two soldiers of the New South Wales Regiment, two males and sixty-eight women prisoners bound for the convict colony of Botany Bay. The voyage had started smoothly but, halfway across the Atlantic, three French prisoners of war who had been forcibly enlisted into the New South Wales Regiment started a mutiny. Killing the Captain, they seized control of the ship and, raising the French flag, changed course for Montevideo, where they claimed the ship to be a prize of war and demanded asylum.

At first, the authorities were highly suspicious of this unexpected interloper but, confronted by so many tearful members of the fairer sex, Latin gallantry came to the fore and after a lengthy enquiry the *Cabildo* graciously granted them permission to disembark, and hastily bundled them off to Buenos Aires. Many of the women made good marriages and became respectable citizens but others, to the annoyance of the Buenos Aires *Cabildo*, reverted to their previous

Argentina: The British Invasion of Buenos Aires, 1806

trade of being talented prostitutes, expert pickpockets and accomplished thieves. Good or bad, they now came under the suspicion of being subversive aliens.

On 25 May, the news reached Buenos Aires that a British Man-of-War had arrived off the coast of Santa Teresa, and had landed a naval officer and five sailors on a beach close to Montevideo. These were quickly taken prisoner but, in retaliation, the British warship HMS *Leda* turned her cannons onto the town and began bombarding the fortress. Having delivered this warning, Captain Honeyman, Commander of the ship, sent another landing party ashore under a flag of truce to negotiate his men's release. Unimpressed by the bombardment or the boat's white flag, Don Rafael Guerra, the Commander of the fortress, to the indignation of the watching English sailors promptly arrested this little party as well. For this blatant contravention of the Rules of War, the Governor and Viceroy would reprimand him. Their admonishment proved of little consequence, as Don Rafael paid scant attention to either. Instructing the ships in the harbour to be manned ready to repulse an attack he prudently ordered them to remain in port, as they were in no way strong enough to take on such a formidable opponent.

On quickly hearing of these alarming events, the Buenos Aires *Cabildo* begged the impressively titled Viceroy Don Rafael Nuñez Castillo Angulo Bullon Ramirez de Arellano, third Marquis of Sobremonte, to take some action, which he refused to do, declaring it was an isolated ship whose crew had landed only to search for water and provisions. He firmly assured the anxious citizens that they had absolutely no cause for alarm, as there was not the slightest question of the British launching an attack.

Now fifty-nine years old, the Marquis had started his

career as secretary to the Viceroy Vertis, who after a suitable time appointed him the Governor of Cordoba, a position he held for the next fifteen years until 1804, when the King appointed him the seventh Viceroy of the Rio de la Plata. Lacking leadership, courage or intelligence, Sobremonte was a typical example of the Spanish aristocrats under whose governance the Creoles were by now sick and tired; it only increased their demands for independence.

Despite all the Viceroy's efforts, the excitement continued to mount and reached fever pitch three days later, when a foreign ship was sighted off Atalaya Point. Still the Viceroy refused to take any action, and as sightings of British ships continued to increase, citizens became caught up in a flurry of terrifying rumours. But despite their repeated warnings the pig-headed Marquis obstinately refused to acknowledge them, although a report on the interrogation of the captured English prisoners had just arrived from Montevideo, confirming that the British were about to launch an invasion.

On 19 June, the Viceroy eventually capitulated to the *Cabildo*'s demands and reluctantly paid his soldiers. A sensible precaution, as their wages were long overdue and the men were becoming restless. He ordered the officers to report every day to the barracks half an hour before sunrise armed, with their horses saddled and ready for action, and then wrote a curt letter to Don Bernardo Velasco, the Governor of Asunción, requesting him to recruit a force of 350 men and dispatch them to defend Montevideo. Each man should be equipped with four horses and receive a salary of ten pesos a month from the day he left Asunción. As there was no mention of urgency in the letter, and the troops could not possibly reach Montevideo until the end of August, it was obvious the Viceroy still believed there was little danger of an attack. Finally, under pressure from the *Cabildo*, he reluctantly placed the militia on the alert.

By 24 June the city was in turmoil, as the attempt to arm the militia had resulted in utter confusion. The cannon balls had been lying in the fortress for years and failed to fit the cannons, while the rifles were in such a poor state it was dangerous to fire them. Only 300 troopers of the cavalry were operational, as those with horses had no saddles and those with saddles had no horses. The Army was untrained, undisciplined and unprepared, but still the Viceroy appeared impervious to the approaching danger, and to the despair of his staff steadfastly refused to believe the enemy had any intention of landing.

24 June 1806 was the birthday of Juan Manuel de Marin, the Viceroy's ADC and future son-in-law and, to celebrate this happy occasion, Sobremonte invited all his family to the theatre to watch a performance of the newly arrived comedy from Madrid, *El si, de las Niñas*. It was a glittering occasion and the cream of Buenos Aires society filled the boxes but despite the intrigues of the plot, the audience's eyes kept switching nervously between the stage and the Viceregal box in search of some sign of trouble. Their patience was eventually rewarded for, just as the play reached its dramatic climax, two mud-spattered officers burst into the Marquis's box to report that a British battle squadron had anchored off Point Quilmes and was in the process of disembarking an army of heavily armed soldiers.

Much to the irritation of the actors, the audience now became infinitely more interested in the drama being played out in the Viceroy's box than in their performance on the stage. But staring fixedly at the performers, the Marquis continued to watch the play and gave no orders for the Church bells to be rung or the alarm sounded and, at the end of the play, the worried audience returned to their homes scared of what disaster the dawn would bring.

They had every right to be, for at seven o'clock next morning three cannon shots blew the citizens from their beds to signal the enemy was advancing, and the Church bells began to peal furiously. Only now did the frightened Viceroy spring into action, and immediately evacuated his wife to Monte Castro (today Floresta) and next ordered the treasure to be dispatched to Lujan. Only then did he turn his thoughts to the defence of the city, to find that the majority of his troops were useless.

The infantry had little idea of how to load their rifles, let alone use them, and the cavalry at best were merely capable of sitting on their horses' backs. Now thoroughly alarmed, the Viceroy frantically dashed off letters to his commanders in the provinces, begging them to send him re-enforcements as quickly as possible. Summoning up sufficient courage, he ventured out of the Fort surrounded by his Cavalry escort and arrived at the Baracas Bridge, at the same time as Corporal Guanes and a platoon of weary soldiers.

The Corporal and his gallant little band of patriots had spent a long and tiring day driving a team of oxen pulling two cannons behind them from the Retiro (a large park about a mile away from the Fort) to the bridge. It had been a frustrating task, as the cannons repeatedly stuck in the mud, and he and his men arrived at the bridge bad tempered and exhausted to find the Viceroy deep in conversation with his staff. Noticing the soldiers standing to one side watching him, the Viceroy barked, 'Take those guns back Corporal they're not needed here!'

The order was too much for Guanes; losing his temper, he indignantly retorted, 'If they are not needed here then, either Your Excellency has lost the battle or betrayed us!'

'Arrest that man and shoot him,' screamed the infuriated Marquis.

'Go on,' replied the equally incensed Corporal, 'I'd sooner die than surrender without having fired a shot!'

Seeing the situation getting out of control, an officer hurriedly ran forward and, drawing his sword, placed it firmly on top of the corporal's bare head, growling under his breath 'Shut up little fellow or you'll give me no choice.' Two soldiers ran quickly forward and, seizing the struggling Corporal, removed him from Sobremonte's sight, to release him a few minutes later among the sympathetic soldiers of the Viceroy's bodyguard. It was an inauspicious beginning to the defence of Buenos Aires.

ELEVEN

THE INVASION

Dusk was falling as Beresford and his men made camp two miles away from the village of La Reducción. The Spanish fires could still be seen burning in the distance but a wide marsh separated the two armies, allowing both sides to pass a peaceful night. Waking early next morning, Major Gillespie looked out of his tent and, materialising out of the mist, saw:

'The enemy drawn up on the further extremity of a deep but verdant morass on a chosen flat rising abruptly many yards above our level like to the steep bank of a river. Nothing could be finer for a defensive position. Early on in the morning, several of their leaders upon steeds richly caparisoned and dressed in fine cloaks or ponchos came down to reconnoitre the borders of the swamp betwixt us, and from there subsequent confidence it may be presumed that they held our menace in derision.'

At first light the buglers sounded the reveille and, at eight o'clock, Beresford gave the order for the Army to advance. Pulling their heavy cannons behind them, his gunners began wading through the marsh and, after a lengthy struggle, managed to manoeuvre two six-pounders onto a ridge to enfilade the enemy's position and left two howitzers behind with the St Helena Infantry to guard the rear.

Seeing the British line preparing to advance, the Spaniards opened fire with a heavy cannonade, but their guns were hopelessly inaccurate, and the shots fell everywhere except on their allotted targets. Weathering this unsuccessful barrage, the Highlanders prepared to attack, and Robert Fernyhough writes,

'Observing this movement, General Beresford gave orders for the whole Army to advance which was promptly and cheerfully obeyed and first taking off our hats, we gave three cheers; the bagpipes of the 71st struck up, and the buglers sounded the charge.'

Kilts swirling, bayonets flashing, the screaming Highlanders hurled themselves at the Spanish line. Charging at the double, with his campaign equipment containing inner and outer sustenance on his back, an excited Captain Alexander Mackenzie fell into a deep hole and was heard loudly vociferating above the battle cries, 'Cut awa ma bag mon! FOR CHRIST'S SAKE CUT AWA MA BAG!'

The awesome spectacle of eight hundred skirted barbarians hurtling towards them, accompanied by the unearthly wail of pipes and Gaelic battle cries, proved too much for the untrained Spanish troops, and their line began to waver. Flourishing his sword above his head, Colonel Pedro d'Arze gallantly stepped forward and gave the order to retreat, and without a moment's hesitation his troops took to their heels and in one magnificent stampede ran as fast as their legs could carry them towards Buenos Aires.

'I ordered a retreat not a rout!' roared the infuriated Colonel as he ran puffing after them, and reaching the safety of the city was heard lamenting, '*Carajo!* (Shit) what will the women say?' Adding reflectively, perhaps to soothe his wounded pride, 'At least I have the satisfaction of being the last man to face the enemy'. Then, in a desperate attempt to defend his order to retreat, he exaggeratedly claimed that the enemy was at least 4,000-strong and he and his soldiers had been hopelessly outnumbered.

The Spaniards' next line of defence was at the Puente

Galvez and, having crossed the river, they began setting fire to the bridge. In the evening the Viceroy, surrounded by a large entourage of officers and aides, arrived to inspect them, and after finishing his inspection ordered the cavalry to accompany him back into the city, announcing that from now on they would come under his personal command. Although surprised by the order, the officers were not unduly worried as they presumed he intended to use them to attack the enemy's flank at first light the following morning.

Collecting up the cannons and regrouping his victorious soldiers, Beresford hurried after them and, as his men reached the Riachuelo, the rain ceased, the sky cleared, and the countryside looked beautiful in the evening sunshine.

Arriving at the river, Beresford took stock of his position and saw the wisps of smoke rising into the air further down the river. Quickly realising their significance, he immediately sent three companies of the 71st to stop the Spaniards from burning down the bridge. They arrived too late and, after half an hour of heavy firing from both sides, the men gave up the struggle and, returning to their comrades, found them camping along the water's edge.

The river was only thirty yards wide and as soon as it was dark a group of Popham's sailors slipped quietly into the water and swam across to the other side. Creeping quietly along the riverbank, they stumbled over some unguarded boats. Sliding them into the water they paddled silently back, and lashing them together constructed a pontoon bridge.

When they woke the following morning, the Spaniards found to their dismay that the British had crossed the river during the night and were now threatening to attack their flank. Having drawn up their line of defence with all the guns and trenches facing the river, they realised their position was untenable and, after only a few desultory exchanges of musket fire answered by a cannonade from the British, their resistance ended. Thoroughly demoralised, they pulled back into the city to seek further orders from the Viceroy, only to discover he had long since left Buenos Aires.

The Viceroy had in fact spent a long and sleepless night overseeing the departure of the treasure, which according to popular rumour contained 9,000 ounces of his own gold, and he and his 2,000-strong cavalry escort were now well on their way to join up with his wife in Monte Castro. However, before leaving, he gave Brigadier Jose Quintana, the commander of the Fort, strict instructions to offer no further resistance and to negotiate the most favourable terms of surrender as he could with the British General. These he insisted should go on for as long as possible to allow him time to reach Cordoba, where after raising an Army he would return and defeat the British invaders.

His order to surrender caused consternation among the Spanish troops for, faithfully obeying instructions, Brigadier Quintana firmly refused to open the gates of the Fort to Captain Murgiondo and his sturdy men, who had arrived hotfoot from the Punta Galvez. Furious at being barred from taking up a defensive position along the Fort's ramparts, Murgiondo sarcastically enquired, 'How the Viceroy could possibly have given such an order, when he hadn't even seen the enemy let alone knew the colour of their uniforms?'

After this sarcastic remark, an angry shouting match began, and Quintana angrily announced, 'Anyone disobeying the Viceroy's orders will be shot!' The threat had no success, the Captain continued to protest and the confrontation only ended when, ordered to hand over their rifles, his frustrated men hurled them on the ground smashing the stocks, leaving the broken pieces lying scattered in front of the Fort.

Following hard on the Spaniards' heels, Beresford and his little Army reached the outskirts of the city at around lunchtime, and halted. Sending for his ADC Lt Gordon, the General ordered him to enter the city under protection of a white flag and demand its surrender. He was to offer the garrison the honours of war and assure the authorities that the citizens' lives and belongings would be respected and, in return for these generous and civilised terms, the Spaniards must immediately hand over the city's treasure into his safekeeping.

His demands produced a serious problem as, without the Viceroy, no one had the authority to accept or decline. After much discussion, the responsibility finally fell on the shoulders of the reluctant *Cabildo*, who like most town councils were more accustomed to the formality of a lengthy discussion, followed by several rounds of votes, before actually reaching a decision.

Realising they had no alternative but to accept this position, the *Cabildo* hurriedly recruited Guillermo Pio White, an American smuggler from Boston who spoke Spanish fluently, to act as their interpreter to ensure they fully understood the British demands and ordered him to beg the General for more time to discuss the matter.

Their appeal fell on deaf ears as the British General dismissed their request outright, firmly declaring that there was no question of waiting any longer for an answer. His men were soaked to the skin and badly needed shelter. He assured them that their answer was immaterial as, no matter what they decided, he intended to enter the city before nightfall and it was merely a question of whether in peace or by the sword. On receiving this frightening reply the *Cabildo*, fully aware of the looting and rape that would undoubtedly take place should these skirted barbarians be permitted to run riot through the streets of the city, immediately capitulated.

At three o'clock in the afternoon of 27 June 1806, under a cloudy sky, Beresford and his triumphant little Army marched proudly down the Calle de la Residencia (today Defensa) with drums beating, colours flying and pipes skirling, into the Plaza Mayor. To give the impression their numbers were greater than they actually were the men marched well apart, and Major Gillespie at the head of his marines declares, 'Many of the balconies were filled with excited ladies waving handkerchiefs and clapping their hands.' While Robert Fernyhough notes, 'The gates were opened to us and our gallant little Army marched triumphantly into the city to be received by the Bishop and the clergy in their robes, as well as the civil authorities of the place'.

It was only now that the watching citizens realised that they had surrendered the city to an Army of less than 1,500 men, and Ignacio Nuñez, an eyewitness to the scene, writes with irony in his memoirs, 'The Viceroy arrived at Monte Castro to fall into the loving arms of the Vicereine, at the same time as the Viceroyalty fell into the loving arms of General Beresford.' Equally enraged, the indignant citizens sarcastically chanted a popular lampoon,

Al primer cañonazo de los valientes
disparo Sobremonte con los parientes!
As the first shot from the cannon sped,
Sobremonte and his family fled.

Then a young lawyer manning the bridge at the Punta Galvez, Manuel Moreno, declares,

'I saw many men in tears in the plaza crying at the disgrace that had befallen them. I too cried more than most at what took place at three o'clock on 27 June 1806, as I watched 1,580 Englishmen that had conquered my country take up residence in the Fort and other quarters of the city'.

The heavens opened; the rain came down in torrents, despair pervaded the city and, as if in sympathy with the inhabitants' mood, the temperature plummeted. Calm to begin with, this mood quickly turned to panic when the news broke that eighty-nine armed convicts had escaped from the Fort, and four lunatics had disappeared from the local asylum, which in the excitement of the moment had been left unguarded.

The streets were empty; the cafes closed as in darkened rooms, people discussed in hushed whispers the events of the day. Most of these conversations centred on the cowardly behaviour of the Viceroy, who had fled the city before a shot was fired. In his defence, those of a generous nature maintained it was wrong to expect too much from a man who in his entire career had never commanded a force larger than a bodyguard, let alone heard a shot discharged in anger.

Light was fading as Beresford and his men took possession of the Fort. This stood on the eastern side of the Plaza Mayor and the empty square seemed eerily silent, except for the strange sound of Gaelic words of command as the sergeants posted their sentries to guard its numerous approaches. And as night fell, little groups of shivering Highlanders could be seen huddled together at the entrance of the empty streets vainly seeking shelter from the freezing wind gusting down the narrow alleyways.

After seeing that their men were safely billeted, Major Gillespie and a small group of English officers set off to dine at Los Tres Reyes, a popular inn situated near the Fort where they were greeted by mine host, the affable Don José

Bonfillo, who politely welcomed them to his humble abode. Several Spanish officers were already sitting at tables eating a supper of bacon and eggs, owing to the inn having run out of beef and the market closed due to hostilities. No animosity was shown between the two adversaries, but the pretty young serving girl taking the English officers' orders looked grim-faced and nonplussed.

Fearing they were the cause of her ill humour, Major Gillespie hurriedly asked his interpreter to assure her that they intended to pay for their supper. This was not the reason for her anger as, banging the plates down in front of the embarrassed Spaniards, she angrily announced in a loud voice for the room to hear, 'Things would have gone differently if we the women of Buenos Aires had been fighting at the front, as we would have smashed the enemy to smithereens'.

Sir Home Riggs Popham, still aboard his ship anchored in the estuary, could scarcely control his emotion on receiving the news of Beresford's success. His gamble had far exceeded his wildest dreams and the casualties had been trifling: one man killed, one man missing, and thirteen wounded. For this negligible loss, a great city had been taken and a vast treasure would soon be safely in his hands. The prize money would be sensational!

TWELVE

BUENOS AIRES UNDER BRITISH RULE

At precisely nine o'clock the following morning, a twenty-one-gun salute rang out across the city, rattling the windows and setting off a chorus of dogs hysterically barking. Seconds later, a thunderous reply came rolling across the water from the ships at sea but, apart from this military fanfare, Buenos Aires remained silent as a tomb.

The streets were empty; the shops and cafes closed; and the normally bustling markets stood deserted. The city appeared devoid of life except for a few stray dogs sniffing optimistically for scraps, as they circled around the Highlanders warming themselves in front of some newly found braziers.

General Beresford, or the 'Governor of Buenos Aires' as he now preferred to be called, spent the morning in conference with the members of the *Cabildo* and the *Real Audiencia* (tribunal). The talks were running far from smoothly, owing to the General's constant demand for the city's treasure to be handed over. His repeated request cast a depressing shadow over the negotiations but, hard as the *Cabildo* tried to evade the subject, Beresford kept returning to it. Until losing his temper, he angrily announced the time for talking was over, and he would sack the city if they did not immediately hand the treasure over.

After delivering this frightening ultimatum he stormed out of the room and ordered his ADC, Captain Arbuthnot, to send Lieutenants Murray and Graham with thirty men of the 71st and a troop of 20th Light Dragoons to overtake the treasure train still wending its way along the muddy road to Lujan.

Shocked by this uncouth behaviour, the mesmerised *Cabildo* for several seconds sat in silence, but his threat to sack the city quickly brought them to their senses. Springing into action, they hastily dispatched a delegation with a letter to the Viceroy in Monte Castro demanding his help. This letter, dated 28 June 1806, clearly shows their disapproval of Sobremonte's behaviour for, although not actually criticising the Viceroy, the opening paragraph begins:

'Excelentisimo Señor

'Having been forced to surrender due to the lack of help or arms to resist, the Authorities now find the City in turmoil, as its so called forces have been useless and having done nothing have abandoned the city to the enemy invaders.'

It then goes on to beg the Viceroy to release the treasure and to ensure he fully understood the danger facing them, the *Cabildo* ordered the delegation to stress that, 'If this was not instantly carried out the British General would let his soldiers run riot through the streets and put the city to the sword'.

Although undoubtedly a coward, the Marquis was not a fool, and receiving this frightening ultimatum he immediately sent a messenger to Lujan ordering the treasure to be handed over to the British, rather naively adding the optimistic rider that it should remain in Buenos Aires. Hi rightly reckoned that the immediate loss of gold and silver could always be replaced, but rebuilding a city would be an infinitely more costly affair. Anyhow, he was confident that, once he had raised an Army in Cordoba, Buenos Aires and the treasure would soon be back in Spanish hands.

Not all of the citizens were un-cooperative and Beresford

found many of the foreign residents willing to assist him in the running of the city. Prominent among these was the American interpreter Guillermo Pio White, who was rumoured to have known Popham from his freebooting days, and the General gave him two important tasks. Firstly, supply the Army with provisions and secondly, find suitable accommodation where his officers could board.

Also seen permanently at the General's side were Thomas O'Gorman and his pretty wife Anita, who was the daughter of Don Esteban Perichon, the French gentleman that Baird had so rudely expelled from Pondicherry. Anita was renowned as being an accomplished flirt with a penchant for men in power. Her Irish husband O'Gorman, or the 'Captain' as he liked to be called, was a well-known fraudster whose claim to fame had occurred the previous year when he had successfully swindled a number of important Buenos Aires merchants out of a large sum of money.

It had been a very unsavoury affair. Trade with England, although officially illegal, was still common practice, so when the 'Captain' offered to load a ship full of their cargo and sell it in London several merchants unwisely accepted his offer. It proved an expensive error, as on its arrival in London his brother immediately auctioned it to pay off their innumerable creditors, and the 'Captain' regretfully informed his clients that His Majesty's zealous revenue officers had seized their goods. He explained there was nothing he could do unless they advanced him further funds to keep the greedy customs officers happy, but not surprisingly the merchants refused to do so, and a legal battle began that continued for the next ten years.

Aided by his intimate knowledge of the city, Guillermo White carried out Beresford's orders efficiently and found the officers comfortable quarters in the wealthier merchants' houses. These dashing young men dressed in their scarlet uniforms and full of the latest gossip from fashionable Europe caused quite a stir among the ladies, some of whom secretly admitted they found them rather more entertaining than their worthy but stolid boyfriends or husbands.

Moreover, Beresford's soldiers were well behaved and discipline was strict. Any soldier caught stealing was promptly flogged, and now that the threat of loot and rape had vanished the city returned to normal. Parties, routs, and balls were quickly organised to which all the English officers were invited and Major Gillespie, who attended most of them, was much taken by the ladies but not so much by the heating system of their houses.

'The fair sex' he declared, 'are interesting not so much from their education than a pleasing address, facetious conversation, and the most amiable temper. It was winter when we were masters of Buenos Aires during which *tertulias* (parties) and dances were given every evening at one house or another. Thither all the neighbouring females resorted without ceremony in their long cloaks, and when not engaged they drew close together seemingly to warm each other on a long form, as there were no chimneys. Fire was only used in extreme cold being brought into the room in a *brazero* that is placed near to the feet over which a stranger never fails to experience a headache from the fumes of the charcoal. No refreshment was offered on these occasions to which few were specially invited, and all even if but slightly introduced were welcome. Waltzes were the vogue and the piano accompanied by the guitar, which all play was the music. No other matron was present, except that of the house who was their sole protectress and everyone departed at ten at night'.

As soon as the fighting was over Sir Home Riggs came

ashore to congratulate Beresford on his success and, more importantly, personally count the treasure which far exceeded his expectations. The revenue alone from the Royal Treasury, the Company of the Philippines, the Post Office and the Tobacco House came to 1,086,000 dollars or the equivalent of over thirty tons of silver, and the arrival of the Viceroy's gold from Lujan added a further 631,684 dollars to the sum. A large quantity of other valuable merchandise such as hides and Peruvian bark, from which quinine was extracted, brought the total up to the magnificent figure of around 3,500,000 Spanish dollars, or roughly the equivalent of £15 million in today's money.

Under the Commodore's watchful eye, the treasure was carefully counted, and once completed the great chests were loaded onto a fleet of shallow crafts and transported out to the *Narcissus*. As soon as the last chest was safely on board, she upped anchor and sailed for England carrying letters from Beresford and Popham urgently requesting Government reinforcements. The Commodore also begged the Admiralty to send him a large number of 'Guernsey Frocks' as his men were suffering badly from the icy weather.

This was not the first report of Popham's success to reach England. This came from the official Commander of the expedition, Sir David Baird at the Cape of Good Hope, who on receiving Beresford's report of his successful capture of Buenos Aires immediately wrote to William Windham, Minister for the Colonies. Windham quickly forwarded the dispatch on to King George III at Windsor, who surprisingly was not best pleased. Writing to Windham in June from Windsor Castle, His Majesty declares, 'Sir David and Popham should be reprimanded for setting a bad precedent by attacking the Spanish population of the River Plate without authority.' Nevertheless, when later informed of the capture of Buenos Aires he seems less aggrieved and in a letter to the Minister dated 13 September admits, 'Its acquisition is an advantage to His Majesty, the Government, and the country.'

Although all appeared to be running smoothly in Buenos Aires, Beresford was a realist and foresaw that, until reinforcements arrived from England, his only hope of keeping control of the city was to win over the goodwill of the people. Having cracked the whip, the time had come to proffer the carrot. So summoning the *Cabildo* to a meeting, he gave them the good news he was sure they had been waiting for and grandly announced,

'From now on you are the free subjects of that benign and best of monarchs His Majesty George the Third, King of Great Britain, Scotland and Ireland,' and to emphasise this happy state of affairs he issued the following proclamation.

'1. Every citizen is entitled to freedom of religion:

'2. No change will be made of those in positions of authority and the Administration of the city will continue under the control of the *Cabildo*; and all legal matters will remain in the hands of the *Real Audiencia*

'3. Citizens' rights will be observed at all times, their property will be respected, and the Army will pay for all its provisions and equipment (not that generous an offer considering all the money the British had stolen).

'4. All the merchant ships and boats confiscated lying at the mouth of the Riachuelo by the British Navy will be returned to their rightful owners.

'5. From now on, Buenos Aires is part of the British Empire, an open port free to trade with whom it wishes, and I am its Governor.'

Although suspecting this proclamation would have little chance of winning over the support of the traditional

Spanish merchants, Beresford hoped the offer of free trade would gain the approval of the younger ones. His surmise proved correct as far as the older merchants were concerned: unwilling to break the family and financial ties binding them to Spain they had little wish to see the market flooded with cheap imports from Europe. However, disappointingly, the smaller merchants were also unhappy. Many had obtained financial help from their elders and feared that, if they accepted Beresford's offer, their loans would be recalled, and the Creoles and supporters of Miranda's Independence party wanted total freedom, not just a change from one rule to another.

Despite these reasonable terms, Beresford's greatest stumbling block was that he would not or could not give those sympathetic to his cause any safeguards from Spanish reprisal should a peace treaty be later signed with Spain. This made it obvious to anyone tempted to accept his proposal that in the event of this occurring the vengeful Spaniards would undoubtedly hang him as a traitor. Unimpressed by Beresford's offer, the *Cabildo*, merchants and people began making plans to overcome his little Army.

After a few days, Buenos Aires returned to normal. The shops raised their shutters; the bars and cafes opened their doors, and the overall feeling of gloom and fear enveloping the city changed to one of intense resentment over the behaviour of the Viceroy and his Army.

Every citizen felt deeply ashamed of surrendering to so small a force, as despite the British Commissariat attempting to conceal the Army's strength by resorting to various ruses such as indenting for more rations than were needed, the crowd watching the Highlanders parade every morning in front of the Fort quickly deduced their number.

Incensed by Sobremonte's behaviour, the *Cabildo*

immediately dispatched a vitriolic report to Spain via the Governor of Montevideo accusing the Viceroy of cowardice, at the same time begging the Governor to send them help as quickly as possible. Bands of resistance fighters began to meet in secret to plan how to remove the invaders from the city. Martin Alzaga, the city's Mayor, co-ordinated them into small cells, and paid each recruit four dollars a day out of his own pocket.

Martin Alzaga, now to play a major part in the reconquest of the city, was born in Galicia in 1755 and, being a Basque by birth, was at first unable to speak any Spanish. Jobs at the time in Spain were difficult to find, so setting off for the Rio de la Plata he arrived in Buenos Aires as a penniless young man to find work as an apprentice in the house of Gaspar Santa Coloma, then the richest and most powerful merchant in the city.

By the time of the British invasion in 1806, Alzaga, through hard work, natural acumen and an advantageous marriage to Santa Coloma's daughter, had risen to be 'Alcalde de Primer Voto' or the equivalent of Mayor of Buenos Aires. He would remain staunchly loyal to Spain for the rest of his life and would wage a constant war not just against the British, but also against all those seeking independence from the mother country.

Dividing his resistance fighters into separate groups, the Mayor gave each one a different task. For instance, Jose Fornaguera, Gerardo Esteve y Lach and Felipe Sentenach, Catalans and engineers by profession, were given the task of blowing up the British soldiers' sleeping quarters in the Ranchero. Quickly requisitioning a house next to the college of San Francisco, they immediately began digging a tunnel under the road to deposit thirty-six barrels of gunpowder under the barrack room floor to blow the Highlanders to kingdom come.

The tunnel was never discovered, but the Highlanders strongly suspected that something suspicious was going on, as a drummer boy kept complaining to his sergeant of being woken in the middle of the night by the weird noises coming from under his bunk. Determined to solve the mystery, Major Gillespie declares, 'Some muskets barrels uppermost were gently secured upon the floor on which pins were placed, so as to be deranged by the smallest concussion. One morning they were found on the ground but although an investigation was ordered nothing was found.'

Less adventurous citizens began to bribe Beresford's men to desert by offering them 20 dollars, a horse, and the promise of a house and wife in the country. This offer held no small attraction as, disappointed by the ban on looting, the soldiers were beginning to appreciate the wealth of the country, and the beauty of the women. The lower classes employed a less sophisticated but more effective mode of resistance: simply making the soldiers drunk, a relatively easy matter, and slitting their throats.

Drunkenness in fact was a perpetual problem. Writing to a Peruvian friend, Don Gaspar Santa Coloma declares, 'When passing by the British barracks, we found everyone except the Captain lying on the ground half-naked and totally drunk. Given only fifty men we could have easily captured the lot.'

The streets and alleyways by now were becoming too dangerous to walk down and Robert Fernyhough dryly notes, 'Assassinations are frequent.' Nevertheless, in spite of all these sinister activities Beresford's greatest problem was not drunkenness but desertion, principally due to the

Spanish priests encouraging his Roman Catholic soldiers to save their souls by abandoning his army of heretics. Adding further to his problems, the ill-disciplined St Helena troops, having little wish to fight or return to their isolated island once the hostilities were over, began to disappear in droves and, in an attempt to discourage them, Beresford ordered four captured deserters to receive 500 lashes each, three of whom died from the flogging.

Alzaga also had his problems, as with the number of resistance fighters rapidly increasing he needed to find houses and warehouses around the city where his men could secretly train and hide their weapons and ammunition. A farmhouse was therefore requisitioned outside the city at Perdriel (near today's Campo de Mayo) where an arsenal was hurriedly assembled. Transporting the weapons there proved a problem, and Jose Fornaguera and his men were nearly caught loading a large number of rifles onto a wagon outside Don Martin Monasterio's house, which was situated half a block from the Plaza Mayor. Because of this, an English sentry stood permanently on guard where the street entered the Great Square which bustled with enemy activity, as troops were sent to search or guard important buildings across the town. Owing to this constant activity, it was decided to move the weapons from the house at eight o'clock in the morning when, hopefully, the British troops would be parading in front of the Fort.

Duly arriving at the appointed hour, the workers were in the process of loading the weapons, carefully wrapped in hides, onto the wagons, when two English officers walking by stopped and demanded to know the contents of the vehicle and where it was going. It was a tense moment and Don Monasterio nervously began to reach for the pistol hidden beneath his cloak, but luckily Fornaguera kept his head. Whipping the horses round, he set off at a smart pace towards the square shouting over his shoulder that he was taking them to the Plaza Mayor and was already halfway down the street before the officers could answer. Seeing him heading for the square, they presumed he was delivering his load to the Fort and continued on their way. Next day, the weapons were delivered safely to Perdriel, where, as will be seen, they would be of little use.

Well aware of these sinister activities, Beresford tried hard to counter them by forming his own network of spies and informers. Intrigue was everywhere and, hoping that a show of military proficiency would impress the spectators and discourage them from any idea of rebellion, every morning he ordered his troops to drill in front of the Fort. And to demonstrate his own lack of concern and ensure his presence was known, every afternoon, accompanied by his staff, he would stroll along the avenues of the city with his personal piper marching in front of him playing cheerful Gaelic airs.

In spite of all his efforts, every day the opposition grew stronger and the cavalry that Sobremonte had removed to Monte Castro slowly began to filter back into the city. The Viceroy offered to double their wages to escort him to Cordoba but they unanimously rejected this, firmly asserting they had been led to believe that their removal to Monte Castro was in order to regroup and counter-attack the enemy the following morning. They indignantly maintained that at no time had any mention been made of escorting him to Cordoba. Anyhow, their uniforms and weapons were sopping wet and, due to having no Commissariat, they lacked any change of clothing. Under such conditions there was no question of escorting him into the interior and leaving their wives and families at the mercy of the barbaric British soldiers.

Not all the inhabitants were anti-British, and Beresford found friends if not allies among the Argentines. Dr Castelli, a follower of Miranda's Independence party, was rumoured to be holding secret talks with the British General. While Francisco Cabello, editor of the newssheet *El Telegrafo Mercantil*, would later be accused of collaborating with the enemy, when obtaining that exclusive scoop every reporter dreams of, 'An interview with General Beresford.' Even Don Pedro Menendez Arguelles, the chief of police, would later be accused of aiding the British when only fulfilling his duty of keeping the peace and public good order.

Alzaga's spies were everywhere, and carefully noted down all these actions so that their perpetrators could be punished at a future date. These, however, were merely minnows compared to the greatest offender of all: Don Martin Sarratea, chairman of the *Campania de Filipinas*, who, in the forlorn hope of retrieving the 1,000,000 dollars stolen by the British from his company's warehouse, gave a magnificent ball and invited all the English officers and their friends. Prominent among the latter were Thomas O'Gorman and Anita, greatly admired by the men and consequently loathed by their wives who rightly reckoned that none of their husbands were safe from her all too visible charms. These were certainly attracting the one-eyed General's attention, as in his arms he whirled her around the ballroom. Anita had a generous nature and was not at all selfish with her favours; at the time she happened to be the mistress of Santiago Linares, soon to make an appearance on the scene.

The ball was a huge success for, although unable to speak Spanish, many of the young British officers could converse with their partners in French or Latin and their elegant manners and dashing uniforms quickly won the ladies' hearts. Romance was definitely in the air, but the ball caused much resentment among those loyal to Spain. Memories were long, as in 1808 the *Cabildo* not only demanded but also impounded 200,000 pesos from Don Martin to contribute to the cost of defeating the British. This was an enormous sum of money and double the amount demanded from any of the other merchants.

On the surface everything appeared to be peaceful, but underneath rebellion was growing, and with Alzaga's recruits increasing daily, secrecy now became a problem. The citizens thoroughly enjoyed discussing all the strange activities they had witnessed the night before over their morning cup of coffee, or glass of wine in their favourite cafe or bar and Beresford's spies carefully noted down all these conversations and kept the General fully informed.

Hard as Beresford fought to stem the mounting unrest, his efforts proved useless. Despite posting notices on the doors of every important building warning that anyone found with arms would be fined 200 pesos, they were little heeded and in desperation he decreed that all those holding positions of authority should publicly take an oath of allegiance to His Majesty King George III.

The *Cabildo* and *Real Audiencia* openly refused to do so, but Major Gillespie, in charge of the operation, declared that three of their members secretly took the oath in his office after it was closed. This stood on the corner of Santo Cristo Street (now Balcarce and 25 de Mayo) and kept strict business hours, opening its doors every morning at ten o'clock except on Saturdays and Sundays, when it was closed all day.

The Spanish officers firmly refused to take the oath, on the grounds they had already given it to the King of Spain and therefore could not be expected to commit perjury. Instead they gave their word of parole not to continue fighting, and from now on took no further part in the coming struggle. This was left to the militia, many of whom, like Manuel Belgrano and Juan Pueyrredon, had already fled the city to join up with Santiago Linares and his Army swiftly approaching from Montevideo.

THIRTEEN

SANTIAGO LINARES

Born at Niort on the west coast of France in 1753, Santiago Liniers de Brémond, called Linares by the Spaniards, was the third son of an ancient aristocratic Poitou family; his elder brother, the Comte de Linier, had attended the courts of Louis XV and XVI, living happily at Versailles until forced to flee to Buenos Aires at the start of the French Revolution.

There were few suitable occupations open to the younger sons of the aristocracy in the middle of the eighteenth century, and the majority either joined the Army or entered the Church. Skilfully combining the two, Linares at the age of twelve became a page in the service of Manuel Pinto de Fonseca, Grand Master of the Knights of Malta.

Although a shadow of its former self, the order was still embarking on forays against the Barbary pirates, and it was on these expeditions that Santiago began his military career. He remained on the island for the next three years, returning to France when just fifteen wearing the Cross of Malta, which he would proudly display around his neck for the rest of his life.

Aided by his maternal uncle, the Comte Brémond d'Ars, Governor of Amboise, he obtained a cornetcy in the Royal Piedmont Regiment in 1774 and for the next nine years remained stationed with his regiment in Carcassonne.

Life in the land of the Cathars was pleasant but dull, and hearing rumours that Spain was about go to war with Morocco he resigned his commission and set off to join the

Spanish Army currently being raised in Cartagena. Arriving there a month later, he found the seaport a seething mass of undisciplined humanity.

Volunteers from every country filled the city; lodgings were crammed to bursting point and positions hard to find. Nevertheless, after many interviews he obtained a post as ADC in the retinue of the Prince de Rohan and, in 1784, he set sail in this great armada of forty-six ships and twenty thousand men to fight the troublesome Moors. Four years later, after bravely serving as a Captain of Marines at the sieges of Mahon and Gibraltar, he was posted to the Rio de la Plata, never to see Europe again.

Once in the Rio de la Plata his fortunes steadily began to decline as he despairingly watched all the major military positions being allocated to the Court favourites of Charles IV, now the King of Spain. No permanent post was forthcoming and, now relatively poor and almost forgotten, he was sent by Viceroy del Pino to act as temporary Governor of the Province of Missiones, accompanied by his second wife, the daughter of Martin Sarratea. It was to be a stopgap position until the official appointee arrived from Spain and, while occupying this position, he became acquainted with Monsieur Esteban Perichon de Vandeuil and his pretty daughter Anita, soon to become his mistress.

Two years earlier the workers in the port of Buenos Aires had been suitably impressed by the sight of Monsieur Esteban Perichon, his wife Juana Magdalena nervously clutching his arm as they descended the narrow gangplank of a newly arrived merchant ship from the Orient. Monsieur Perichon was indeed an imposing figure as, being of noble birth, he was elegantly attired in the habit of a gentleman of the ancient regime, suitably befitting someone that had held an important post in Pondicherry until forced to flee by the arrival of Major General Baird and his marauding sepoys.

After this unhappy experience, Monsieur Perichon settled on the Isle de Bourbon and in 1781 moved on to Mauritius where his daughter Anita was born. For the next twelve years, his fortunes steadily flourished, but in 1793 ill fate struck again with the arrival of a ship carrying on board the representatives of France's new Revolutionary Republic, forcing him to flee again.

Monsieur Perichon was now faced with the serious problem of selecting a new country to live in, only to discover there were few suitable venues left where a *ci-devant* aristocrat could comfortably settle down. The Far East was unsafe; North America and Canada too young; and England out of the question after his disagreeable experience in India. Carefully taking all these factors into account, Monsieur Perichon finally settled on Argentina, which being under Spanish rule was reasonably civilised, and more importantly far from the escalating conflict in Europe.

Five handsome offspring, Juan Bautista, Eugenio, Esteban, Luis and Ana Maria, all aged between twenty and twenty-five, followed their parents at a suitable distance down the gangplank, and behind them stretched an impressive retinue of servants. Thirty sweating slaves brought up the rear of this lengthy procession, carrying on their shoulders a large assortment of chests containing Madame and Anita's jewel cases; Monsieur Perichon's cellar and cigars, in fact everything a lady and gentleman could possibly need to maintain a suitable standard of living in this uncivilised backwater of the Spanish Empire.

After a leisurely stay in Buenos Aires, where he was hospitably entertained by the French community, Don Esteban in 1800 bought a tobacco *estancia* three miles outside the little town of Corrientes not far from Candelaria, the capital of Misiones where Santiago Linares was now the acting Governor. The families soon became friends and, when Monsieur Perichon returned to Buenos Aires in 1803, Linares followed a few months later on the arrival from Spain of the designated Governor of the Province. Sadly, on the long journey back to the capital Linares's wife died of a fever, and now alone in Buenos Aires with just his children he slipped into impoverished obscurity.

It was not until 1805, when an English fleet was sighted in Bahia, did Viceroy Sobremonte appoint him commander of Ensenada de Barragan, a small garrison post on the shores of the River Plate, and here, at the age of fifty-three, his fortunes were about to change dramatically.

The following winter, sighting Popham's battle squadron sailing unmolested up the River Plate, Linares immediately sent a messenger to alert the Viceroy of the approaching danger. The mission proved fruitless, as Sobremonte paid no attention to the warning and the messenger returned a few days later to inform Linares that the capital had surrendered, and that Lt Groves with a platoon of soldiers was on his way to demand his parole and take command of Ensenada.

Heeding his warning, Santiago hurriedly left the garrison and, with the help of Anita Perichon, or her husband O'Gorman, obtained a letter of safe conduct from General Beresford allowing him to enter Buenos Aires. Ostensibly to visit his children staying in the house of their grandfather, Don Martin Sarratea.

Once inside the city he surreptitiously inspected Beresford's Army and, as a professional soldier, quickly recognised that although small in number, the British troops were by and large organised and well disciplined. This left him three options. Either he could obey the Viceroy's orders and report to Cordoba; join Martin Alzaga's freedom fighters and remain in Buenos Aires or enlist in and help raise an Army in Montevideo.

The choice was not difficult to make, as the Viceroy's military skills were nonexistent and even a well-trained Army under his command would inevitably be defeated. While Martin Alzaga's resistance fighters, although undoubtedly brave, were undisciplined and unruly, and his military experience told him that only a professional Army had any hope of defeating the British, which could be found only in Montevideo.

Secretly slipping out of the city on the night of 10 July, he set off for Montevideo and arriving there four days later immediately sought an audience with its Governor, Don Ruiz Huidobro. Describing this eminent personage, a contemporary gentleman unkindly commented, 'His body pervaded more scent than a perfume shop' but tactfully discounting this idiosyncrasy, Linares begged the Governor to raise an Army, and dispatch it as quickly as possible to Buenos Aires to aid the citizens in their fight for freedom.

His request placed Ruiz Huidobro in a quandary, as he had just received a message from the Viceroy ordering him to send all his available forces to Cordoba and, at the same time, he had to consider the defence of Montevideo. A large British Army was rumoured to be on its way from England to reinforce Beresford, and to send troops to Buenos Aires would greatly weaken his city's defences.

It was a difficult decision to make, but fortunately the citizens and the *Cabildo* solved the problem for him, as the entire city voted for troops to be sent immediately to the relief of Buenos Aires. The merchants, citizens and militia all unanimously volunteered to join it, which was surprising, as there had always been a distinct rivalry between the two communities. For a long time, Montevideo had resented being dominated by the larger and richer Viceregal city of Buenos Aires, as was later shown in 1828 when Montevideo and the Banda Oriental turned down Belgrano's offer to join Argentina, and broke away to become Uruguay.

In the end, the Governor's own personal ambition probably played a major part in his final decision. As the second most senior officer in the Province he quickly realised that, with Sobremonte's popularity obviously on the wane, should his troops be successful there was a distinct possibility of his becoming the next Viceroy.

With this happy thought in mind, he ordered an Army to be raised and appointed Santiago Linares to command, as his experience and knowledge of the terrain were infinitely superior to that of Gutierrez de la Concha, the naval Captain currently in command of Montevideo's forces. Diplomatically, he made Gutierrez second-in-command of the expedition, and placed him in charge of the flotilla of boats to transport the Army across the River Plate.

On 22 July 1806 the sun shone, the bands played martial music and the cheering crowds lining the streets enthusiastically waved their flags as in full dress uniform, mounted on a prancing white charger, Santiago Linares led his troops through the gates of San Pedro and set off on the road to Buenos Aires.

Although a large number of volunteers had offered to join his expedition Linares, believing in the old maxim, 'Battles are won by disciplined soldiers rather than enthusiastic masses', selected only a small force to accompany him. These consisted of a company of artillery, a company of infantry, three companies of Dragoons, and two companies of *Blandenegues* (a frontier force), which combined with 372 militia brought his Army's strength up to approximately 980 men. At the last moment this was further increased by the arrival in port of the notorious French corsair Hypolite Mordeille and his band of bloodthirsty pirates.

Nicknamed 'Maincourt' owing to his lack of one hand, Mordeille and his men probably offered their services more from the lure of booty than from any French or Spanish patriotic feelings, but needing every experienced fighter he could lay his hands on, Linares was only too happy to accept their offer.

The hundred-mile trek to Colonia del Sacramento took much longer than expected as, from moment they left Montevideo, torrential rain fell unceasingly, making the roads almost impassable. Every hundred yards the gun carriages sank deep into the mud and had to be laboriously extracted by teams of swearing men and sweating horses. It was not until 31 July that Linares and his little Army finally reached Colonia.

Over the previous weeks, Beresford's spies had kept him well informed of the steady build-up of arms and troops at Perdriel, and realising the situation was becoming dangerous, the General decided attack would be his best form of defence. So, on the night of 1 August, Beresford and his staff visited the theatre where they ostentatiously showed themselves off in the Viceroy's box to throw Alzaga's spies off the scent. Then, returning to the Fort at midnight, the General set off for Perdriel at the head of 500 soldiers, pulling behind them six cannons whose wheels had been carefully muffled in skins to avoid waking the townsfolk.

Security at the farmhouse was lax and, although numbering over a thousand men, there was no overall Commander, no sentries posted and the cannons had been left unloaded. Making matters worse, a large consignment of wine and women had arrived the previous day to entertain the troops, and the happy recipients were now in no fit state to defend themselves, let alone the camp. Beresford's dawn attack took the hung-over soldiers completely by surprise, and the resistance was chaotic.

Colonel Olavarria, in charge of a squadron of 200 *Blandenegues*, flatly refused to allow fifty of his men to join Pueyrredon's cavalry in a counter-attack. He claimed that he had come only to escort Linares to Buenos Aires and, anyhow, as a professional soldier he was in no way prepared to take orders from an officer in the Militia. Despite his refusal, Pueyrredon's gauchos bravely charged the British line and, describing their attack, Thomas Howell writes,

'Those who faced to the right came galloping across our left flank near, which were posted two howitzers and immediately that they got clear of the flank they wheeled short round to our rear in the most irregular manner possible. About five of them were mad enough to make a dash at one of our ammunition carts, which was bringing up the rear quite unprotected being loaded only with the grain for the mules. This they succeeded in carrying off, desperately wounding one of the drivers with a sword in several places and one of his legs had to be instantly amputated. Our light infantry quickly faced about, and dashed after them but could not save the fellow'.

As always, Beresford was in the thick of the battle and was lucky to escape with his life. When slipping unperceived behind the rear of the right flank of the 71st, Pueyrredon and one of his gauchos suddenly charged straight at him. Seeing their approach, the General attempted to draw his sword but found to his dismay that it refused to budge as the blade had rusted in its scabbard. Luckily, Captain Arbuthnot standing next to him spotted his predicament and, keeping one at bay, Colonel Pack with his customary coolness engaged the other, allowing Lt Mitchell time to call up a file of grenadiers who, opening fire at close quarters, brought the rider to the ground. In this hopeless state of confusion, the Spaniards were quickly routed and Beresford returned triumphantly to the city, bringing with him a German Roman Catholic deserter from the Cape who had been captured staunchly operating his gun after the crew had fled. Found guilty of desertion by a court martial he was duly sentenced to be shot, but the Bishop of Buenos Aires, administering the last sacrament before the execution, was profoundly shocked when during this solemn service the British guards flatly refused to remove their hats. Despite his indignant protests, they firmly kept them on their heads and refused to take them off, declaring it would be contrary to King's regulations to remove them. The unfortunate victim met his death bravely and his last request was that his parents should be kept unaware of the circumstances that caused it.

The reappearance in Buenos Aires of Beresford and his troops caused consternation among the citizens, as rumours had reached them that he and his men had been defeated. His return only increased their determination to eject the British from the city, and the atmosphere now became decidedly threatening. Sensing menace in the air, Thomas Howell ominously writes,

'I am inclined to think that from this day on we shall be in continual hot water with them… God grant that we may receive a reinforcement to enable us to put a final check to their proceedings.'

Although the defeat at Perdriel was a serious setback, matters on the coast were progressing better for, after successfully fending off an attack from an English sloop, Gutierrez de la Concha and his barges had safely arrived at Colonia. The weather was cold and foggy with poor visibility, precisely the conditions that Linares needed to avoid Popham's watchdogs. With *pampero* (a strong wind) blowing he therefore ordered the crossing to begin, and boarding their barges his men set off across the estuary. The bad weather continued all the following day, keeping the English sailors occupied in stopping their ships from being swept onto the sandbanks, and it was not until the morning of 5 July that they finally reached Olivos. Disembarking from their boats, the men quickly regrouped and were soon joined by Pueyrredon's cavalry and the routed troops from Perdriel.

FOURTEEN

LA RECONQUISTA

Now only two miles away from Buenos Aires, Linares received two urgent messages. The first from the Viceroy ordering him not to advance any further until he and his Army arrived from Cordoba, and the second from Felix Sentenach and the Catalans begging him to postpone his attack until they had blown the Fort to kingdom come. It was obvious from these demands that both parties were anxious to be the first to claim a victory over the English: the Viceroy to redeem his name, and the Catalans to become the dominant party in Buenos Aires.

Having little faith in the Viceroy, or any intention of waiting for the pyrotechnics of the Catalans to succeed, Linares ordered his men to continue the march and the Army pitched camp for the night on the outskirts of the town in the Corral de la Miserere, the city's municipal slaughterhouse.

Day and night, an endless stream of volunteers was now pouring out of the city to join him, and the arrival of the scattered troops from Perdriel brought the Army's strength up to around 3,000 men. It was time to launch the attack so, following the etiquette of war, Linares sent Hilarion Quintana into the city to demand the British surrender.

Setting off early next morning, the tall Brigadier strode importantly through the empty streets towards the Fort. Energetically waving a large white flag over Quintana's head, a corporal followed close behind him and in front of him marched a small boy proudly banging an enormous drum in time to the Brigadier's steps. The contrast of the tall officer, tiny boy and huge drum tickled the watching British soldiers' sense of humour, and gave them infinite amusement.

As expected, Beresford haughtily dismissed Linares's demand to surrender, contemptuously declaring, 'I will defend this position at the point of the bayonet as long as I consider it necessary.' Receiving this reply, Linares ordered the advance to continue and the Army pitched camp for the night in the Retiro, the large park a mile distant from the Fort.

Inside the city the scene was one of total confusion, as nervous citizens frantically tried to organise their families into groups and send them to the safety of the country. Others rushed to retrieve the arms and ammunition from their hiding places and tension, already high, now reached breaking point. Serious incidents began to break out all over the city and, rather worse for wear in the inn of Los Tres Reyes, Major Gillespie drew his sword on Monsieur Gicquel, a well-known French busybody just returned from Linares's camp who, inadvertently or on purpose, spat a grape pip in the Major's direction. Taking umbrage at what he considered an insult, the Englishman instantly demanded satisfaction, and only Don Bonofillo's rapid reaction saved blood from flowing. Grabbing an enormous club, which he kept secretly hidden behind the bar, the Innkeeper waved it threateningly over the antagonists' heads, bringing both contestants rapidly to their senses.

This was not the only case of aggression. The bullfighter *Alcadio El Nato* (the snub-nosed one), getting drunk in the Calle de Cabildo lost his head and, attempting to seize the rifle out of a British sentry's hands, stabbed Lt Sampson of the St Helena Corps coming to his rescue.

On the evening of 11 August Linares drew up his plan

of battle for the following day, which included using the boats that his men had crossed the river in to stop Popham from supporting Beresford from the sea. All through the night shots continuously rang out across the city and, at three o'clock in the morning, Colonel Pack, Major Tolley and Colonel Campbell, with three companies of the 71st, crept silently out of the Fort and attempted to launch a counter-attack.

The plan was simple. Tolley and his party would advance along the riverside and attack the enemy from the front while, taking another route, Pack and Campbell at the same time would attack them from the flank and rear. Despite their careful planning the attack failed, as the people living in the houses around the Fort were on the alert. Spotting the soldiers crossing the drawbridge, they immediately raised the alarm and drove the attackers back into the Fort.

Without doubt, 12 August 1806 is one of the most momentous days in the history of Buenos Aires, as down the present day streets of Florida, San Martin, and Reconquista marched Linares's troops. Out of the houses spilled Martin Alzaga's freedom fighters and over two thousand armed men filled today's avenues of 25 de Mayo, Hipolito Yrigoyen and Rivadavia. Down the latter strode the one-armed buccaneer Mordeille at the head of his bloodthirsty crew, whose coloured bandanas, shining brightly in the sunshine, added an aspect of Carnival to the proceedings. Following behind them came a screaming mass of excited citizens, and all Linares's carefully laid plans vanished into thin air as the avenging mob advanced on the hated invaders.

Drawn up in front of the Fort, as if on Horse Guards Parade, Beresford's soldiers stared impassively to their front. While standing behind their guns, strategically sited at the mouths of the streets converging on the Plaza Mayor, the

British gun crews waited with glowing braziers by their side ready to light the fuses.

A long building with colonnades called the Recoba split the square in half, whose arcades were manned by the 71st, and behind it waited the St Helena Regiment ready to enfilade the rear entrances. Snipers filled the windows of the nearby *Cabildo*, and riflemen poured a relentless fire down on the advancing mob from the rooftops of the houses surrounding the Fort.

The battle was fierce, and for a while the British soldiers staunchly held their ground, but the gun crews struggled to keep up a continuous fire. Although well trained, reloading the cannons was a lengthy process, as the barrels needed to be swabbed out after each shot before another charge of powder could be safely rammed down the muzzle. Then, due to its violent recoil, the gun had to be realigned and sited before another shot could be fired. Hard as the gun crews strove, the impetus of the advancing crowd proved too great, and one by one the guns were overrun. After inflicting many casualties, the 71st were driven out of the Recoba and, despite a desperate struggle, the *Cabildo* fell. Taking up a position on the rooftops of the high buildings surrounding the Fort, the Spaniards poured a blistering fire down on the unprotected British troops standing in the open below. Thomas Howell describing the scene writes:

'This unremitting fire continued from every direction until about one o'clock, when I observed the General who was walking under a wall near my company to be extremely agitated at beholding so many fine fellows carried into the Fort killed or wounded. At this time, there was not a church or house that could in the smallest degree command the market square but was filled with men that were enabled to take deliberate aim being perfectly secure from our fire.'

Stationed safely out to sea on board the *Diadem*, watching the battle unfold, Sir Home Riggs Popham was outraged to see the Spaniards mounting a cannon on the roof of the Cathedral. Writing to William Marsden at the Admiralty on 25 August, he indignantly complains,

'… Reinforcements crowded the tops of all the houses commanding the great square from the back streets, and our troops were soon considerably annoyed by people they could not get at. The enemy commanded the castle in the same way with the additional advantage of a gun on top of one of the churches, which I consider an indelible stigma upon the character of the Bishop not only from his situation but also from the profession he made!'

Sword drawn, his face and gold braid uniform black with powder, the one-eyed General gallantly urged his men on and, for a time, they bravely kept the crowd at bay. But when Captain Kennet – his ADC standing beside him – fell to the ground fatally wounded, Beresford realised the situation was hopeless and, commanding his hard-pressed men to retreat into the Fort, ordered them run up the white flag and cease firing.

Into the Plaza Mayor surged the excited crowd screaming, 'Death to the English', 'Slit their throats,' and other threatening cries and, running forward, Mordeille's bloodthirsty pirates threw their scaling ladders up against the Fort's walls. Clenching their cutlasses firmly between their teeth, they began swarming up them and, Robert Fernyhough bemoans,

'Never shall I forget the scene that followed the hoisting of the flag of truce and the advantage gained over us. About 4,000 ragamuffins rushed into the square brandishing their knives, and threatened us with destruction. The savages paid no regard to our flag of truce and were firing in all directions.'

The white flag meant nothing to the uneducated mob and a hail of bullets greeted anyone rash enough to raise their head above the parapet to parley. Seeing the situation rapidly getting out of control, Jean Baptiste Raymond, one of Mordeille's lieutenants, ran to inform Linares of the dangerous situation. Hurriedly sending for Hilarion Quintana, he ordered him to rush to the Fort, and accept the British surrender to avert a massacre.

Fighting his way through the milling crowd, the Brigadier reached the Fort, and mounting the ramparts to address the mob unwisely raised his head above the battlements without giving a sign or warning. A volley of musket fire greeted his sudden appearance and executing a rapid somersault, he dived for cover below the parapet. A feat of gymnastics that may have ruined the solemnity of the occasion, but undoubtedly saved his life.

Cautiously raising his head above the parapet, he shouted at the mob to cease firing. It had little effect and bravely standing up, he bared his chest and commanded the mob to shoot him first, if they were determined to continue firing.

Order was only restored when a Spanish flag, found hidden in a locker, was hurriedly run up the flagpole to replace the white flag, and seeing the Royal colours flying once again over the Fort the crowd's mood instantly changed from vindictive fury to happy euphoria. People cheered and others wept for joy, as Beresford and his defeated troops, carrying their wounded on stretchers behind them, dejectedly marched out of the Fort to surrender to the Argentine General. A disconsolate Captain Fernyhough gloomily writes:

'We hung down our heads sorrowfully and instead of carrying our swords erect, we dropped them by our sides and arriving at the *Cabildo* delivered up our arms. This was the most distressing scene I ever beheld and there was scarcely a dry eye amongst us. Some of the men, when they came to deliver their muskets threw them on the ground cursing the day they ever took them in their hands.'

From that day onwards the terms of surrender would be a source of controversy. Beresford strongly maintained that these had been conditional, and that Linares had agreed to:

'Grant the British the honours of war, and having laid down their arms permission to board the transport ships for England

'The ships should be provisioned for the voyage, and guaranteed safe passage home. While the wounded should be cared for in the city's Hospital, until healthy enough to be repatriated to England

'All British subjects' property would be respected.'

The Spaniards on the other hand insisted that the surrender had been unconditional, which had been shown by Beresford raising the white flag and surrendering his sword. They firmly maintained that Linares had only signed a conditional surrender written in English on 17 August and predated to the 12th, out of the kindness of his heart to save Beresford from suffering the same fate as Admiral Byng. Anyhow, they insisted it was immaterial what Linares had signed as he had no authority in the first place to negotiate the terms of surrender, so whatever these had been they were obviously invalid.

Once the English officers had given their word of parole, they were treated kindly and billeted with the same families whose houses they had been staying in before the battle. While the other ranks were held in their former barracks in the Fort and the wounded were either nursed in private houses or transferred to hospitals to be cared for by the Bethlehemite friars.

When the roll was called the numbers differed. The British estimated they had lost three hundred, and the enemy four hundred men dead or wounded. The Spaniards claimed the same figure in reverse but irrespective of who was right it had been a fierce and bloody battle, and the following days passed gloomily to the non-stop sound of tolling bells, as the dead were laid to rest. The English officers, including two of Beresford's ADCs, Captain Kennett of the Royal Engineers and Lt Mitchell of the 71st Highlanders, were buried with full military honours; considered heretics, the other ranks were interred in the ditch in front of the Fort, or in the Barranca del Retiro, the Rinconada de Rocamora and the Paseo del Bajo.

In a moving ceremony on 23 August 1806, after ten days of religious and civil celebrations, Santiago Linares laid the captured colours of the 71st Highlanders at the foot of the altar to the Virgin Mary in the Church of Santo Domingo where they hang today. Forty-four days of British rule was finally over.

FIFTEEN

A SUCCESSFUL ENTERPRISE

News of Beresford's success reached London seven weeks later, and the city went wild with excitement. Bonfires lit up all the parks; windows rattled from the continuous thunder of celebratory cannon fire, and rockets blazed across the night sky turning the heavens into a kaleidoscope of glittering colours. Cheering crowds of drunken spectators filled the streets and, all over the country, civic dinners were held during which long patriotic speeches were made and congratulatory toasts copiously drunk. The jubilant citizens embarked on a never-ending round of celebrations and Popham and Beresford were hailed as national heroes. The festivities continued for several weeks, and equalled if not surpassed those held the previous year to celebrate Lord Nelson's great victory at Trafalgar.

Always commercially orientated, Popham in his dispatches home enclosed pamphlets advertising the potential value of his newly opened market, which not only gave their readers helpful suggestions on the needs of the country, but also a long list of all the products they could buy there. Never one to miss a chance, he also dispatched a large number of ponchos and other native clothing for the manufacturers of Manchester to copy, rightly reckoning that anything South American would soon become the rage. Lt Colonel Fletcher Wilkie, commenting on this propaganda, dryly remarks,

'This well-known commercial letter from the Commodore set every broken-down clerk and supercargo on the "qui vive" emptying all the stores in Manchester and Liverpool, and sent us as much long cloths, printed calicoes, and sheeting that would have reached across the Pampas to Santiago. All of which arrived too late for the fair.'

The London merchants suffering hard times, and frustrated by Napoleon's recently imposed blockade, had gloomily watched their export trade drop from ten million pounds a year to barely two. Thrilled by the news of this new and potentially lucrative market, they rushed to load their ships with every conceivable kind of merchandise. No shipper, merchant, or investor intended to miss out on what he was now convinced would be a highly profitable trading bonanza, and strongly urged his neighbours to follow suit.

Fanned by euphoric articles in the press, the excitement spread like wildfire and, on 7 September 1806, *The Times* proudly announced, 'Buenos Aires now forms part of the British Empire,' and two days later assured its readers, 'There can be hardly any doubt that the whole colony of *La Plata* will share the same fate as Buenos Aires, and from the flattering hopes held out to the inhabitants in General Beresford's proclamation, they will see that it is to their interest to become a colony of the British Empire.' Finally on the 25th, it enthusiastically declared, 'Buenos Aires is the breadbasket of South America. Its camps and pastures support thousands of cows, sheep, pigs, and horses.' Then, perhaps to titillate its male readers, it further added, 'Moreover, the women are considered not only charming, but also the most beautiful in the whole of South America.'

Equally delighted, *The Morning Post* fervently pronounced, 'The drooping spirit of commerce is revived,' and filled its pages with numerous advertisements including one from a certain Mr Potter, who assured his investors that he had 'A large quantity of Light Stays made up that will suit the climate of Buenos Aires.'

Everything from silk hats, designed especially for the Spanish market, to pianos, stockings, and furniture crammed the holds of every available ship, and among this diverse selection of merchandise were a large amount of inferior goods that the more shady entrepreneurs hoped to unload on the supposedly gullible natives.

On 18 September, excitement reached a climax with the arrival in Portsmouth harbour of the *Narcissus*, carrying on board the Spanish treasure. An enthusiastic crowd rushed to watch the great chests being carefully unloaded onto a long line of waiting wagons and, greatly impressed, *The Courier* gave its readers an eyewitness account of the proceedings,

'Thirty sailors dressed in the same uniform as they attacked the Spaniards on shore have it under their charge. These set off for London preceded by a brass field piece that they intend to fire a salute with on their entrance into the principal towns along the road. The Royal Marine Band marched at the head of the wagons that were decorated with the Spanish flags taken at Buenos Aires along with three British colours with R.B on them meaning, 'The Royal Blues' the corps of seaman being so-called by Sir Home.

Two days later this impressive procession reached the outskirts of the London and mustering in St James's Square at eleven o'clock on Saturday morning 20 September, the Loyal Volunteers set off to escort the treasure into London. Arriving at Clapham three hours later they found eight magnificently decorated wagons drawn by six large horses waiting for them. A multitude of pennants, blue ribbons, and coloured flags adorned each wagon, written on which in large letters was the word 'Treasure'.

A Royal Marine sergeant proudly carrying the Viceroy of Peru's standard marched in front of the first wagon and carefully draped over the second were the enemy colours taken at Buenos Aires. Blue naval ensigns covered the remainder.

After listening to a suitable number of orations and fuelled by a considerable amount of libation, the procession set off towards the City, and at various points along the route the band of the Loyal Volunteers struck up 'God save the King,' 'Rule Britannia' and other patriotic songs.

A delirious press enthusiastically reported, 'Every Briton's heart rejoiced at the scene.' After stopping for more refreshment and speeches at the Admiralty, the procession continued its way up Pall Mall to St James's Square, where once again it halted to be presented with a pair of colours inscribed with the words, 'Buenos Aires, Popham, Beresford, and Victory.'

Seated in a post-chaise graciously acknowledging the spectators' cheers, Captain Donnelly of the *Narcissus* led the procession as it continued its way towards the City where the treasure was safely deposited in the vaults of the Bank of England.

Over the following days, the absentee conquerors were showered in honours and rewards, and the Committee of the Patriotic Fund at Lloyd's generously voted to give Popham and Beresford two suitably inscribed vases each valued at £200. Not to be outdone, the City of London presented the absentee Commodore with a magnificently jewelled ceremonial sword as a token of their gratitude.

Despite of all the festivities, adulation and brouhaha, one important section of the establishment remained ominously silent: His Majesty's Government was markedly nonplussed.

Over the previous eight years, Spain's relationship with France had been steadily deteriorating and, by now, she had become an unwilling ally in Napoleon's never-ending war against Britain. Not only had she lost all her ships and at least a thousand sailors at Trafalgar, but each year she also contributed or was supposed to contribute three and a half million pounds sterling towards the cost of the war against Portugal, Europe's last remaining seaboard open to English commerce. Not only were her finances in poor shape but her Government was also fed up with their alliance with France, and because of these circumstances the 'Ministry of all the Talents' was in the middle of negotiating a secret peace treaty with the Spaniards, and Popham's unforeseen action terminated any hope of this agreement ever being ratified.

The Prime Minister Lord Grenville was furious, and immediately recalled Baird and the Governor of St Helena to England. The first to receive the Government's censure for authorising Popham's expedition to leave the Cape of Good Hope, and the second for lending Popham his militia.

Equally annoyed, the Lords of the Admiralty sent urgent dispatches to Montevideo ordering the Commodore to return home immediately and face a court martial scheduled to be held on 6 March 1807 at Portsmouth.

Popham's rash gamble had been totally unexpected, and the Cabinet now found itself in an embarrassing position. To leave Beresford and his popular Army to their fate was clearly out of the question and would be little short of political suicide, but to send reinforcements to Buenos Aires could scupper any hope of renegotiating the agreement with Spain.

Confronted by this dilemma, William Windham, Secretary of State for War and the Colonies, reluctantly agreed to send two expeditions to South America and chose two able officers, Brigadier General Sir Samuel Auchmuty and Colonel Robert Craufurd to lead them.

Born in New York in 1756, Samuel Auchmuty was therefore an American by birth but he had strong British connections as his grandfather was a distinguished Scots lawyer who had immigrated to Boston early in the reign of William III. While his father, after being educated first at Harvard and then Oxford, had been appointed the assistant minister of Trinity Church in New York and in 1764, when Samuel was only eight, put in charge of all the churches in the city where, being a staunch Royalist, he firmly continued to read the prayers for the king. But with the demands for independence rapidly rising, Lord Stirling on taking over command of New York ordered him to stop this inflammatory practice and, incensed by His Lordship's demands, the Reverend Auchmuty promptly locked the doors of all his churches. Retiring to New Jersey, he left strict orders that no further services should be held until the prayers could be read again uncensored. Hearing a few months later that the British had re-captured New York, Samuel's father managed to slip through the American lines and, returning to the city, found his churches burnt to the ground and all their records destroyed. This loss, combined with the exposure undergone in evading the American sentries during his return to New York, was too much to bear, and brought about his demise.

At the outbreak of war, the Reverend Auchmuty and his grandfather sent Samuel to fight as a volunteer in the 45th Regiment (The Worcestershire and Sherwood Foresters) and after distinguishing himself at the battles of Brooklyn and White Plains, he was promoted to ensign and the following year to Lieutenant without purchase.

After Lord Cornwallis's disastrous defeat at Yorktown, the war came to an end and, in 1781, he returned with his regiment to England to find, like many officers past and present, it was impossible to live on his Army pay. To solve this vexing problem he changed regiments in 1783, and joined as adjutant the 52nd Foot (The Oxfordshire Light Infantry) who were about to leave for India where life was reputed to be less expensive.

It was a fortunate decision for, while fighting in the war against Haidar Ali, he was promoted to Captain in the 75th (The Gordon Highlanders) and met Lord Cornwallis, now the Governor General. Remembering him from American days, His Lordship offered him a position on his staff, which he gratefully accepted, and by 1800 had risen to the rank of Lt Colonel. Promoted to Brigadier five years later, he took part in Baird's expedition to take Cairo and remained in Egypt as Adjutant General of the Army of the Nile. He returned to England in 1803 to be knighted, and appointed Commandant of the Isle of Thanet. It was while occupying this position that he received Windham's order to go to the relief of his old Egyptian comrade in arms, William Beresford, in Buenos Aires.

On his arrival in Buenos Aires, Windham ordered Auchmuty to place himself and his four-thousand-strong Army under Beresford's command and, should the General have surrendered, he was to do his best to reverse the position. In the event of this proving impossible, he must establish a foothold on the coast, and wait there for the arrival of a further three thousand troops due to leave England three weeks later. Windham gave Auchmuty the following dispatch to deliver to Beresford:

'You are not accountable for the expedition and your conduct is approved. We have long been restrained from invading Spanish South America by fear of exciting a revolt against Spain, which could only be controlled by a British force of superior strength. It is with this view, as much as with that of securing valuable possessions, that your force has been so much increased.

'Use your judgement and your troops principally to avert the evil of such a revolt as we have mentioned, making none but unavoidable changes in the Government. Under no circumstances should you pledge His Majesty's Government to conditions, which it might be unable to make good. We can only assure the inhabitants of our protection so long as our troops are there, and our desire is that they shall never suffer from their amicable disposition to us.'

After receiving these orders, Auchmuty set off for Plymouth only to find more instructions waiting for him from the War Office. These included a long letter discussing the wool bearing animals of South America.

The Government was obviously taking the matter seriously, as they had sought the opinion of the President of the Royal Society, Sir Joseph Banks, then the most eminent botanist of the day, as to where he could find llama, vicuna and guanaco, and likewise whether they could be shipped back to be farmed in Great Britain. Sir Joseph replied that he considered Puerto Deseado the best place to find guanaco and llama but doubted whether vicuna would be suitable to raise in Great Britain, as the quality of the wool was definitely inferior at sea level, and the animals could be farmed only on the highest ground. Having dealt with this correspondence, Auchmuty loaded his ships with sufficient stores for the journey, and embarking his men set sail on 9 October for South America.

Windham's other appointment of Robert Craufurd to be the leader of the second expedition was more controversial, and caused considerable umbrage among the senior Generals, who strongly resented being superseded by such a low ranking officer. It was indeed an unprecedented step to appoint a Colonel, a junior one at that, to command an Army normally headed by at least a Lieutenant General and, in an attempt to stave off any criticism, Windham hurriedly promoted Craufurd to the rank of Brigadier General.

Despite their complaints it proved an astute choice, as Robert Craufurd quickly gained the reputation of being not only a brave and capable commander, but of also of having the worst temper of any officer in the British Army. Nicknamed 'Black Bob' on account of his permanent five o'clock shadow, those unlucky enough to witness this frightening phenomenon reported that his face turned even blacker, as his rage increased and his voice would quickly rise to a high-pitched squeak.

Like many other officers at the time, Craufurd in 1801 became a Member of Parliament for East Retton, and as a young man he had accompanied his elder brother, Colonel Sir Charles Craufurd, to Austria where he had been sent as British representative to the Court of the Archduke Charles. During his stay there, 'Black Bob' became not only fluent in French and German but also a great admirer of the Austrian Army's training methods, which centred on iron discipline and the lash, and he would remain a stickler for discipline and good order for the rest of his life. This made him not only unpopular with the men but also with his brother officers.

Writing home three years later to his family from the Peninsula, Captain John Leach of the Rifle Brigade declares, 'He (Craufurd) is a damned tyrant and a great blackguard, who has proved himself totally unfit to command a company much less a division.'

Despite these harsh words, a glittering career lay ahead for Craufurd that would be terminated by a French sniper in 1812, when storming the walls of Ciudad Rodrigo.

To say the least, Windham's orders to Craufurd were imaginative, and clearly demonstrated the Government's total ignorance of both the political and geographical state of South America. First, he should capture Valparaiso and from there conquer the whole of Chile and should this fail he was to set up a base on the Pacific Coast and from there establish an uninterrupted chain of military and commercial posts to Buenos Aires.

It was an idiotic plan, which totally discounted the fact that Chile's coastline stretches for at least 3,000 miles and the distance from Valparaiso to Buenos Aires, even by the shortest route, is over 1,000 miles across the second highest range of mountains in the world. It likewise failed to explain the major issue of how Auchmuty and Craufurd, with a combined force of only six thousand men, could possibly conquer and hold Chile, Buenos Aires and Montevideo, all at the same time.

Nevertheless, the Government had made its decision and on the shoulders of these two competent young officers rested their grossly over-optimistic hope of not only conquering Argentina but Chile as well.

SIXTEEN

MALDONADO

THE CAPTURE OF MONTEVIDEO, FEBRUARY 1807

Auchmuty and Craufurd's convoys were not the only ones on their way to the Rio de la Plata for, unbeknown to the British Government, a third force of two thousand men under the command of Lt Colonel Backhouse was already on the high seas heading towards South America, having been dispatched by Sir David Baird from the Cape on his receiving Beresford's report of the capture of Buenos Aires. Colonel Fletcher Wilkie, then only a Captain and a member of the expedition, ruefully comments,

'He was only too happy to bid farewell to the Cape as after his unhappy experience under General Dundas, Baird had been determined not to follow in "Old Pivot's" footsteps and allow his men and officers to become idle. Sir David had in military slang been bitten by a mad adjutant or rather inoculated with the pacing-stick drill and retained two sergeants of the 59th to teach us the mystery of standing on one leg. We were put to school directly, and began this operation at five in the morning and continued for two hours then guard mounting followed by regimental parade and courts-martial etc. At two we dined in order to be ready at four to repeat the goose-step until six, then our own regimental parade in the evening after which it was dark. No pretence whatever except sickness could get leave from these parades, and the invalids when they recovered pulled up all their arrears of guards and drill, and one or two never recovered during our stay. These operations began before the Dutch garrison had embarked and they reproached themselves for having let the place be taken by a set of recruits: "You see" said they "the officers are even sent to drill."

'I will further venture to say that no officers could excel those of the Cape at this sedentary species of gymnastics, as we had often to stand on one leg against a southeast wind when a civilian could hardly stand on two. Until we were complete in this noble art, so useful to a man in after life, we had not a moment to ourselves and knew no more of the colony beyond the lines than we did of Sierra Leone!'

Backhouse and his little expedition were the first to arrive at the mouth of the River Plate, where they were greeted by the disturbing news that Beresford and his Army were now prisoners of war and Buenos Aires was back in Spanish hands. It was a severe blow to his confidence and, now far from England and the Cape, the Colonel was feeling decidedly lonely in this strange unfriendly land. He had little idea what action the Government or Baird wished him to take, so it was a great relief when contact was established with Commodore Popham and his fleet. After a lengthy discussion, the Commodore advised him to land his men at Maldonado, today a suburb of the fashionable beach resort of Punta del Este. Taking his advice, the Colonel began disembarking his men on Maldonado's lengthy beach, and the sudden appearance of two thousand British soldiers took the six hundred Spaniards living there completely by surprise. They were astonished at the speed of the British infantry's advance as, having left their knapsacks on board their ships, the soldiers were among them in a flash. After only a short exchange of musket fire, they quickly surrendered and, next day, Backhouse and his men captured the island of Goretti along with the thirty-two guns guarding the harbour. With his base now firmly established, he and his men spent the next three months obtaining horses and supplies for the arrival of the Army that Popham assured him was on its way from England to join them.

Needless to say, Sir Home had an ulterior motive in persuading the Colonel to occupy Maldonado as, lacking a natural harbour for his fleet to shelter in, he omitted to mention the fact that the landward side of the island was almost impossible to defend against an enemy counter-attack. Luckily for the Colonel, this failed to materialise, but Sir Home held no great opinion of Backhouse, noting in his journal, 'Not that I expect he will trouble me much, unless he is aroused by others from his natural torpitude.'

Despite all his scheming, Popham remained on station for only a short time, as on 3 December the *Sampson* arrived in port carrying on board Admiral Stirling with orders from the Admiralty to take over command of the squadron and presented Sir Home with the following letter:

'Whereas, we think fit that you shall forthwith return to England you are required to furnish Rear Admiral Stirling by whom you will receive this dispatch with every information he requests … and having so done so, take your passage to England accordingly in such ship as the Rear Admiral shall appoint'.

The last part of the order was to cause Stirling a considerable amount of trouble, as he wanted to send Popham back aboard the *Sampson*, sailing to England via St Helena and the Cape of Good Hope. The Commodore flatly refused to board her declaring, 'He would be humiliated and insulted for his defeat at these places' and insisted on returning home on a brig sailing directly to England. Stirling firmly pointed out that this little ship had no room for another passenger and a heated correspondence began between the two naval officers that continued for over a month, until Sir Home reluctantly capitulated and announced, 'He would return aboard the American brig *Rolla* as a private gentleman at his own expense.' Much to the Admiral's relief, the Commodore left the Rio de la Plata on 27 December, allowing him time at last to concentrate on drawing up his plans for the coming invasion.

SEVENTEEN

THE SIEGE OF MONTEVIDEO

Sealed in their leaky transport vessels, Samuel Auchmuty, the 95th, 40th, 80th Regiments, three Companies of 71st, and eight troops of the 17th Dragoons set off from Plymouth on 9 October 1807, and after a long and weary journey arrived in Rio de Janeiro to receive the unwelcome news of Beresford's defeat.

This meant that from now on Sir Samuel was in charge of the operation and free to make his own decisions. First on his agenda was the welfare of his troops. Many of whom had been on board their ships for over six months, and were now in poor shape. In an attempt to get them fit, he sent a number of companies ashore to exercise and, although pleased to be back on *terra firma*, the soldiers were not over enthusiastic at the prospect of the drill, as it was now the middle of summer: humidity high, and the temperature over 100 degrees in the shade. Their good humour, however, quickly returned when, after drilling up and down for around an hour, they were reviewed by Princess Carlotta, wife of Dom João the Regent of Portugal, who graciously presented each soldier at the end of the parade with a pumpkin and an onion before they returned to their ships.

The convoy spent the next week taking on provisions, and upping anchor on 5 January set sail for the Rio de la Plata and arrived at Maldonado two weeks later to find Backhouse and his men in serious trouble. The situation had deteriorated badly since their arrival, and the Colonel and his men were now under constant threat from over four hundred horsemen that surrounded their camp and made it difficult for them to obtain any provisions.

These ferocious gauchos were putting up an irritating and successful form of resistance and, describing their tactics in his report to the War Office, Auchmuty writes,

'They ride up, dismount, fire over the backs of their horses, mount again, and gallop off. All the inhabitants are accustomed to this sort of warfare, and every inhabitant is an enemy.'

Adding further to his frustration, the cumbersome equipment of the English Dragoons was far too heavy for the native horses to carry, making them incapable of driving off the enemy and pursuit out of the question. The situation was very unsatisfactory and, after consulting Admiral Stirling, Sir Samuel decided to throw caution to the wind and abandon Maldonado without waiting for the reinforcements to arrive from England, and attack Montevideo.

So, leaving a small garrison behind on the island of Goretti, he re-embarked his Army, and on 13 January 1807 set sail for Montevideo. Arriving at Playa de Buceo three days later, the fleet anchored in a small bay nine miles west of the city close to the Caretas Rocks, today called Puerto Manzo.

All the time, the Spaniards had been shadowing the fleet's progress along the coast, and as soon as the British troops began to disembark they found a formidable force confronting them. But just like the previous year at Quilmes, the enemy seemed reluctant to offer any opposition and the 95th who landed first, suffered only two casualties: a bugler killed and Lieutenant Chawner wounded.

The Spaniards seemed mesmerised by the sight of Auchmuty's troops and their reluctance to attack was put down to fear of retaliation from the heavy guns of the fleet now lying close into shore. In his autobiography published in London in 1881, Sergeant William Lawrence of the 40th declares,

'The enemy was on the banks about fifteen thousand strong to oppose us, which put a nasty taste into our mouth and there seemed nothing but death or glory for us. The signal was hoisted from the Admiral's ship and we started for the shore amid the fire of the enemy's artillery. They killed a few of our men and sank some of the boats but as soon as we struck the shore we jumped out, and forming line in the water fired a volley, charged, and soon drove them from their position on the bank. Even as early as then, we found the Spaniards not very difficult to encounter. In case of a retreat, our boats were still within our reach but having gained the victory, we had no need of them stopping where we were on the banks all the night.'

Lt Colonel Bourke, Major Tucker, and Brigade Major Roache along with the 95th, 38th, and Light Brigade were the first to land, and quickly pushed their men a mile on inland to leave room on the beach to unload the supplies and stores. They were closely followed by Colonel Gore Browne with the 40th, who took up a defensive position on the surrounding high ground and sent scouts forward to reconnoitre the land beyond the beachhead. Over the following days the stores were safely landed and, once this operation was completed, the General gave the order to advance and the Army set off for Montevideo, whose church spires shone brightly in the distance.

Perched on the top of a rocky peninsula, Montevideo in 1807 was a compact walled city, roughly oval in shape and covering an area approximately a mile from north to south, and half a mile from east to west. Although surrounded on three sides by water, any idea of attacking the city from the sea was out of the question as the high vertical cliffs were un-scalable, and any ship approaching them would inevitably be smashed to pieces on the jagged rocks around their base. The only way of attacking the city from the sea was by entering the harbour, but as this was heavily defended by a mass of gun emplacements any chance of success was remote.

The small fort of St Philip guarded the western side of the city and the Citadel protected the east. This was a formidable building standing on a great salient surrounded by a deep ditch with four strong bastions. A high wall encircled the city with two heavily fortified entrances: one across a drawbridge in front of the Citadel, and a smaller one five hundred yards further to the south. Mounted along the ramparts and connected by a covered way were over a hundred and thirteen pieces of artillery; twenty four of which defended the Citadel and forty more the landward side, and garrisoning the town were six thousand brave but ill-trained Spanish troops. Dominating the whole city were the two lofty towers of the Cathedral, a large red brick building with a vast cupola situated in the centre of town; Montevideo was a formidable objective.

Although slightly smaller in number than the Spanish Army, Auchmuty's soldiers were better trained but, after their long sea voyage, the men were far from fit. The 47th (The Lancashire Regiment) were definitely in poor shape and a company of the 71st little more than children. While the best that Auchmuty could say about the 87th (The Prince of Wales's Own Irish Regiment) were, 'They were fine boys.' Fortunately, the 38th (1st Staffordshire Regiment), the 44th (2nd Somersetshire Regiment) and the 17th Light Dragoons were in excellent shape and, from now on, Auchmuty would rely on these and Admiral Stirling's sailors and marines to bolster his Army.

Don Ruiz Huidobro, its fragrant-smelling Governor, was in charge of Montevideo's defence and, although rather nervous, he strongly believed the city could withstand a British attack. His troops had just returned from Buenos Aires brimming with confidence after defeating Beresford's Army and the city walls were well defended; the powder magazine full of ammunition and the stores sufficiently stocked with food to resist a lengthy siege. So seeing Auchmuty's Army approaching he confidently sent his cavalry out to meet them, and out of the city's main gate trotted two thousand horsemen, who advanced on the British vanguard.

Seeing them approach, Auchmuty's soldiers quickly formed squares and briskly drove them off. Realising they could achieve nothing more without the support of infantry, the Spanish cavalry wheeled around and, after setting fire to the houses outside the walls, retired back into the city. One large house they left intact, which was presumed to belong to an important town official and which Auchmuty would later use as a forward observation post.

Drawing his Army up on a high ridge overlooking the city, Sir Samuel ordered the artillery to be unloaded from the ships, including a number of naval guns which were difficult to manoeuvre due to their wheels being designed to run over the smooth decks of a ship and not the rough ground now confronting them. Weighing around two and a half tons, each gun first had to be unlimbered and manhandled from the beachhead to the front and then laboriously re-assembled and sited.

Next morning, the cocks began to crow and as the sun came up Montevideo came alive to the sound of martial music. Bugle calls echoed through the narrow streets and drums began to beat, as out of the main gate sallied Colonel Bernard Lecoq of the engineers, marching proudly at the head of 2,362 infantry, closely followed by the Marquis of Sobremonte and his 1,700 cavalry.

Separating into two columns, they advanced on the English redoubt which put up a fierce resistance. Under their accurate fire, Sobremonte and his cavalry soon gave way but the infantry still came on, and seeing a picket of four hundred men about to be overrun, Colonel Gore Browne sent Major Campbell and three companies of the 40th to their support. The Spaniards bravely stood their ground but, in the end, the bayonets of the 40th proved too strong. Seeing the Spanish line begin to waver, Sir Samuel threw in the Light Battalion to attack their flank and the impetus of the charge was such that the column broke. Dropping their weapons, the Spaniards ran for the safety of the city hotly pursued by Auchmuty's men.

Not yet seventeen and experiencing his first battle, Thomas Howell, a soldier of the 71st, describes his return from the charge in his memoirs published in Edinburgh in 1819:

'As the battalion to which I belonged returned from the pursuit, we passed in our way to the camp over the field of dead. It was too much for my feelings and I was obliged to turn aside my head from the horrid sight. The birds of prey seemed to contend with those who were burying the slain for the possession of their bodies. Horrid sight! Men who in the morning exultingly trod forth in strength whose minds only fettered by their bodies seemed to feel restraint now lay shockingly mangled and prey to animals, and I had been an assistant in this work of death! I almost wished I had been a victim.'

After this action, later called 'The Battle of El Cristo de Cardal', the siege began in earnest. Bringing all their cannons to bear on the city walls, the British bombarded them unceasingly for the next ten days until finally, on 2

February, a breach was made next to the town's main gate. Unfortunately the six guns on either side of the breach had to be left intact as, owing to the length of this bombardment, the Army was nearly out of ammunition.

The time had come to launch the attack so, as protocol insisted, Sir Samuel sent a messenger to the Governor demanding his surrender. As expected this was defiantly rejected, so Auchmuty began to draw up plans on when and where to launch the attack. After a lengthy discussion with his officers, it was agreed that the major assault should go in at the breach at first light the following morning, and at the same time another party would wait at the smaller gate for it to be opened from the inside, once the breach had fallen.

A 'Forlorn Hope' was quickly mustered, which consisted mostly of men from the 44th (East Essex Regiment) and a sergeant of the 38th placed in charge. Choosing an officer to command proved more difficult, as there were many volunteers and a heated argument broke out among the young officers as to who had the right to lead. Lt Everard of the Queen's (The 2nd Regiment of Foot) on attachment to the 38th firmly insisted the position should be his, as he belonged to the senior regiment and, after a long and passionate discussion, he was finally granted the honour.

This suicidal command was much sought after by junior officers who, lacking the funds to purchase their promotion, knew that if lucky enough to survive they would automatically be granted it on the field of battle. In fact, during the Peninsular War, the 'Forlorn Hope' was so keenly competed for that sergeants often fought as privates, and some soldiers even offered their comrades as much as £20 for a place in the assault. In the end only seven men of the 'Forlorn Hope' were lucky enough to survive the siege of Montevideo, one of whom was Lt Everard, who would later go on to command the 14th Regiment (The Buckinghamshire) during the Peninsular War.

No moon shone, the night was still as, at three o'clock in the morning, the 'Forlorn Hope' crept silently towards the breach, unaware that during the night the Spaniards had camouflaged the gap with leather skins filled with rubble. The entrance was now so well hidden that the 'Forlorn Hope' twice passed by it in the dark and, hearing the men blundering around under the city's walls, the Spaniards opened fire. Their first cannon shot struck only one man but the second killed twenty-five of the thirty soldiers following behind and, for the next fifteen minutes, the 'Forlorn Hope' stumbled blindly around in the dust and smoke searching desperately for the entrance. Suddenly out of the dark came a cry from Captain Renny of the 40th that he had found it, which were his last words as seconds later he was killed mounting it.

It was indeed a formidable obstacle, as the entrance was so small that only three men abreast could pass through it at one time. Once through this narrow gap, a twelve-foot drop confronted the attacker, behind which waited a battalion of Spanish infantry supported by a battery of light cannons.

Ignorant of the danger that lay ahead, Auchmuty's soldiers began feverishly pulling down the hides and Captain Dickinson of the 95th, struggling up the fallen masonry, found it impossible to keep his footing, as he slipped and stumbled over the bodies of his dead and wounded men. From either side, cannons pounded the besiegers and, blinded by the smoke and dust, Major Gardner and Captain Harry Smith with the remainder of the 40th twice missed the breach, and passed under the heavy fire of the murderous guns. Sergeant Lawrence, scrambling desperately through the smoke and rubble declares,

'The ladders were placed against the hides of earth, and we scaled them under a heavy fire from the Spaniards. We found the earth better stuff to encounter than stone and although our poor Captain fell in the breach whilst nobly leading on his men, we succeeded in forcing our way into the town, which soon was filled with the reinforcements following behind us. We drove the enemy from all the batteries and massacred with the sword and bayonet all whom we found carrying arms.'

With his leg shattered by grapeshot, Colonel Vassal of the 38th lay dying on the ground but still managed to cheer his soldiers on as they poured through the breach. Many were wounded by falling on each other's bayonets and, having miraculously passed through the breach unscathed, Captain Dickinson died minutes later charging at the head of his company up the city's empty streets. Following his orders, Major Campbell swung left with the grenadiers of the 38th and 87th, and began knocking out the gun batteries running along the ramparts.

The 87th (The Royal Irish Fusiliers) and a company of the 95th safely reached the smaller gate undetected and, getting bored of waiting for it to be opened from the inside, threw their scaling ladders up against the wall, and began climbing up. Drowned by the noise at the breach, they took the Spaniards by surprise and opening up the gate the waiting troops came pouring through, and the battle was over. During this encounter, the Irishmen captured a Spanish flag, which they proudly called 'The Flag of Montevideo', and hangs today in their museum in South Armagh.

By eight o'clock, the entire town was in British hands except for the Citadel whose Commander, despite being shot in the breast and bayoneted in one arm, stubbornly refused to surrender. It was not until a group of sharpshooters of the 95th climbed to the top of the Cathedral's towers and began pouring down fire on the Citadel below with their new Baker rifles that the defenders finally raised the white flag and surrendered.

By midday the looting was brought under control and, once order had been restored, the residents ventured nervously out of their houses to inspect the damage done to their city. This in fact was minimal, as apart from the damage at the breach Auchmuty's soldiers were well disciplined and, unlike future sieges in the Peninsular War, the looting insignificant.

Without doubt it had been a hard-fought battle and the casualties were high on both sides, especially at the breach where the enfilading fire had mowed down over four hundred men. The armchair Generals of the day would later blame Auchmuty for this, insisting that he had used far too much ammunition bombarding the whole front instead of concentrating on knocking out the cannons on either side of the breach before launching his attack. It was an unfair criticism, as by then the Army had almost run out of powder and shot and, in the end, his critics were forced to admit it had been a famous victory.

When the roll was called the Light Battalion, with sixty-three men killed and eighty-four wounded, had suffered the most casualties, followed by the 38th with twenty-seven dead and a hundred and twenty-one wounded, nine of whom were officers. Lockjaw (tetanus) soon began to take its toll and, lacking any knowledge of the remedy, many with only minor cuts later died from this dreadful disease, including Colonel Brownrigg of the Light Battalion whose uncle at Horse Guards was soon to play a part in the coming campaign.

With eight hundred dead, five hundred wounded, and

two thousand taken prisoner, the Spaniards had also suffered severe losses, but the majority of their troops managed to escape in little boats across the harbour to Rat Island and, for this, Popham and the Navy were unfairly blamed as the ships too had almost run out of ammunition.

Auchmuty's men had undeniably fought bravely and the crossfire at the breach would certainly have daunted any less well trained troops. But considering their men had neither the training nor experience of the British, the Spaniards had also put up a brave resistance. One well known casualty of the battle was the Commander of the Citadel who, dying from his wounds, turned out to be none other than the one-armed buccaneer Hypolite Mordeille, last seen leading his pirates through the streets of Buenos Aires. His new role as Commander of the Fort had obviously suited him and was certainly more respectable than his previous one, when as the dreaded 'Maincourt' he struck terror into the hearts of every merchantman sailing the seven seas. The British officers greatly admired his stubborn defence of the Citadel, and buried him with full military honours in Montevideo's graveyard.

Despite the large number of casualties, the siege had been a brilliant success and, to ensure the Governor and his staff had no chance of escaping, Auchmuty hurriedly embarked them onto a ship leaving for England. Now, short of men and ammunition, all he could do was consolidate his position and wait for the arrival of the promised reinforcements from England.

Although the siege of Montevideo had been a bloody affair, the *Cabildo*, writing on 27 August 1807 to Colonel Gore Browne, the military Commandant of the city about to leave for England, expressed their gratitude for the behaviour of his soldiers after the battle.

'Estimado Señor'

'The moment is approaching when the armies of his Britannic Majesty must evacuate this place and you Sir! Being on the eve of departure, this *Cabildo* is anxious to testify the joy inspired by the prospect of the former event, and the regret occasioned by the latter. This *Cabildo* would be ungrateful were they not to make public the virtues of you and Sir Samuel Auchmuty. You Sir, entered the City with the General commanding the troops at that moment when the *Cabildo* was assembled in the Capitular Hall, and preserved by your exertions that death with which all were threatened by from the fury of the soldiers.

'You Sir, received the sword and insignia of justice from our hands but returning them immediately into our possession directed that we should retire to our Hall, and placed a respectable guard in order that we might be secure from the smallest insult.' The letter then goes on to thank the Colonel for controlling his troops' looting:

'The victorious troops thinking themselves of a right to the property of the citizens began some of them to plunder but what Sir, except your rectitude and firmness could have been able to restrain so great a number of soldiers and marines in the midst of a city whose inhabitants were either slain; wounded prisoners, or fugitives. In effect two hours after the assault, this place was deserted; a profound silence reigned in all the streets and not a soul was seen save only the scattered bodies of the dead and wounded with their arms. You Sir! seemed to have been struck with consternation, as you permitted no drum or any instrument of martial music, nor cannon to interrupt the melancholy silence of those first mournful days. All the citizens' property and effects remained secure, as if they themselves guarded them and some trifling excess that was committed by some of your men in the first moments of confusion was publicly chastised upon the same day in the square by a severe lashing. It was alone at the entreaty of some of us that you Sir, had the goodness to spare two soldiers who were condemned to die. Whatever thing however small it might be that was found in the possession of any soldier or sailor was remitted to this *Cabildo* for it to be restored to its owner should he appear. Every family was respected and the pride of the victorious troops who had just conquered and entered through fire and blood became tranquilised in an instant from that moment without occasioning the smallest disorder. In these sentiments of admiration and gratitude, we now bid you a farewell and our earnest prayers for a prosperous voyage, and a happy restoration to your country of which you are so bright an ornament do most sincerely accompany you. May God preserve your Excellency for many years.

'Signed: The Members of the *Cabildo.*'

EIGHTEEN

MONTEVIDEO UNDER BRITISH RULE

Left behind to guard the camp with the other conscripts of the 71st, Thomas Howell took no part in the storming of the city. Nevertheless, he leaves an interesting description of the inhabitants and everyday life in Montevideo during the British occupation.

'We marched into Montevideo the day after the assault where I remained for seven months. It is a most delightful country were it not so hot. The evening is the only tolerable time of the day. The sea breeze sets in about eight or nine o'clock in the morning, which mitigates the heat a good deal; yet I suffered much. It was now the middle of December (it was in fact January). Summer had commenced with all its sweets on a scale I had no conception of, neither can I convey any of it in words. We had the greatest abundance of every article of food and as the summer advanced the choicest fruit; indeed even more than we could consume and at length we loathed it. I was billeted upon a young widow who along with her aged father did all in her power to make me comfortable.'

The widow was highly superstitious and not in the least surprised by the news of her husband's death during the siege as she was quite convinced he had been bewitched. Returning home a day earlier from partridge shooting he had encountered an old Indian sitting by the side of the road, who seeing the dead partridges in his bag immediately demanded to be given some. This her husband refused to do; the man had promptly cursed him, and because of this, she was not at all surprised to hear of his being killed during the siege, and firmly believed it to be the reason for his death. Thomas continues:

'She behaved to me like a mother, and to her I was indebted for many comforts. Never, shall I forget Maria de Parades. She was small of figure yet elegant in appearance and like the other women of the country, very brown with sparkling eyes as black as jet. Her teeth were equal and white and she wore her own dark hair dressed, as the fashion of the country in plaits down her back, which was very long and of flossy black. Her dress was plain and a black veil covered her head with her mantilla tied in the most graceful manner under her chin. This was the common dress of all the women, and the only difference being in the colour of their mantillas and shoes, which they often wore of all colours except for the veil that was sometimes white. The men wore the cloak and hat of the Spaniards but many of them had sandals, and a great many wanted for both shoes and stockings.' Despite Maria's comely looks, Thomas found,

'The native women (Indians) the most uncomely I ever beheld. They have broad noses, thick lips, and are of a very small stature. While their hair, which is long black and hard to the feel is frizzled up in front in the most hideous manner, and hangs down their backs below the waist. When they dress, they stick in it feathers and flowers, and walk about in all the pride of their ugliness. The men are short of stature, stoutly made, have large joints, and although brave, are indolent to excess. I have seen them galloping about on horseback almost naked with silver spurs on their bare heels and perhaps an old rug upon their shoulders. They fear no pain and I have seen them with hurts ghastly to look at, yet they never seemed to mind them. As for idleness, I have also seen them lie stretched for a whole day gazing upon the river and their wives bring them victuals, and if not pleased with the quantity they would beat them furiously. This is the only exertion they ever make, readily venting their fury upon their wives. They prefer flesh to any other food and eat it almost raw in quantities, which a European would think impossible.'

Life in Montevideo was relatively peaceful, except for Maria de Parades and her father Don Sancho's determination to convert Thomas to the Catholic Religion. Equally determined to save his soul from damnation, their Father confessor repeatedly came to visit him but by now the Highlander had learnt some Spanish, and firmly told the zealous priest, 'Hay muchos caminos al cielo' (There are many roads to heaven).

Despite persistent rumours that the Viceroy was advancing on the city with a large Army, all appeared quiet in Montevideo and, to ensure he was swiftly informed of their approach, Auchmuty ordered outposts to be stationed in all the villages and towns around the neighbouring countryside which could not only protect the roads leading into the city, but their officers could also encourage the local inhabitants to bring their goods into the city and sell them in the market. He then dispatched two hundred men to garrison Canalones, a town twenty miles north of the city, and a company twenty miles further on to occupy St Lucia.

The sudden arrival of the Viceroy and his Army was certainly a serious threat but Auchmuty's greatest worry was desertion. This was a perpetual and irritating problem, as he found it difficult to win over the goodwill of the people and persuade them to join him without the reverse occurring. For in spite of all his efforts to stop them, the citizens were successfully persuading his soldiers to join them, which was not altogether surprising, as by now the soldiers had discovered the country to be attractive, the women pretty, and the money offered them to change sides substantial. A disapproving Sergeant Lawrence indignantly complains,

'A sergeant and corporal of the Spanish Army came in disguise and tried to enlist any of our men that would join their service. Unfortunately, one of my own regiment, a sergeant named Goodfellow tempted by the heavy bounty they offered accepted their proposals. Another case of desertion was an officer's servant, who went away with the greater part of his master's clothes taking with him a Spanish lady. He was lucky enough to get off safe, and nothing was heard of him afterwards.'

To counteract the depletion of his forces and keep his men occupied, Auchmuty decided the time had come to put the aim of the expedition into operation. This was the rescue of Beresford and his men, and for this to succeed he needed a base closer to Buenos Aires from which to launch his invasion. He therefore dispatched Colonel Pack and the Light Battalion with three companies of the 95th to capture Colonia del Sacramento, which they successfully achieved.

All appeared to be running smoothly, but this radically changed on 10 May, with the arrival in port of the *Thisbe* carrying on board Lt General John Whitelocke and his second-in-command, Major General John Leveson-Gower. These two officers would soon become famous as two of the most incompetent Generals ever to lead a British Army.

NINETEEN

GENERAL JOHN WHITELOCKE

Owing to the steady build-up of troops in the Rio de la Plata area, the British Cabinet in February 1807 decided that an Army of this size needed a more senior officer to command it. Up to now, it had been quite content for Auchmuty and Craufurd to lead their respective forces but, with the two about to combine, they felt such a formidable force needed a more experienced officer to lead it.

Why they chose General John Whitelocke remains a mystery. Nevertheless, rumours were legion and one more scurrilous than the others maintained that, due to the strong support he was receiving from the Duke of York, he was in fact a Royal bastard. Apart from a slight Hanoverian resemblance, there was little basis for this assumption, but it was well known that the Duke was a close admirer of Whitelocke's wife and some hinted that, due to this attraction, the Field Marshal selected him to command this Army.

Minister for the Colonies Windham's own choice lay between General Sir John Stuart and Robert Craufurd, while Lord Grenville, the Prime Minister, favoured Sir George Prevost, who had shown his ability facing Villeneuve's predatory raid on Dominica in 1805, but in the end he was dismissed as being too old.

Windham's other choice, General Sir John Stuart, was a vain, flighty, superficial officer who had recently returned in glory from the Sicilian campaign, where he had shown himself incapable of planning any major operation. His success had been entirely due to the competence of his

Brigadiers, Cole, Kemp, Oswald, and Ross; all of whom would later make their names during the Peninsular War. However, as the senior officer, it was Stuart who gained the kudos, and in gratitude for his services the King of the two Sicilies created him the Count of Maida at the end of the campaign, and the General was now parading his newly acquired title in front of London society, 'As if he was a modern day Alexander the Great.'

As Commander-in-Chief of the Army the Duke of York had the final say and, turning down Stuart for reasons already mentioned and Craufurd for lack of seniority, instead chose John Whitelocke, currently the Inspector-General of Recruiting, a position requiring no great military skill and certainly not one to inspire the confidence of the average soldier.

Trained at Lochee's Military Academy, Chelsea, John Whitelocke was a bluff, corpulent, stubborn officer who firmly believed that coarse manners, blunt speech and rudeness denoted a tough soldier. He was convinced these attributes, combined with swearing like a trooper, would make him popular with his soldiers, when in fact his crude behaviour and arrogant manner made him disliked by his officers and men, who easily saw through his act.

Commissioned as an ensign in 1778, Whitelocke would fifteen years later make his name during Admiral Villeneuve's attack in 1793 on Port-au-Prince. When a Lt Colonel, he sent his ADC with a letter to the French General offering to pay him £5,000 if he persuaded his men to lay down their arms and surrender. General Laveaux, the officer in question, was an aristocrat of the old school who, reading the letter, politely asked the young officer who brought it if he knew its contents. The young man innocently replied he had not the slightest idea, and the General declared, 'Then

I congratulate you on your luck Sir! For if you had, I would have immediately given orders for you to be hanged from the nearest tree!' He then challenged Whitelocke to a duel for his insulting behaviour, which the Englishman refused to accept.

During his military career, Whitelocke had served in many regiments including 36th, 60th, and 13th Foot, and had fought without distinction in India, Egypt and the Cape of Good Hope. His brother officers therefore greatly resented his appointment, which caused a considerable stir, and General Lord Henry Paget (future Earl of Uxbridge – later to lose his leg at Waterloo) angrily declared,

'How the devil such a man as this could be chosen? For independent of manners which are coarse and brutal, he is notoriously known to have the greatest antipathy to the smell of gun powder!'

Lt Colonel Fletcher Wilkie likewise had his doubts, and scathingly writes 'Without scarcely an idea beyond the limits of a drill ground, he had the most pure and perfect contempt for the opinion of others.'

Despite his many critics, Whitelocke had two strong supporters: his brother-in-law Sir Robert Brownrigg (uncle of the Colonel killed at Montevideo) who held an important position in the War Office, and Lord Granville Leveson-Gower, brother of the Duchess of Beaufort. Although not actually a member of the Cabinet, His Lordship was an intimate friend of the Duke of York and as such was held in high regard by London society.

Not only renowned as a menace to his neighbours out shooting, Lord Granville was also famous for being a danger to the ladies, and his relationship with Lady Bessborough, sister of Georgiana Duchess of Devonshire, was common knowledge and had already produced two illegitimate children, one of whom became a Bishop. Their bond would last a lifetime, as in 1809 he married Lady Harriet Cavendish ('Harry-o'), Georgiana's daughter and Lady Bessborough's niece, and hence became not only part of the Devonshire set, but also her Ladyship's nephew-in-law.

Good-looking, and famous for his winning manners, Lord Granville had happily indulged in many other affairs, including one with Lady Hestor Stanhope, William Pitt's niece, and it was strongly rumoured that the Prime Minister appointed His Lordship as Ambassador to St Petersburg in 1804 only to terminate this embarrassing liaison.

Despite his attractive personality, not all of Lord Granville's encounters were successful, as he received a firm rebuff from that celebrated *demi-mondaine* Harriet Wilson. One morning, hearing the young Duke of Leinster mention that Lord Granville was considered very good-looking, she immediately invited him to an assignation in Marylebone Fields. Their meeting was not a success for, writing in her famous memoirs the irrepressible Miss Wilson declares,

'Lord Granville's looks failed to come up to my expectation, and he was therefore made to suffer. But I conceived that having brought a man up to Marylebone Fields on such a terribly hot day, it would have not been fair or Ladylike to have dismissed him until I had given his talents and power of pleasing a fair trial. I therefore walked him up to the top of Primrose Hill then towards Hampstead and back again to Great Portland Street.

'At last His Lordship made a full stop and taking off his hat to wipe his face declared, he could go no further as he was quite unaccustomed to walking and the sun was so very oppressive. He therefore entreated that I would permit him to accompany me immediately to my house, if only to sit down and rest or otherwise he apprehended a stroke of fever or sudden death!' Lord Granville's ploy had no success, as Harriet firmly assured him, 'I was sorry, very sorry, and hoped such a fatal consequence would not follow our little bit of rural pleasure. While at the same time, I could only express my regrets and frankly declared to him that he was not in the least the sort of person I wanted!'

Several years later they would meet up again in Paris, where Lord Granville was now the British Ambassador. Despite at first receiving a stern rebuff Harriet, probably with the help of a little blackmail, successfully persuaded him to forward her memoirs to her London publisher in the diplomatic bag.

Lord Granville's appointment as Ambassador to France proved a great success and he soon became popular with the *Beau Monde*. Famous for his skill at cards, and considered one of the best whist players at the time, the Parisians greatly admired his addiction to high play and flatteringly called him, 'Le Wellington des joueurs.'

During the intrigue and struggle to obtain command of the expedition to South America, Lord Granville struck a bargain with General Whitelocke that in exchange for his support, influence and diplomatic skill, should the General be selected to command the Army he would appoint His Lordship's nephew, Major-General John Leveson-Gower, to be his second-in-command. After receiving the appointment, Whitelocke duly kept his part of the bargain. It proved a disastrous choice, as Leveson-Gower was if possible even stupider and more arrogant than Whitelocke.

Known as a drawing room soldier and a 'go-onner', not a 'follow-onner,' he had little military experience and when only twenty had purchased a Colonelcy in the 63rd. Disloyal throughout the whole of the South American campaign, he never ceased to dispute Whitelocke's commands, criticise Auchmuty and veto Craufurd and Colonel Pack's sensible suggestions. General Sir Harry Smith, then a lieutenant in the 95th, suffered under Leveson-Gower's behaviour throughout the campaign and describes him in his memoirs, 'As an overbearing disobedient man that ought to have been dismissed the service.' Winter was approaching as the three British Generals – Whitelocke, Leveson-Gower and Auchmuty – waited impatiently in Montevideo for the arrival of the fourth, General Craufurd and the Light Brigade.

TWENTY

THE VOYAGE OF THE LIGHT BRIGADE

Due to the ever-increasing escalation of trouble spots around the world, the Government in 1806 ordered detachments of troops to be stationed aboard ships docked in various ports along the English Channel. This had several advantages: firstly, they could be deployed at a moment's notice, secondly it saved the expense of building barracks to billet them in and, lastly, it solved the problem of desertion. British soldiers had a reputation of getting drunk and causing trouble among the local population so, by keeping them at sea, this inconvenience was also eliminated. Another two years would pass before the Duke of Wellington formed the first Military Police unit during the Peninsular War, in a vain attempt to stop his soldiers, fuelled by an excess of cheap or stolen liquor, from killing, looting and other misdemeanours.

On receiving Windham's orders, Craufurd immediately set off for Falmouth and arriving there on 24 October found the town bustling with activity. The inns were full to bursting point and anxious officers packed the shops, buying their wives clothing and provisions for the lengthy voyage. All day long the agents of the Commissariat scurried up and down the quays stocking the ships with supplies while at night, the dreaded press gangs lurked down darkened alleyways patiently waiting to pounce on any unsuspecting merchant sailor or country bumpkin leaving the pothouses worse for wear.

Craufurd's first order: 'Officers' wives should immediately leave the ships, as the coming expedition would be far too dangerous' was very unpopular, and produced a considerable amount of ill feeling. Many of the officers had already spent their pay on buying their wives food and clothing for the journey and would now be forced to spend more money on sending them to stay with their relatives or friends in the country. They angrily declared that Craufurd should have given this order earlier but, with hindsight, all admitted the order had been right though at the time it was greatly resented.

Waiting impatiently for his arrival, Craufurd found the 5th, 36th, 45th, 88th Infantry Regiments, five companies of the 95th, two squadrons of the 6th Dragoons, and two Batteries of the Royal Artillery. Many of the men had been on board their ships since the end of July and, although the officers had tried hard to keep them fit, in the confines of the ships it had been a losing battle.

The General spent the next two weeks personally inspecting every ship to ensure his men were properly quartered and had sufficient victuals for their long sea voyage. He was pleasantly surprised to find that almost every detail had been covered and even the hulls of the transport ships had been sheathed in copper to increase their speed, an expensive operation normally reserved for only Men-of-War.

Satisfied with his inspection, he ordered the convoy to set sail on 12 November, and to the sound of regimental bands playing patriotic tunes, cheering spectators, sobbing wives and girlfriends, the ships sailed out into the English Channel to carry out the Government's optimistic order of conquering an area double the size of Europe. Stretching out behind the convoy followed a long line of merchant ships, whose optimistic owners were determined not to miss out on making their fortunes in Popham's newly found land of *El Dorado*.

For the next three days, the weather remained fine and the sea calm. But despite the Channel resembling a millpond, most of the soldiers were sick before the convoy passed the Lizard as travelling in a troopship was an unpleasant experience. Dom Domingos Coutinho, the Portuguese Ambassador at the Court of St James, writing a year later from Brixham to his friend Viscount Stanhope on his way to take up his position as British ambassador in Rio, begs him, 'To prevail upon Canning, the Foreign Secretary, and make one more attempt to represent to him the indecency of sending me with troops for the Cape of Good Hope, who are such bad sailors, that even the East India Company will not allow them to sail with their fleet.'

Colonel Tarleton, 'The Green Dragoon,' and hero of the American War of Independence, also emphasises the danger of travelling in a troopship. In a long speech to Parliament on 4 Feb 1791 in defence of the slave trade for the benefit of his constituency of Bristol, he produces the following alarming statistic,

'The number of slave deaths in the Liverpool ships has never exceeded five out of a hundred, whereas the average in the regiments sent to the Indies or America is about ten and a half soldiers in the hundred.'

The weather suddenly changed on the 15th, and a severe storm struck the convoy, carrying away the main mizzenmast of the *Juliana*, the headquarter ship of the 36th (The Herefordshire Regiment). Eleven ships vanished in the night that would reappear again at around noon the following day, but the wind continued and by the 19th reached gale force, blowing the convoy apart again. The frigate *Nereide* and a merchantman vanished off the Cape Finisterre and the sea became so rough that the store ship *Campion* began to leak and over five foot of water had filled her hold before the source was discovered and successfully blocked.

Captain Stopford, third son of the Earl of Radnor and Commander of the convoy, was greatly relieved to see the *Nereide* reappear on the horizon a few days later. He had been convinced that she had either sunk or was so badly damaged that she was struggling back to England for repairs. In fact, the opposite had occurred for, blown off the coast of Portugal, her Captain had spotted a Spanish corvette and a Portuguese merchantman battling their way along the coast and, unwilling to let good prize money slip through his fingers, had immediately set off in pursuit. His chase had been successful and both ships could now be seen safely on tow behind the *Nereide*.

Steadily the weather began to improve and, sailing past Madeira on 6 December, Craufurd sent the Commissary-General with a brig and store ship into port to purchase wine, sugar, and, more importantly, fresh lemons to combat the scurvy already attacking the troops. Twenty days later, this little party caught up with the convoy and began distributing their purchases among the ships. The wine at £45 a pipe was considered cheap at the price. As well as being drunk, two freshly caught dolphins were gently poached in it, and the resulting touch of *haut-cuisine* declared delicious.

Up to now, the journey had been long and tedious, but life cheered up as the ships approached the line and the decks were cleared for the traditional ceremony to take place.

Three sailors, dressed in old sacks with painted faces and powdered wigs of oakum to represent Neptune, Amphytrite and her assistant, demanded their customary dues from those crossing it for the first time. The officers escaped lightly by agreeing to donate a half a gallon of rum to each member of Neptune's court but, unable to be so generous, the soldiers were forced to endure the following ceremony.

'Seated on a pole stretched across a tub filled with water, they were forced to kiss an axe covered in tar and some other evil smelling mixture. This concoction was smeared over their faces, and they were then shaved with a blunt razor. To end this hilarious entertainment, the pole was suddenly snatched away; the victim fell into the tub and to the enjoyment of the spectators given a good ducking.' A delighted watcher gleefully reports, 'This ceremony ended with a drunken frolic at the expense of many a black eye and bloody nose.'

The weather slowly began to get hotter, and Private George Bee of the 5th, writing home to his brother in Lincolnshire in his rather shaky spelling, declares, 'We set sail and crost the lion on 29 March (it was in fact the middle of December) wear the sun is Right up and Down and not a Bet of shader.'

The expedition finally reached Porto Praya on St Jago, the largest of the Cape Verde Islands, on 14 December and, as the harbour came into view, a thirteen-gun salute greeted its arrival which, as protocol demanded, the *Spencer* duly returned.

Windham's instructions to Craufurd were to take on fresh victuals, and wait here for the arrival of Admiral Murray and his squadron who would then escort them on to the River Plate.

Supplying a convoy of this size abroad was a complicated exercise, and care was needed on how it should be done. No communication was allowed with the shore until an agreement had been reached with the tradesmen on a fair price for the articles that the fleet required, as a failure to do so could easily lead to the shopkeepers grossly overcharging, and result in unpleasant and frequently physical arguments.

Early the next morning, Craufurd and his staff came ashore to negotiate the details and on disembarking was flattered to be welcomed by a twenty-two-gun salute. Obviously, the Portuguese Governor was regretting his previous day's rather meagre thirteen-gun salute and in no way wished to risk offending the Commander of what he now could see was a very formidable force. Negotiations began immediately, and once the arrangements had been completed Craufurd gave the signal for the waiting ships to come ashore and the bay exploded into a frenzy of activity. Fifty longboats with their sailors straining on the oars raced to shore spurred on by the ship's pursers, eager to obtain first choice of what the market had to offer. Behind them at a more leisurely pace came a long line of supply boats carrying on board the ship's butchers, who once on shore immediately began slaughtering the newly purchased cattle.

Always conscious of his men's health, Craufurd gave orders for the troops to be fed meat four times a week. This was not as good as it sounded as the quality of the beef was poor but the market stalls abounded with other delicacies, such as goats, turkeys, fowls, tropical fruits, and some long leafed cabbages and lettuce which the pursers eagerly seized on. Those lucky enough to reach the shore first bought everything at two thirds of the regulated price, as not all the tradesmen had been informed of the agreed rate. The shopkeepers quickly compensated for their temporary loss as by the time the fleet left the island, they had trebled the price of everything on offer in their shops.

Having replenished the ships with victuals, next came the laborious task of refilling the ships' casks with water. This was organised by regiment and the great barrels were landed on a suitable sandy beach. From there, they were trundled to a valley about half a mile away where two ship's pumps extracted water from a well into a long wooden trough. Four hoses then delivered it into the casks and despite the locals pessimistically forecasting the water would run out, eight hogsheads were filled every day.

Next on Craufurd's agenda was the defence of the ships lying in port. Throughout the voyage, there had been repeated rumours that a French squadron out of Brest was pursuing them and, should this appear, the sixteen Portuguese guns guarding the bay would be of little use as their mountings were in such a poor state that they could scarcely withstand the shock of firing a salute, let alone a cannonball in earnest. To rectify this danger, Craufurd ordered a number of cannons to be unloaded from the ships, and once on shore his artillery officers began sighting them at strategic points around the harbour.

After this he quickly formed a police force to maintain peaceful relations with the locals and instructed them to arrest the occupants of any vessel attempting to land on the island after sunset. Apart from the possibility of sabotage, the General had no intention of allowing his men to sneak ashore and desert, or worse, get drunk and upset the locals.

His fears proved prophetic but it was not the men that got inebriated but the officers. The future General Sir Samuel Whittingham writing in his memoirs, rather self-appreciatively declares,

'Captain Whittingham's knowledge of languages was very useful to the Brigadier-General not only in official matters but also very agreeable to the donna and her two lovely daughters in whose house he was quartered. For as the Staff Officer of the force, he had to settle a serious affair that was the result of the wanton midnight freaks of some wild British officers who, obviously having over-indulged in the local wine, insulted the Portuguese Governor, Don Antonio Contiñho and his guard.

'The Hon Captain — was madly determined to force the Governor *into a bag*, which he had obtained especially for the purpose and it was only with difficulty that he was dissuaded from carrying out his scheme. To his credit, the Governor took it in good heart for after accepting Whittingham's and the offender's apologies he hospitably invited them to dinner'. Whittingham fails to mention whether the Captain succeeded in his efforts but regretfully adds, 'Sorry I am to say, I never saw my countryman to less advantage!'

On the morning of 31 December, the 5th (The Northumberland Regiment of Foot) and the 30th (The Queen's Lancashire Regiment) came ashore to practise for the following day's New Year parade. But due to the ever present fear of desertion, the men were not trusted to remain on land and in the afternoon were rowed back to their overcrowded ships.

The New Year's parade proved a huge success and, at the first sound of the fifes and drums, the shops and markets quickly emptied. An excited crowd of spectators rushed to watch the smartly dressed soldiers march up and down in their highly polished boots, and an English officer watching their enthusiasm rather patronisingly remarks, 'The locals were more accustomed to seeing a ragged assembly of ill-disciplined men in scruffy uniforms, armed with useless weapons marching up and down out of step.' Equally unimpressed by the aspect of the natives, Private George Bee dismissively writes, 'The pepoll was all black and nothing to cover their privats'.

Craufurd's original plan was to land all the regiments and

exercise them in rotation. But, in the end, only four took the opportunity before orders were given for the Army to prepare to leave the island. However, after holding a Council of War with his senior officers, Craufurd cancelled the order in the hope that Admiral Murray and his escort might still arrive and, realising that this could be their last chance of obtaining supplies, the pursers hastily boarded their long-boats and sped ashore to scour the countryside for further provisions despite their highly inflated prices.

The Army had now been stuck on the island for nearly a month, and at the end of the week the General's patience finally ran out. Tired of waiting for the errant Admiral to appear, he gave orders for the ships to get underway and the fleet sailed out of Porto Praya, leaving behind in the harbour two schooners and a French vessel from Senegal that was on her way to Martinique with a cargo of slaves.

The forty men, women, and children on board were indeed a pitiful sight but, due to Porto Praya being a neutral port, Captain Stopford was forbidden to seize her. Permanently kept in chains, each slave had an area no larger than a coffin to lie on and, with no sanitation, the stench from this leaky schooner of less than thirty-five tons could be smelt several leagues away whenever the wind blew from her direction.

Once out to sea, Captain Stopford, having accomplished his mission, fired a farewell salute and the two seventy-four-gun battleships swung north for England, while the remainder of the fleet, led by the *Nereide*, continued their journey south towards the Cape. For the next two weeks the friendly trade winds carried them gently south, then another severe storm struck the convoy, carrying away the main mast of the store ship *Ware*, and the *Campion* again began to leak.

By now the old ship was seriously holding up the convoy

and, fed up with the delay, the Commodore ordered her stores and troops to be dispersed among the other vessels. Once this had been completed he ordered the *Campion*'s Captain to reach the Cape as best he could, and her crew watched in disbelief as the fleet disappeared over the horizon, leaving them frantically manning the pumps to escape a watery grave in Davy Jones's locker.

Over the following days the weather gradually became calmer, and a pleasant relief to the boredom of the voyage came on 2 February, when over the horizon appeared a British sloop on her way to Buenos Aires. This brought them their first news from Europe since leaving Falmouth two months earlier, and more importantly a message from the Admiralty advising Craufurd that Admiral Murray and his fleet would be waiting for him at the Cape, still three weeks away.

The storm had seriously upset their timetable and the General now announced that the convoy would not be putting into another port before reaching the Cape, and the pursers began to worry as most of the fresh food embarked at Porto Praya had almost run out. One ship gloomily reported,

'All they had left to eat were three goats (nearly starved); two pigs; half a dozen turkeys, and a cow that supplied them with milk, which they were reluctant to hand her over to the butcher as although very thin, she still produced a little milk.'

The vegetable situation was little better, and an effort to catch some fish ended in failure, when the tackle was discovered to be rotten. The situation was serious, and after a lengthy discussion it was decided that a system of food rationing should be introduced, and two days were allotted each week when only ship's rations should be eaten.

It was bad news as these consisted of weevily biscuits and salted meat, both of which tasted vile and had provided little nourishment. Describing this unappetising fare in his memoirs, Baron Jeffrey de Raigersfeld, serving a year earlier as a midshipman at the battle of Trafalgar, writes,

'The biscuit served to the ship's company was so light that when you tapped it upon the table it fell almost into dust, and out of it crawled numerous insects called weevils. These were bitter to the taste, and a sure indication that the biscuit had lost its nutritious particles. But if instead of these weevils, large white maggots with black heads made their appearance then the biscuit was considered to be only in its first state of decay. These maggots, although fat and cold to the taste, were not bitter unlike the biscuits that became hollow and crumbled with age. The meat in contrast grew so hard that the sailors could carve it into fancy articles, such as little boxes that were capable of taking a high polish like fine-grained wood.'

Being mostly beef or pork, the meat was often several years old and preserved in caked salt; it had to be soaked for at least a day in water before being cooked. Even then, it tasted very salty and wine, which once had been prolific, was now strictly rationed, forcing the troops to drink the stagnant water. Disease soon began to affect the men; diarrhoea ran rampant through the fleet, and four soldiers, an officer and a hospital mate died of dysentery.

Morale was low, but spirits rose a few days later when a shoal of flying fish jumped from and landed on the decks. Hastily grabbing an assortment of cooking pots and buckets, the excited sailors rushed to scoop them up and although little bigger than herrings they were a pleasant change from the weevily biscuits and solid chunks of salty meat.

On 17 February Table Mountain finally came into view but, due to first becoming becalmed and then battered by storms, rough seas and conflicting orders, the fleet failed to make harbour until two weeks later. While waiting out to sea for the weather to change, the convoy had a pleasant surprise when over the horizon under full sail appeared the *Campion*. Having kept further to the west of the convoy, the old ship had fallen in earlier with the Trade Winds, enabling her to catch them up but, once back with the convoy, she soon began to drop astern. Nevertheless being bereft of cargo, as soon as the wind picked up she sailed ahead and made harbour five days before the rest of the fleet, much to the delight of her Captain still smarting from being so cruelly abandoned.

Craufurd found Admiral Murray and his escort waiting in port for his arrival, who gave him the bad news that Buenos Aires had been re-taken, and Beresford and all his men were now prisoners-of-war. He then presented Craufurd with fresh instructions from the Cabinet ordering him to abandon the original plan of invading Chile, and join Auchmuty in the River Plate as quickly as possible.

TWENTY-ONE

CAPE TOWN AND ST HELENA

The following weeks passed pleasantly, as the ships were loaded with provisions and the officers spent happy hours exploring Cape Town and the surrounding countryside. Nevertheless, owing to the perpetual threat of desertion the men were not trusted to come ashore and were firmly held on board their overcrowded ships.

A year had passed since Baird's invasion; the town was beginning to prosper and although possessing only one inn, 'The British Hotel,' an officer writing home assures any future visitor that 'No genteel stranger need feel at a loss for accommodation, as the best families in the place will receive him in their house as a boarder, or lodger on very moderate terms.'

Cape Town had many attractions to keep the officers entertained, including a lion and lioness, which were kept in a cage behind the Fort and, having once belonged to the Dutch East India Company, the Government gardens were pretty and well kept. Every Sunday the regimental bands played light music underneath the trees and this pleasant sound attracted the ladies of the town to promenade along their shady paths in the cool of the evening. Describing these women, Major Gillespie rather rudely remarks,

'The Cape women were pretty in their youth, and had good figures that unfortunately turned to fat as they grew older showing that they were closely allied to the Dutch. They were very fashion conscious but according to information obtained from a gentleman resident, their morals left much to be desired!

'The gross manner of living in Cape Town doubtless promotes the corpulency of its inhabitants. It is not unusual to see a married lady, nay even the unwedded, to sup on fish swimming in the fat of sheep's tails appropriated for the purpose of frying; a second course of beefsteaks with onions, and after a bumper of hollands (gin) dive into bed'. Colonel Fletcher Wilkie likewise writes,

'The Cape girls are pleasant and good tempered nymphs enough, possessing good figures. Many of them have handsome countenances but their extreme fairness throws an air of insipidity over them, such as may be remarked in women of very fair skin in England. It is said that this pallid look they encourage by drinking vinegar, and look on rosy skin as a blemish. I asked a Cape girl of what she thought of Miss N… whose beautiful complexion I alluded to when speaking of Brazil. Her answer was that the young lady looked as if she had been drinking brandy! Perhaps this extreme desire for fairness arises from the contrast it forms with all the shades of brown and black, and denotes pureness of European blood.'

Food was abundant; the markets overflowed with vegetables but beef although plentiful was considered of inferior quality owing to the cattle being fed on rank and sour grass. Mutton, on the other hand, was excellent, fat, and with a delicate flavour. The flocks were large, and the sheep famous for the formation of their tails, which had a solid lump of fat about eight inches wide at their base. Weighing about eight pounds, this was used as a substitute for cooking butter, and made excellent dripping that the slaves spread on their bread out working in the fields.

Poultry and game were expensive and a young ostrich could cost as much as two or three guineas a pair; while more exotic animals, like a lion or leopard, could be purchased for around seven guineas. Corn was plentiful, so the bread was good. The same could not be said about the wine for, although deemed passable, the white wines were not impressive, and only the red wines of Constantia considered drinkable; but having only a small production these were scarce. The best Cape madeira cost five shillings a gallon but other wines although cheaper were considered unsafe to drink.

Being mostly Dutch or of Dutch descent, the European population did little work, relying on their slaves to do it for them. A British officer on the expedition observes,

'The slaves were taught every trade and were let out of their quarters each day in the same manner as horses and cattle are released from their stables or barns in Europe. The males are roughly treated, but the females well looked after on account of their breeding potential'.

Owing to a virulent epidemic of measles brought by a cargo ship from Mozambique, slaves were scarce and prices high. The outbreak was so serious that during Craufurd's stay around eight hundred people died from the epidemic. Seven thousand white inhabitants lived in the town and nearly double that number of slaves and, because of this difference in numbers, the fear of an uprising was always present. A strong and watchful police kept the slaves at all times under constant supervision and the strictest of these were the emancipated slaves and Hottentots who, armed with swords, stood on every street corner to ensure there was no trouble. Owing to the darkness of their skins, the slaves were forbidden to walk through the streets at night without carrying a lighted lantern and, if caught without one, the offender was instantly thrown into jail.

Capital punishment was frequent but, much to the Dutch residents' disapproval, the British had banned execution on the wheel and replaced it with hanging, which they declared was a far lesser deterrent as the natives were superstitious and firmly believed that St Peter would never accept them into heaven with mutilated limbs.

When Baird captured the Cape the previous year, it had been in a sorry state and many of the inhabitants had barely sufficient clothing to decently leave their houses. This had changed thanks to the profitable export of bullion and paper money was now the only currency, which greatly benefited the British soldiers. Being paid four shillings and eight pence a week in sterling they could profitably change the silver coin into notes at a premium of six shillings and five pence.

Having replenished his ships with victuals and water, Craufurd and the Light Division left the Cape on 5 April and, escorted by Admiral Murray and his squadron, continued their journey to South America. The weather remained fine, the sea calm, the wind favourable, and two weeks later the forbidding Island of St Helena rose slowly out of the sea to greet them. Its dark precipitous cliffs bristled with gun batteries and as the ships drew slowly closer, they could see intermittent flashes of light flickering from point to point to signal to the gun emplacements around the island the approach of an unknown stranger.

Ignoring these threatening signs, the fleet sailed around the Island's northernmost point and passing under an impressive rock came to anchor in front of Jamestown, the capital and only town on the island.

The high cliffs surrounding the harbour sheltered it from the wind and a mass of notices covered the seafront that sternly announced, 'No vessel or person should land without first presenting their credentials to the authorities'. To ensure that no one could claim ignorance as to where they should present their papers, one notice larger than the others stood next to a great gun emplacement covering the port's anchorage. This had written on it in large white letters the word, 'BOAT,' in French, Dutch and English, so that no one could claim ignorance of its meaning.

This warning was not to be taken lightly, as the Captain of the *Diadem* had discovered the previous year when proceeding to his anchorage in St James's Bay. Believing the regulation not to apply to a Royal Naval Man-of-War, he had been startled out of his wits when a shot flew across his ship's bows, followed swiftly by another even closer to remind him that no one was exempt from this order.

It was not the only hazard. The sea was rough and approaching the landing place dangerous. One boat capsized in the swell and only the rapid assistance of the other boats saved its occupants, still valiantly clutching their papers, from being devoured by the horde of hungry sharks which permanently circled the bay waiting for some succulent morsel to satisfy their perpetual hunger.

Only forty-seven square miles in size, St Helena was an important victualling station for ships trading between England and India. It had been in the hands of the East India Company since 1659, and was therefore considered a British colony and came under the administration of a British Governor and an executive council. Jamestown, its capital, had none of the charm of Cape Town and was very small – possessing only one street, which gradually wound its way up through a long narrow gorge flanked on either side by steep rock faces. Neat rows of thatched English cottages stood on either side of this solitary thoroughfare that steadily became more dilapidated as the visitor progressed. Halfway up the hill stood the barracks and next to them the hospital, the chance of coming out of which alive was reckoned very slim. At the end of the road, a long flat plateau stretched across the top of the island dotted with country houses that their owners retired to when there were no ships in the harbour.

The little town had only two amenities: a small plain church and a playhouse, which during Craufurd's stay was disappointingly closed as, either dissatisfied by the size of their audiences or appreciation of their performance, the actors had recently returned to England. Living on the island were two thousand white men of English descent, and roughly double that number of slaves. This number could fluctuate for, just as at the Cape, an outbreak of measles was decimating the population so badly that during the convoy's stay only a few officers and the Commissariat were permitted to go ashore.

Wood was scarce, so fuel was a perpetual problem, and the islanders frequently had to break up the old gun carriages to keep their stove and fires alight. The climate was also very changeable, as in winter it rained incessantly and fog covered the island. While in summer it was extremely hot and clouds of flies unremittingly attacked the inhabitants. Even more unpleasant, a large horde of rats infested the island, which eight years later would cause General Bertrand's wife Fanny considerable anguish, when exiled on the island in attendance on Napoleon.

The defence of the island lay in the hands of the St Helena Corps, who were employed by the East India Company. Normally numbering around 900 undisciplined soldiers, these were fewer than usual owing to Sir Home Riggs Popham having removed a hundred and eighty a year before to take with him to Buenos Aires. Gun emplacements covered every inch of the ground, along with numerous signal stations carefully sited on prominent positions around the island to keep the gun crews in touch with each other.

Lost in the middle of the Atlantic Ocean, St Helena was an impenetrable fortress; the ideal place for the allies to exile the Emperor Napoleon to after the battle of Waterloo, and ninety years later Field Marshal Smuts and his Generals at the end of the Boer War.

Having filled the ships' holds with fresh provisions and water, Craufurd and the convoy left the island on 25 May and, eighteen days later, the lofty towers of Montevideo's Cathedral appeared on the horizon. The Light Brigade's journey was over, but many of the men had been on board their ships for over nine months, and only the butchers and troops that had paraded five months earlier at Porto Praya had set foot on land since leaving England. The men of the Light Brigade were in poor shape, and totally unfit for the campaign that, only three days later, General Whitelocke would order them to embark on.

TWENTY-TWO

WHITELOCKE'S INVASION PLANS

With the arrival of Craufurd and the Light Brigade, General Whitelocke's Army was finally complete, and with Craufurd's invasion of Chile definitely abandoned, Lt Colonel Sir Lancelot Holland (Craufurd's brother-in-law) cheerfully declares,

'General Whitelocke behaved in a very handsome manner by offering General Craufurd leave to go home immediately, or the command of a Brigade in the coming attack on Buenos Aires. Accepting the latter, the Commander in Chief gave him the 36th, 45th Regiments and a Grenadier Company for his Brigade.'

Sir Lancelot optimistically continues, 'There were also orders for our staff to return to England immediately after the fall of Buenos Aires, which gave me great satisfaction as I felt sure of soon setting out for England.'

Before leaving England, Whitelocke had received the following orders from 10 Downing Street signed in the absence of Windham by the Secretary of State, Lord Howick, the future Earl Grey.

'Sir—It having been thought advisable that an officer of high rank, as well as approved talents and judgement, should be sent to take command of his Majesty's forces as are at this time employed or likely soon to be employed in the southern provinces of South America. I am therefore to inform you that his Majesty has been graciously pleased to make choice of you for that purpose, and you are to prepare forthwith in a vessel to the south of the river Plate and there to take upon you the said command.'

He then informs the General that he is placing around 9,000 troops under his command, consisting of Sir Samuel Auchmuty's force of 5,380 men; Colonel Backhouse's 2,000 men already there and the 1,600 men travelling with him. This number would be further increased by another 4,212 men should Admiral Murray successfully meet up with Craufurd at the Cape. If not, Craufurd following his orders to conquer Chile would be rounding Cape Horn and he left it to Whitelocke's discretion to order him to return to the River Plate, or continue with the original plan. Even without Craufurd, the Government considered this force adequate for any purpose Whitelocke might have in view, and should Craufurd and the Light Division appear he was to,

'Detach at the very earliest moment in which you will judge it safe to do so, the 89th and any other regiment that you may think are strong enough to spare after your first operations, who are to proceed to the Cape and from thence to India. With the force above stated, you will execute the service entrusted to you in the reduction of the Province of Buenos Aires under the authority of his Majesty.' Windham then specifically ordered Whitelocke not to:

'1) Annoy or distress the enemy. The occupation of such stations. or portion of territory as being once subject to his Majesty's arms, could not be easily recoverable. Moreover, it would require for the preservation of them a body of troops more considerable than it may be conceived this country would be willing to spare. The number certainly ought not to exceed that now placed under your command.

'2) The greatest care must be taken in whatever part his Majesty's authority shall be established, and the most earnest endeavours used to conciliate the good will of the inhabitants. Abstain from everything that can shock their religious opinions or prejudices by respecting their persons and property by a removal of those restrictions and impositions of which they most complain, and by making them feel in general the beneficial influence of his Majesty's government, as compared with that under which they were before placed.

'3) The principal to be observed must be to abstain as much as possible from everything that can infringe upon the rights, privileges, and established usages of any class of inhabitant. Do not; introduce into the government any other change than that which must necessarily arise from the substitution of his Majesty's authority for that of the King of Spain. Individuals it may be necessary to change but in doing so the preference should as much as possible be given to the native inhabitants over persons born in old Spain. All those instrumental in promoting or executing the insurrection against General Beresford should be carefully removed, and either sent to Europe or placed in some situation where their machinations may no longer be dangerous.

'His Majesty will not surrender but with great reluctance possessions to which he attaches so much value, and would in no case consent to such surrender without providing for the security of those who from the attachment shown to his Majesty might be fearful of having rendered themselves obnoxious to the displeasure of their former Government'.

Windham further encouraged Whitelocke to raise a native Army but like any parsimonious Government of today added the proviso, 'A strict regard must be kept on economy.' The orders grandly end by announcing, 'The honour of the country is at stake and under all circumstances, General Beresford and his Army must be freed.'

As can be seen, the Government gave the General an

impossible task. Not only was he to conquer a country and capture a city without damaging the people's possessions but when doing so, not to upset their feelings. Secondly, under no circumstances must he guarantee British protection to anyone supporting him should the Government later sign a peace treaty with Spain, and lastly recruit a native Army of malcontents using the minimum amount of expense to pay and equip them.

Keeping these impossible instructions in mind, Whitelocke began work on his invasion plans and like Popham before him, soon realised the invasion would have to be an entirely military operation. The River Plate was far too shallow for a Man-of-War to sail in close enough to shore to bombard the enemy position but once his troops had landed the Navy could be useful in supplying them with provisions. He therefore needed to find a suitable landing place, which presented a problem, as information on the area was difficult to obtain. So he sent Captain Thompson and Lt Colonel Bourke aboard *The Fly* to reconnoitre the area. They returned a few days later to report,

'We examined a considerable extent of the coastline for at least sixty miles eastward of Ensenada, and as far as six or seven miles westward of Buenos Aires. The result of which examination was that we believed that there was no place where the troops could land under cover of the smallest ships of war, except at the Ensenada de Baragan. We were particularly anxious to ascertain if a landing could be effected to the westward of the city but Captain Thompson was decidedly of the opinion that the navigation was too intricate to render it at all safe to conduct a fleet of transports to that point.'

They further reported that the Spaniards had mounted a new gun emplacement overlooking the narrow landing beach at Quilmes, where Beresford had landed the previous year. However, Ensenada appeared devoid of defences and had the advantage 'Of beach nearby where the water was sufficiently deep to allow the landing craft into shore, and wide enough to disembark a large number of men at one time.'

This settled the question, and Whitelocke announced that Ensenada de Baragan should be the main landing point.

Having chosen a landing place, he next needed to find a route from there to the capital which also presented a problem, as the ground stretching two miles inland from the beach was only just above the water level of a large number of springs running down to the sea. Normally dry, this area, due to the rainy season having begun, was now under two feet of water but once across the flooded area the ground rose gradually up to a narrow ridge twelve or fifteen feet above sea level that extended west to the village of Reducción.

Through the middle of the unwelcoming swamp ran the River Riachuelo, whose wooden bridge at the Punta Galvez the Spaniards had destroyed the previous year in front of Beresford's Army and was rumoured to have now been rebuilt. Nothing was known of the countryside between Ensenada and Reducción, as undercover reconnaissance was out of the question, as few officers could speak Spanish so that even in disguise they would be easily detected, and have their throats cut by the extremely hostile natives. Likewise, a larger force would be more easily spotted and, once outnumbered, inevitably suffer the same fate.

Despite intensive enquiries, little information about the terrain or people could be gleaned from the inhabitants of Montevideo as, being over a hundred miles away, few citizens had any interest in going there. To find a solution to this knotty problem, a meeting was held and a staff officer suggested a priest might be bribed to accompany an officer to reconnoitre the ground. His bright idea was quickly vetoed when it was pointed out that there was no way of guaranteeing the prelate could be trusted. In the end, all that was known about Ensenada was that it was twenty miles from Reducción and Buenos Aires lay nine miles further on.

The other way of reaching the city was by marching along the shoreline but Whitelocke dismissed this route as the tides could be difficult. Instead, he elected to cross the marsh onto the higher ground and from there his troops could either follow the ridge to Reducción and cross the newly repaired bridge over the Riachuelo, or ford it higher up where the waters narrowed. This route had one major problem. Few farmhouses existed along the way in which his men could shelter from the wintry weather before reaching the suburbs of Buenos Aires but, on the plus side, the plains abounded with wild cattle that could be easily caught by bringing native lasso men from Montevideo. On the minus side, once caught there was little wood to make a fire to cook the meat on.

Transport was another serious problem. Horses were hard to find, and those obtained in Montevideo were either unbroken or too puny to pull the heavy gun carriages. Despite having three regiments of Dragoons at his disposal, Whitelocke could barely mount three squadrons of cavalry, all of whom he badly needed in this wide and open country.

To counteract the lack of transport, the General ordered his men to carry three days' rations in their knapsacks, which ought to be sufficient for them to reach Reducción where they could obtain fresh supplies from Admiral Stirling's ships now anchored off Point Quilmes. As he omitted to inform the Commissariat, the Army had actually landed before the Quartermaster-General discovered that he was not five, but thirty-five miles from Buenos Aires, and the only transport he had with him were half a dozen mule carts to carry the supplies off the beach. Whether through incompetence or neglect, this difficulty of provisioning the troops and the posting of orders was a problem that Whitelocke would fail to overcome throughout the whole of the coming campaign.

All that remained was to choose a date to launch the attack, which also presented a problem. The rainy season had begun and, although not as ferocious as the monsoons in India, should his men be exposed for any length of time to the elements the casualties from sickness would be high.

Asked for his opinion, Colonel Pack declared they should postpone the invasion until the spring, when the weather would be better. His sensible suggestion was curtly dismissed as this would give the enemy time to reinforce the town's defences, turning it from an open city into a fortified one.

Food stocks were running low; supplies hard to find and this crucial factor tipped Whitelocke into deciding the attack should be launched at once. He therefore ordered the Army to embark, and nine thousand soldiers began mounting the gangplanks of their ships. Trundling behind them: 3x24-pounders, 3x12-pounders, 5x4-pounders; 2xSt Helena 3-pounders; 2x12-inch mortars, and 5 howitzers along with sufficient ball and powder for two hundred rounds for each gun. Twenty thousand carbine cartridges and 40,000 rounds of rifle ball for the 95th's new Baker rifles were then carried on board, and carefully deposited in the ships' magazines along with eight wagons to carry the ammunition in.

One last decision remained. Should Colonia be kept as an

advanced station or be abandoned? Whitelocke himself was debating whether to transport the main Army to Colonia and wait there for Reducción to fall, and then land his men fresh and only nine miles away from the capital. Colonel Pack, already there, declared it should be kept as a supply base but, for some unknown reason, Whitelocke left the final decision to Leveson-Gower. Who arriving at Colonia, after only a cursory inspection, ordered the troops to be evacuated and the guns spiked, which settled the question.

By the evening of 16 June, everything was in place to launch the attack when Don Pedro Jose de Pando, a Captain of Hussars and aide-de-camp to Santiago Linares, arrived under the protection of a white flag to offer an exchange of prisoners. Describing their meeting, Sir Samuel Whittingham, who happened to be dining with General Whitelocke at the time, writes in his memoirs,

'General Whitelocke rejected the proposal altogether, and invited the Captain to dinner. In the course of the evening, he desired him to say to General Liniers that after the abusive letters he had addressed to his predecessor Sir Samuel Auchmuty, he could not possibly enter into any correspondence whatsoever.'

Having arrogantly dismissed the welfare of Beresford and his soldiers, Whitelocke ordered the ships to sail and two days later the soldiers set off on one of the most disastrous campaigns in the history of the British Army.

TWENTY-THREE

LA DEFENSA

After the defeat of General Beresford's Army, the inhabitants of Buenos Aires settled back to enjoy a continuous round of festivities. Civic celebrations, jubilant parties and religious ceremonies carried on for several weeks and many eminent citizens not only opened their houses but also their wallets to the brave defenders of their city. Prominent among these grateful patriots were Don Francisco Martinez de Hoz and his wife, who in honour of the conquerors gave a magnificent banquet and personally served their guests. They generously presented $25 to every soldier and sailor, along with fifteen endowments of $1,000 to the daughters of all those soldiers that had died during the battle.

As the celebrations drew slowly to a close, the citizens attempted to return to their previous way of life only to find it impossible, as their world had changed. On one thing, however, they unanimously agreed: that under no circumstances should the cowardly Viceroy ever be allowed to set foot in their capital again, and many declared he had done more damage to Spain than the enemy, a view strongly supported by the *Cabildo*.

The Viceroy's banishment brought with it many problems, for as head of state he was imbued with the powers of a sovereign. This meant that any legislation, tax or levy proposed by the *Cabildo* or *Real Audiencia* needed his signature to make it legal and they were forced to dispatch all their documents for him to sign. Finding the Viceroy was a difficult and lengthy operation, as he was continually on the move, hovering around the outskirts of the town and visiting him could lead to unpleasant encounters. One group of civic dignitaries was most incensed when a band of armed and suspicious citizens rudely stopped them, convinced that the Viceroy was travelling in disguise among their entourage or hiding in the baggage.

In order to find a solution to this knotty problem, the *Cabildo* dispatched Juan Martin de Pueyrredon and Juan Pedro de Velasquez to Spain, and ordered them to give Charles IV an eyewitness account of all that had taken place since the arrival of the British. They should describe to him in detail the heroic retaking of the city by its brave and loyal citizens, and at the same time emphasise Sobremonte's cowardly and inept behaviour. Unbeknown to the *Porteños* (citizens of Buenos Aires), a similar delegation had just arrived at court from the *Cabildo* of Cordoba sent by the Viceroy to complain of the seditious actions and rebellious behaviour of the citizens of Buenos Aires.

With the reports of the enemy's approach increasing daily, Linares began to draw up his plans for the defence of Buenos Aires. All able-bodied men were ordered to enlist in the militia and citizens from the same birthplace, or country of origin, began to join together to form regiments who took their names from the region that their members came from. For instance, the Buenos Aires regiments grandly called themselves '*Los Patricios*,' and the men from the North, '*Los Arribeños*.' While the newly arrived immigrants from Spain named theirs from the provinces they came from, such as *Andaluces, Catalanes, Asturianes* and so on. On 6 September, Linares summoned the citizens to a meeting in the Plaza Mayor and in a stirring speech appealed to their patriotic instincts and in stimulating words beseeched them,

'To arise invincible Cantabrians, intrepid Catalans, valiant

Asturians, Gallegos, Andaluces, Aragoneses, all of you that are proud to call yourselves Spaniards and are worthy of such a name. Unite in a true and immortal struggle, and defy this despicable enemy who not content with despoiling our cities, country, and ancient customs, now threatens to invade and occupy our peaceful coasts of America.'

Moved by his rousing oratory, the response was immediate; the citizens rushed to enlist and within a short time the Army surpassed 8,000 men, roughly consisting of two thousand cavalry, six thousand infantry, and a special battalion of Indians, half-breeds and slaves.

News of the approaching invasion quickly spread across the continent, and Peruvians, Chileans and Paraguayans flocked to defend their neighbour from the Anglo-Saxon invaders. Volunteers began to arrive from all over the country and, escorted by their braves, ten Indian Caciques (Chieftains) rode in from the pampas to hold a meeting with the *Cabildo* to assure them of their unshakeable loyalty. The Indians in their customary fashion embarked on a lengthy diatribe that lasted for several hours, and ended by them offering to raise twenty thousand warriors, each with five horses to defeat the red-coated devils. The Mayor, not to be outdone, gave an even lengthier response thanking them for their generous offer and tactfully ending by presenting them with bags of yerba mate, sugar, *aguardiente* (alcohol), all of which were graciously accepted.

As the Army grew, so dress became important, and each regiment began to design their own uniforms. These were styled in the latest of fashion and an army of tailors, seamstresses and wives laboured night and day to complete their colourful and flamboyant designs. Plumes, hats and boots were soon at a premium and the shops and stores quickly ran out of suitable material, while the metalworkers struggled to manufacture and engrave sufficient buttons to adorn their elegant tunics. So proud were the *Cabildo* of their finely dressed warriors, that they ordered engravings and drawings to be distributed among the public and one elaborate set was sent to the King to demonstrate the loyalty and affection of his subjects.

Officers were elected by their men, which although a new and democratic system did not always lead to a successful outcome. Many of those chosen to command their regiments were either popular figures, or rich merchants who had little knowledge of military strategy and still less of how to train a bunch of raw recruits in the skills of warfare.

Dressed in gaily-coloured uniforms and brightly plumed headgear, handsome young men filled the avenues and squares and without doubt, the most elegant of these were Pueyrredon's Hussars who irrespective of expense were dressed in the smartest of uniforms. The city soon began to resemble a vast military encampment, and their Commanding Officers so keen in training their newly formed regiments that they begged the *Cabildo* to close the cafes, bars, and shops between six and eight o'clock to ensure their men arrived punctually on parade and more importantly sober.

Patriotic spirits were running high, and this young and exuberant Army at times got carried away by the excitement of their military fervour. This happened on the Feast of Corpus Christi, when seven thousand infantry and cavalry with drums beating and banners unfurled marched proudly through the city's streets. In order to increase the solemnity of the occasion, the authorities unwisely ordered a cannon to be mounted at every corner of the city's most important streets to fire a salute as the procession passed. Although this was thought a good idea at the time, the plan proved a disaster as the loud explosion blew out the windows of the neighbouring houses, scattering shards of glass and splinters all over the adjacent street and pavements. The enraged and deafened owners vehemently complained to the *Cabildo* at this unnecessary damage and demanded instant compensation, as glass at the time was not only scarce but also very expensive.

It was not the only regrettable incident to take place that day. As carried away by the solemnity of the occasion, the Galician Regiment when marching past the figure of Our Lord failed to lower their newly presented colours and the Bishop of Buenos Aires, considering this an outrageous act of blasphemy, descended from his seat and solemnly advancing into the middle of the road imperiously raised his right arm, bringing the procession to a jolting halt. In strident tones, he demanded the regiment to lower their colours, which the *Gallegos* defiantly refused to do, proudly announcing to the assembled crowd 'They lowered their colours to no one.' As the Bishop's demands steadily increased so his tones became harsher, until begrudgingly the regiment lowered one colour. It was still not enough for the infuriated prelate who refused to move, until they finally lowered the other. It was the regiment's first battle, and first defeat, routed by Christ's army in the form of the bellicose Bishop.

Cannon and rifle fire echoed incessantly across the city over the following days and nights. Sometimes to celebrate the presentation of colours or herald the end of a parade but more often discharged in error. Watching these events unfold with disapproval, the veterans of the Viceroy's Army never ceased to criticise every move the *Cabildo* or Santiago Linares made. Like most old soldiers they held little respect for their civilian leaders, and even less for the newly raised militia who they refused to help, firmly declaring they had given their word of parole and were in honour-bound to keep it. However, when the invasion actually started, many of them offered to escort the convoys entering the city or volunteered to guard the boundaries of some distant frontier.

The Viceroy returned from Cordoba at the beginning of October. Carefully bypassing Buenos Aires due to his unpopularity, he set off to defend Montevideo and, arriving at Puerto de las Conchas to cross the river to Colonia, was extremely vexed when 400 of his Cordovan Army promptly deserted. Never having seen such a vast expanse of water before, these untrained recruits certainly had no intention of risking their lives by embarking on it and, delighted by their mutinous behaviour, the Buenos Aires citizens sarcastically cheered them as they passed through the city on their way back to Cordoba.

News of the fall of Maldonado, and that Montevideo was coming under constant shelling, reached Buenos Aires at the end of November. It appeared that the worst of these bombardments had occurred on the last day of October when the wind being favourable, the entire British fleet sailed close into shore and fired over 3,000 shells at the town, until forced to stop by the turning tide.

The Montevideo batteries stalwartly returned their fire, and the women and children acting as powder monkeys, bravely scurried up and down the ramparts carrying ammunition to the guns. The Governor gallantly strode the ramparts cheering on his brave defenders in contrast to the cowardly Viceroy, who keeping his head well down below the parapet scuttled up and down behind the sweating gunners.

By now Sobremonte's behaviour had become intolerable, as wherever he went he caused trouble. First, he fell out with Ruiz Huidobro over a proposal to attack Maldonado, and then sent orders to Buenos Aires that General Don

Pedro d'Arze, now famous for his turn of foot at the Puente Galvez, should be placed in command of the newly formed Regiments. His final order that 'the militia's new uniforms were far too gaudy and should be changed for something more sober' was a step too far, and the infuriated citizens began to search for a way to bring about his downfall.

Every action the Viceroy took was intended to usurp the position of Santiago Linares, Martin Alzaga and the *Cabildo*, in the hope of replacing them with his own supporters. He even went so far as to write to the Principe de la Paz, Manuel Godoy, the Queen of Spain's lover, complaining of the *Cabildo*'s behaviour which he declared was not only traitorous but also a serious threat to Spanish rule throughout the whole of South America.

The final straw came after the battle of El Cristo del Cardal when, abandoning Montevideo, the Viceroy and his cavalry hurriedly sought refuge fifty miles away at Las Piedras. Although furious at the time of his cowardly departure, the citizens were also relieved to see him go, as most of his soldiers had returned home to Cordoba and been replaced by a band of ruffians who were more intent on looting the citizens' property than protecting it.

The Marquis's behaviour had by now become so contentious that, on 10 February, a Council of War was held in Buenos Aires to vote on whether to suspend him from his position as Viceroy. Ninety-eight of the town's most important officials attended to hear Don Bernardino Rivadavia expertly put the case for the prosecution. After castigating the Viceroy for his behaviour, he diplomatically submitted that the Marquis was too ill to govern. This point was immediately seized on by Sobremonte's supporters who responded that the Viceroy for his age was in remarkably good health.

Magnificently attired in his clerical robes, the Bishop of Buenos Aires refused to vote on such a thorny question, firmly announcing it was not a matter for the clergy. Santiago Linares also abstained on the grounds that the Viceroy had appointed him to lead the Army and, therefore, it would be disloyal for him to vouch an opinion. The speeches continued all day, and the debate became increasingly heated as both sides made their point: the *Real Audiencia* in favour of the Viceroy, the *Cabildo* against him. It was a dangerous debate in which to take part, and each speaker soon realised that not just the Marquis's future was at stake but also their own. Memories were long, and should he back the losing side, his words would be remembered and retribution inevitably follow.

The assembly waited in suspense for the votes to be counted, and a great cheer went up when it was announced that the Marquis should be removed from his official position as Viceroy, Governor, and Captain General of the Rio de la Plata. After making this epic announcement, the President of the Court assured the defeated *Real Audiencia* that the Viceroy would be treated with the utmost decorum and as a sop to their wounded pride diplomatically placed the reins of Government in their hands, until the Sovereign made his decision on the country's future ruler.

Most of the citizens were happy with the verdict, but not with the notion of leaving Sobremonte at liberty, and the *Cabildo* sent Manuel Ortiz Basualdo and Martin Monasterio with two companies of infantry and one of cavalry to arrest him. After a brief struggle he was successfully apprehended and placed under house arrest in the suburb of San Fernando, until orders as to his future arrived from Spain.

Without doubt the arraignment of Sobremonte is one

of the most momentous days in the history of Argentina, as it not only heralded the dawn of democracy but also Argentina's first major step towards independence.

TWENTY-FOUR

BANISHMENT TO THE PROVINCES

With the fall of Montevideo, the *Cabildo* quickly realised the British Army would soon be hammering at the city's gates and began to draw up plans on how to resist. Their greatest worry was the persistent rumour that the streets were swarming with spies. The nervous citizens became convinced that their ever-day movements were being reported to the enemy in Montevideo and first to come under suspicion were the so-called neutral American merchants, who the citizens insisted should be immediately expelled from Buenos Aires, or at least be evacuated to the provinces along with every other foreigner.

Owing to his close association with General Beresford, Guillermo White was immediately arrested and banished to the frontier from where he soon disappeared, probably aided by Anita Perichon, whose position as Linares's mistress gave her ample scope to help him to escape. Hurriedly returning to Montevideo, he found his business thriving thanks to the arrival of the English merchants. The news of his arrival soon reached Buenos Aires, along with an ominous report that on 1 June he had been seen in deep conversation with the English Generals.

Blood curdling and chilling tales of what the British intended to do on their arrival in Buenos Aires abounded in the bars and cafes. One popular rumour averred that 'Those lucky enough to survive the sacking of the city and slaughter of its inhabitants were to be forcibly incorporated into regiments and shipped to India under the command of

150 British officers brought from England especially for the purpose'.

Nervous tradesmen began to panic and to avoid a financial disaster should the English sack the city, Jose Carafe & Sons dispatched all their high quality cloth and stock to Potosi. Others of a less pessimistic nature sent theirs to Cordoba, which being closer was less expensive.

Also causing the *Cabildo* anxiety were the number of English prisoners of war who they had refused to allow to embark on Popham's ships as agreed on by Linares in his treaty with Beresford. Admittedly when signing the document, Linares had written under his signature 'Si yo puedo' (if I'm able). His warning was proving prophetic as the *Cabildo* firmly asserted that as Linares had no authority to offer such terms in the first place, whatever these had been they were clearly invalid.

Nevertheless, they were now bitterly regretting the decision as, once the English officers had given their word of parole, they were at liberty to walk freely about the city and every day fair-haired young ensigns could be seen promenading along the streets and avenues with pretty young ladies on either arm. This unattractive behaviour not only annoyed the gentlemen and the girls' parents, but also irritated the authorities who strongly suspected the officers of spreading disruptive ideas such as free speech, Parliamentary democracy, Magna Carta, and, that ultimate danger of all, independence. Remarking on this state of affairs, Major Gillespie declares,

'An evident partiality existed on the part of the females to English officers over that shown to that class of their friends. The only bar to the closest connection was the difference in their creed, that if only sacrificed the ladies would have viewed the military rank of their admirers as a minor consideration, and much priestly eloquence was exerted in this Holy struggle.' One lady married a cadet in the St Helena corps, who was a voluntary convert and soon after received a Captain's commission in the Buenos Aires Army.

Such was the female passion for music that the ladies invited the master of the band of the 71st to become their teacher. Many pupils enrolled in his classes and, being an excellent composer, his little productions were keenly bought and the ladies did their utmost to retain him when the officers were banished to the country. In this they failed but he amassed sufficient money to ensure his comforts while a prisoner of war.

The authorities also accused the British officers of encouraging the citizens to adopt strange foreign manners such as shaking hands with strangers, linking arms when walking down the street and – that most pernicious habit of all – offering their arms to the ladies. Renowned for their heavy drinking, the British officers were also accused of instructing the citizens to toast each other at table and, among other strange customs, of introducing the odd habit of having their plates changed after every course.

Religion was another major problem. Anti-Catholic feeling in Britain was still strong and an angry crowd of citizens threatened to beat up an English officer who firmly refused to remove his hat as the procession to Nuestra Señora del Rosario passed by.

As these incidents increased, the authorities grew steadily more worried and finally reached the conclusion that the city would be safe only if they banished the hundreds of British prisoners to the provinces. This presented a problem, as many of Beresford's soldiers had been persuaded to desert and were now training their newly formed militia, which made it difficult to choose exactly whom to send. But by

3 September the problem had been sorted out and, under command of their sergeants, the British rank and file were split into six groups and loaded onto wagons to begin the long journey inland. Four hundred were sent to Cordoba, two hundred each to Mendoza, San Juan and Tucumán, and another two hundred to Santiago del Estero and San Luis. The wounded remained in Buenos Aires to be cared for by the Bethlehemite friars.

The journey inland was long and hazardous. Writing a month later to the *Cabildo* of Buenos Aires, the shocked Governor of Santiago del Estero reported, 'The men of the 71st have arrived here practically naked, as their uniforms have been stolen on the way to outfit a regiment of *Migueletes* (Spanish light horse)'.

During their ten-month stay in the provinces, the prisoners inevitably came into contact with the local people. The majority were content to settle down, but the 71st who had been sent to Cordoba refused to obey their guards' orders and, after causing a considerable amount of trouble, were split into two groups, one of which was sent to Alta Gracia and the other to La Carlotta.

Steadily the number of enemy ships blockading Montevideo began to increase and despite the British having given their word of parole, the nervous *Cabildo* became convinced that they were also a threat to the city's safety. They strongly suspected them of passing information through Beresford's old spy network to Auchmuty in Montevideo and, by October, the situation had become so worrying that the *Cabildo* decided the officers were a serious threat, and should also be banished from the city.

Rumours of their decision soon reached the ears of Major Gillespie who, along with several other officers, invited their hosts and Creole friends to a farewell lunch at the Tres

Reyes. After finishing their meal, they bade a fond farewell to their Creole friends, and especially to Don Bonfillo and his hospitable family, and set off for the Plaza Mayor where they found a vast number of the King's horses saddled and bridled waiting for them and were officially informed they were about to be evacuated to the provinces. Outraged by the order, General Beresford vehemently protested that the Argentines were breaking the terms of surrender but his remonstrance proved of little value. Politely brushing aside his protests, the *Cabildo* calmly assured him that in no way was this a violation of the Treaty but, on the contrary, a necessary precaution for his own and the officers' personal safety. Unable to find a suitable answer to this reasonable statement, the indignant General climbed reluctantly into the back of a hired carriage and, staring fixedly ahead with his ADC by his side, led the procession out of the city. Seated on a long line of wagons with their luggage beside them, his officers followed behind, escorted by a regiment of cavalry.

Educated, well mannered, and mostly bachelors, the British officers had made good friends with the Argentine families in whose houses they had been billeted. At the risk of being accused of treason, their hosts freely admitted they were sad to see them leave and it was rumoured that several young ladies cried themselves to sleep that night, sobbing inconsolably into their pillows.

After the turmoil of the city, life in the country was most enjoyable and stationed on various *estancias* around Lujan, San Antonio de Areco, and Capilla del Señor, the officers spent happy days hunting, fishing, shooting and playing cricket. The evenings were equally entertaining, thanks to the continual round of routs and balls given by the local gentry.

Writing to the Buenos Aires *Cabildo*, an astonished Don Jose Gamboa, Mayor of Lujan, declared that on Don Felipe Otalora's *estancia* alone near Areco, the officers fished; pursued ostriches; hunted stags and wild boar, and in four days killed the impressive figure of 500 head of game. More disturbingly, he also reported that they were holding daily meetings, and strongly suspected them of being in contact with the enemy as they seemed well informed of all that was going on in Montevideo. He ends the letter by rather enviously reporting that the officers were also receiving a large number of food parcels full of tea, chocolate, fine wine, and other similar delicacies, sent by the charitable ladies of Buenos Aires.

Good horsemen and hard men to hounds, the officers soon became proficient in handling the lasso and bolas, and were only too happy to help their hospitable hosts in the work on their *estancias*. On the face of it, life in captivity appeared to be running smoothly but, beneath the surface, resentment lingered and unfortunate incidents occurred at times to cast a shadow over this country idyll.

Colonel Pack and Captain Ogilvie, peacefully riding home one evening through the streets of Lujan, were surprised to be waylaid by an unknown peon who taking them to one side whispered in their ear; he had an important letter for them that could be delivered only in private. He therefore suggested that they should ride out along the Buenos Aires road to a quiet place in the country, where he could deliver it to them unobserved.

Overcome by curiosity, the two officers agreed but, approaching a desolate spot, the man slowly dropped behind and surreptitiously removing his bolas from his saddle attempted to lasso them. Thomas Howell writes:

'Colonel Pack twice extricated himself from the rope and

Ogilvie once and not succeeding with his lasso, the man rode up close to the Captain and discharged his pistol into his back. Ogilvie was dangerously wounded by the ball, which went through his shoulder-blade and touched his lungs.'

Thomas appears to be quoting the official report, as there are other versions of the incident. One of these declares that discreet inquiries being made the following day in Lujan as to the motive for the assassination, revealed that an infuriated husband, strongly suspecting the gallant Captain of attempting to seduce his wife, had ordered his removal. It came as no surprise to his friends and brother officers, as the Captain had a reputation of flattering the ladies by presenting them with gifts of handkerchiefs and little trinkets, 'a gallantry that greatly irritated their fathers, and even more their husbands'.

Despite every effort to save him, Captain James Frederick Ogilvie died a fortnight later and the coroner's verdict was, 'Killed by persons unknown.' General Beresford read the funeral oration and, considered a heretic, the Captain was buried with full military honours behind the church wall at Villa Lujan.

It had been an unlucky campaign for the Captain, as not only had he been badly wounded bravely defending the Recoba but, after the *Reconquista*, an indignant citizen accusing him of insulting behaviour challenged him to a duel and shot him in the shoulder. His brother officers now greatly mourned his loss, and proudly announced that he was the first and only officer in the campaign to fall a victim to Venus and not Mars.

The rumours continued to persist that the General and his officers appeared well informed of the English movements in Montevideo, and the *Cabildo* now became convinced that Beresford's old spy network was still in operation. In fact it was probably the *estancia* owners themselves that were keeping the officers informed, anxious to guard their interests should the British be successful and rightly reckoned that it could hardly be classified as traitorous behaviour to give the officers information known by one and all.

Seriously worried by these disturbing reports, the *Cabildo* sent orders to Captain Manuel Fontes in charge of the prisoners to escort the General and his staff further inland to Catamarca, a little town lying in the shadow of the Andes. Fontes was in the process of carrying them out when Captain Saturnino Rodriguez Peña and Captain Aniceto Padilla overtook him on the road and informed him that the order had been rescinded. He was now to hand the General over to them to escort back to Buenos Aires.

The Captain was suspicious and refused to part with his prisoners without first seeing the order in writing; something neither officer could produce. After a lengthy discussion, and probably swayed by Peña's position as one of Linares's adjutants, Fontes released them and, as darkness fell, the General, Colonel Pack and the two Argentine officers mounted their horses and vanished into the night to reappear two weeks later in Montevideo.

Who organised Beresford's escape remains a mystery but there are many theories. Most of which centre around Saturnino Peña's behaviour, as it was well known that only a few days before he had held a secret meeting with Martin Alzaga, and some thought that the Mayor was hedging his bets – hoping to make an amicable agreement with Beresford, should Whitelocke's Army be successful. Others believed it to be the work of the Independence party, as Peña was known to be one of Miranda's followers. Santiago Linares was also rumoured to have had a hand in it, determined to honour his word over the terms of surrender, which the *Cabildo* had forced him to break. Even Anita Perichon came under suspicion three years later, when she was accused of being in the pay of the British.

Irrespective of who planned the escape, the Argentines were incensed by Beresford and Pack's behaviour and accused them of breaking their word of parole. On the other hand, the British officers insisted that their actions had been legitimate as the Argentines had broken the terms of surrender drawn up between Beresford and Linares.

Both sides took the matter seriously and, on their arrival in Montevideo, Beresford and Pack were ordered to attend a Court of Inquiry to judge if in any way they had compromised their word of parole. Not surprisingly, the court exonerated both of them of the charge but the controversy continued for many years, and both sides were convinced they were right.

TWENTY-FIVE

THE BATTLE FOR SAN PEDRO

On his arrival in Montevideo, Beresford refused to join Auchmuty's Army, firmly announcing that he had given his word of parole to Linares and was not prepared to break it. He was, however, willing to give Sir Samuel all the information he needed, and strongly advised him that his mission was doomed to failure, as the Argentines would never accept British rule without the promise of protection should a peace treaty later be signed with Spain. While those in favour of a break with the mother country wanted total independence and not just a change from one rule to another.

Colonel Pack for his part strongly maintained that, as the Argentines had broken the terms of surrender, his word of parole was no longer valid. It therefore could be no reflection on his honour if he accepted command of the battalion of troops about to be sent to attack Colonia. His behaviour infuriated the Argentines, and when captured again in the coming battle he was lucky to escape with his life.

News of the approaching invasion soon began to spread, and neighbouring countries rushed to offer their assistance. Don Fernando Abascal, Viceroy of Peru, sent a message to the *Cabildo* explaining that although personally unable to leave Lima, he intended to send the Marquis de Aviles with a large number of troops. He made only one condition: that Aviles should be placed in command of the Army and given the powers of a Viceroy.

The Marquis de Aviles by now was a doddering old man

definitely nearing senility, who had once commanded the armies of Chile and Argentina. After this he had been made Viceroy of Peru, a position in which he had proved singularly inept. The Peruvians aptly nicknamed him '*Inabiles*,' a pun on '*Habil es*' meaning 'Able he is' to '*Inabil es*' (Able he isn't'). Now old and infirm, he spent most of his time in Church concentrating his thoughts on the next world rather than the present one. Despite this sombre travail, the *Real Audiencia* gratefully accepted the Viceroy of Lima's generous offer but, having suffered sufficient disasters under the rule of such ancient Spanish dinosaurs, the *Cabildo* firmly rejected it.

When the news reached Buenos Aires of General Beresford's mysterious escape, tension in the city began to mount and, making matters worse, the *Real Audiencia* and *Cabildo* were now permanently at each other's throats: the former supporting the Viceroy and his Army, the latter in favour of Santiago Linares and the militia. Every day, more and more problems arose to face the authorities, such as should they arm the slaves? Ought every foreigner be imprisoned or at least be banished from the city?

After much discussion, it was reluctantly agreed that the slaves should be issued with knives, which was a brave decision, as these could easily be turned against their owners not only during the battle but also after it. Faced with these knotty problems, the *Cabildo*'s nerves finally ran out and they announced that every foreigner residing in the city should immediately be exiled to the provinces, which once again produced a problem. Many of the British deserters had or were in the process of joining the militia, which made it difficult to rule exactly who to send. For instance David Frost, an Anglo-American living in the house of Don Bernardino Rivadavia (now a Major of Hussars), adopted a neutral position by becoming a bandsman in Don Bernardino's regiment. Others followed suit, and the authorities found it increasingly difficult to categorise exactly who to expel.

Another serious problem was the carrying of arms. Almost every day, citizens were injured by these being accidentally discharged, and several soldiers were killed in drunken squabbles between rival regiments. In an attempt to stop these incidents, General Balbiani ordered all the rifles and powder to be housed in the Fort but the Colonels flatly refused to obey the order, insisting that their men should at all times be ready for active service. In the event of a sudden attack, it would take far too long to withdraw the weapons from the Fort.

The unwelcome arrival of the *El Estella del Sud* 'The Southern Star' from Montevideo added further to the *Cabildo*'s worries. This newspaper, printed in English and Spanish, was a clever piece of British propaganda, which first pointed out the advantages of living under British rule and then frightened its readers by grossly exaggerating the strength of the British Army occupying Montevideo. To further whet the reader's appetite, it filled its pages with mouth-watering advertisements for all the luxuries they could buy in Montevideo, along with an endless list of sought-after items supposedly arriving from London at any moment.

The excitement reached fever pitch on 1 March with the arrival in port of the *Chartwell*, flying a white flag, and carrying on board Major Campbell with General Auchmuty's demand for the surrender of the city. After being carefully blindfolded he was escorted to the Fort, and presented Sir Samuel's letter to Santiago Linares which strongly advised the Argentine General to surrender, saving the city from being destroyed, and its inhabitants from inevitable bloodshed and loss of life. He magnanimously offered the Argentines the same terms of surrender as General Beresford had proposed a year earlier.

The Major also brought several other letters with him, including one from the *Cabildo* of Montevideo. This bitterly complained that due to Governor Ruiz Huidobro's lack of leadership, the populace and Army had been allowed to run riot, resulting in the fall of the city and causing its citizens unnecessary loss of life. Especially as the English were behaving fairly, and had kept their promise to allow freedom of religion. Moreover, Auchmuty's soldiers were under not only control but also respecting private property and the General had released all the married prisoners. The citizens bitterly regretted not having accepted the British terms in the first place as this would have avoided a vast amount of unnecessary bloodshed and damage.

The Major also brought a letter from Ruiz Hudobro, written before sailing for England, for Santiago Linares confirming that the English General was faithfully honouring the agreement to look after the 200 wounded Spanish troops. Lastly he brought a personal letter from General Beresford to Martin Alzaga, explaining that he felt justified in making his escape as the Argentines had violated the terms of surrender. He assured the Mayor that he had no intention of breaking his word of parole, and was therefore embarking on the first ship leaving for England.

The *Real Audiencia* and the *Cabildo* dismissed Auchmuty's offer to surrender, and Martin Alzaga wrote a lengthy reply to Beresford refuting his accusations of violating the terms of surrender, and politely ended by wishing him a safe journey home.

Having completed his mission, Linares courteously invited Campbell to dinner, and on his return to Montevideo the

Major reported to Auchmuty,

'So many people were in Linares's office that there was hardly enough room to open your letter. Some tried to read it over his shoulder and others from the side. It was obvious that the General was not in control of the situation and had little authority, as in the middle of a discussion at the dining room table he ordered the diners to keep quiet, and no one paid the slightest attention!'

It was not the only excitement, as four days later the alarm was raised when two English merchant ships were sighted sailing two leagues apart off Point Quilmes. As soon as it was dark, a flotilla of gunboats slipped quietly out of the harbour and surrounded the nearest ship, which promptly surrendered. The crew were carefully interrogated and declared that they had arrived directly from London and had no idea that Buenos Aires was no longer in British hands. A Portuguese sailor on board also disclosed that, before parting, the two ships' Captains had made an agreement that whoever landed first would fire two rockets into the air to signal to the other it was safe to come ashore.

Armed with this important information, the Argentines returned to port and as soon as it was dark fired two rockets into the air and, as the clocks chimed midnight, a launch with muffled oars approached the pier and out of it stepped the shadowy figures of four marines, five passengers, and the pilot.

The *Guardia*, who had been ordered to watch the harbour, by now had become bored of waiting and, convinced that nothing was going to happen at so late an hour, were now safely tucked up in bed. For over half an hour, the little group of Englishmen wandered aimlessly through the unlit streets unchallenged and hopelessly lost until, spotting a light shining in an upstairs window, the English Captain plucked up the courage to knock on the door. Saluting the owner who opened it, he politely inquired where he could find the General's palace or villa.

Confronted in the middle of the night by a British officer in full naval uniform, the startled gentleman kept his head and, pretending not to understand a word the stranger was saying, made frantic signals behind him to his watching wife to send for help. Realising the dreadful danger they were in, she immediately dispatched a servant to alert the *Guardia* who, woken from their slumbers, rushed to arrest the frustrated Englishmen still standing outside the house, waving their arms in the air and gesticulating wildly in a desperate effort to be understood.

Early next morning, the Argentines duly raised the Union Jack and believing it to be the signal that all was well, the Captain of the other ship sailed into port and was promptly arrested. The whole affair had been a huge success and, when valued, the captured cargo exceeded half a million pesos and contained among other things gunpowder, cannons, muskets, rum, beer, and a large trunk full of periodicals, which kept the ladies entertained for several weeks.

Although delighted by the outcome, some pessimistic citizens were horrified by the length of time the enemy had been allowed to stroll unhindered through the streets without being challenged, and the merchants of doom prophesied that this boded ill for the future.

Autumn had now arrived; the leaves were turning brown, and with the coming of the cooler weather, the time had come to go on the offensive. Linares therefore dispatched Colonel Elio with 500 militia to retake Colonia and generously offered a 4,000 pesos reward to any man capturing that despicable perjurer, Dionisio (Denis) Pack.

His choice of leader proved a disaster, as Elio was an

impetuous and inexperienced officer newly arrived from Spain who had already shown his military incompetence when confronting Beresford's troops at the Punta Galvez. Without first ascertaining the capability or fitness of his men, he immediately set off for Colonia. Arriving there just before daybreak the next morning, he rashly ordered the attack to begin and, as the nervous recruits crept quietly towards the enemy lines in the dark, one of them tripped over a rock and accidentally discharged his rifle into the air. The loud report alerted the English sentries who instantly responded with a fusillade of musket fire. Never having faced such a volley before, the terrified recruits turned about and ran back through their ranks. Mistaking them for the enemy, these immediately opened fire and in the panic that followed the entire force took their heels and ran as fast their legs could carry them, vanishing over the horizon.

Aghast at the sight of his men rapidly disappearing over the skyline, Elio beat a hasty retreat to San Pedro and next day sent a lengthy report to Linares angrily declaring he could do nothing with these cowardly soldiers, some of whom had astonishingly covered over fourteen leagues in less than five hours. He plaintively writes, 'So far I have lost eight men dead and sixteen wounded, but it is difficult to know for certain what the final count will be as more than three quarters of my troops have vanished!' He then bitterly complains that his men, especially the Catalans, were insubordinate and begs Linares to send him some marines, or at least a contingent of veteran soldiers. He ends the letter by pathetically announcing, 'At the moment, I have less than a hundred men on whom I can rely to face the enemy.'

Unbeknown to Elio, the battle had been a close run thing, and but for the warning shot his men might well have succeeded in overrunning the British position. Writing later in his memoirs, Sir Samuel Whittingham disparagingly remarks,

'One particular night a column of Spaniards that had crossed the river from Buenos Aires stormed this post, and were near to carrying it by surprise had it not been for Scott and his guard of Riflemen who most bravely defended the breach until the troops had got under arms. The enemy was not pursued as their numbers were unknown and the night was dark but why this breach was not repaired, one cannot say. Except that in those days our Commanders understood little of the art of war and sat themselves down anywhere in a state of blind security without using every means to strengthen their posts. Experience has taught us better'.

Over the following months, Colonel Elio fought a continuous and heated battle; not against the enemy but against his own men. The mutinous Catalans were the worst offenders: they flatly refused to obey any of his orders and remained stubbornly insubordinate. Under such circumstances, the men's confidence in their commander soon began to wane and some of the more mutinous troops threatened to return to Buenos Aires. The Colonel satisfactorily dissuaded them from this irresponsible behaviour by turning two cannons on them just as they were about to leave, resulting in a rapid change of heart.

Much to Elio's delight, a naval officer, Lt Don Pedro Ramon Nuñez, arrived at San Pedro at the end of May bringing with him reinforcements, including a regiment of *Patricios* and a squadron of Hussars. Morale, already low, now hit rock bottom as the Colonel promptly promoted Nuñez to be his second in command, over the heads of Lt Colonel Francisco Albin and Don Ramon del Pino (the veteran commander of Colonia's cavalry) who strongly resented being placed under the command of such a junior officer. However, the final battle for Colonia came a month later, but this time it was the British that launched the attack.

Stationed only twelve miles away at Colonia and hearing rumours of the increase in Spanish soldiers at San Pedro, Colonel Pack decided the time had come to launch an attack before the Spanish numbers became too great. Setting off under the cover of darkness with three companies of riflemen, the 40th Regiment, two six pounders and three Light Companies, he arrived in sight of the Spanish camp just before daylight the following morning to find the enemy drawn up on an elevated piece of ground.

A deep and narrow river ran in front of their position but, ignoring this advantage, Pack's men jumped into the water and fighting their way to the other side scrambled up the bank, quickly overrunning the seven Spanish guns mounted on the ridge above them. Describing the attack, Sergeant Lawrence declares,

'We found a river in our way which fortunately was not very deep, so we waded through it under heavy fire from the Spanish cannons that killed two of our men whilst in the act of crossing. As soon as we were over, we formed line and advanced towards the enemy who lay on some fine rising ground to our front. They had some few pieces of cannon with them and opened fire with both cannon and musketry but every shot seemed to rise over our heads and I don't think that volley killed a single man.' He cheerfully continues 'They left a nice breakfast cooking for us in the shape of fowls, geese, turkeys, beef, rice and calavancos (though the latter were too warm with cayenne pepper, and garlic), all of which the enemy had to leave in his hurry.'

Still resenting the way the Spaniards had treated the 71st on their way to imprisonment in Cordoba, Colonel Pack ordered his men to strip the prisoners of their belongings, and the men immediately began relieving the Spaniards of their clothes, boots and money (about two thousand dollars). After completing this operation, the entire party set off for Colonia dragging behind them the gun carts loaded with the wounded, the prisoners hobbling along barefooted behind them.

As the triumphant party marched into Colonia, the sailors aboard their ships anchored in the harbour, seeing the number of prisoners and captured cannons, gave three cheers and fired a salute in the Colonel's honour. After posting the pickets and incarcerating the prisoners safely aboard a ship lying out to sea, Colonel Pack and his men retired to the comfort of their quarters and celebrated their splendid victory.

Next morning the Colonel relented and ordered his soldiers to return everything taken from the prisoners the day before. He generously offered a fair price for them, declaring that he had only ordered their removal to show how badly the Spaniards had treated his men on their long trek to Cordoba. After this he embarked Lt Colonel Raymond and Captain Augustin Sosa, both whom were seriously wounded, onto a fast ship so that their wounds could be properly attended to in Buenos Aires and sent the following dispatch to Auchmuty,

'For the loss of forty-eight men, sixteen of whom including Major Gardner were killed when a captured enemy ammunition wagon unexpectedly exploded, I have captured eight guns; killed over a hundred and twenty Spaniards, and double that number of wounded, many of whom were officers'.

Although little more than a skirmish, the battle for San Pedro was an important encounter, as it clearly showed that in open country the British Army would always have the advantage over their Argentine opponents. An important factor that Whitelocke and Leveson-Gower failed to recognise when, ten days later, they made the grave mistake of attempting to defeat the enemy in the narrow streets of Buenos Aires.

As dawn broke on Friday 24 June 1807, the citizens of Buenos Aires woke to see stretching across the skyline the awesome sight of an entire British battle squadron under full sail, as one hundred and sixteen warships – frigates, gunships and landing craft – their sails shining dazzling white in the morning sunshine, passed majestically in front of the city to vanish over the horizon towards the rising sun.

Almost a sense of relief overcame the populace, now that the waiting was over, but suspense quickly turned to action as the militia ran to take up their arms, and put into practice all they had learnt in the past few months. Hundreds of volunteers crammed the Plaza Mayor to be aroused by yet another of Linares's stirring speeches, which firmly denounced Beresford as a coward, Popham as a pirate, and Pack as a perjurer. Smartly dressed in their brand new uniforms, the Army paraded in the Retiro to hear the Bishop of Buenos Aires fervently urge them to take up arms against these heretical invaders and assure a place in heaven. Now confident the Almighty was on their side, this Army of patriots marched proudly out of the city to take up a defensive position on the banks of the Riachuelo. Not to be outdone, the *Cabildo* entered into a twenty-four-hour session to resolve any unexpected emergency that might suddenly arise which instantly occurred, when it was discovered that Linares had taken almost every soldier with him, leaving the city totally undefended. A worried Martin Alzaga hurriedly dispatched a messenger to the Punta Galvez urgently requesting Linares to return a suitable number of troops, not just to keep public order but, more importantly to guard the *Cabildo* and *Real Audiencia* from the approaching invaders.

TWENTY-SIX

ENSENADA DE BARRAGAN

Montevideo was cold, and Thomas Howell, comfortably billeted in Maria de Parades's house, describes the violence of the weather.

'The nights were frosty with now and then a little snow, and great showers of hail that fell as large as beans. In the day, dreadful rains deluged all around and sometimes we had thunder and lightning. One night the side of which the town is built re-echoed the thunder as if it would rend in pieces, and the whole inhabitants flocked to the churches or kneeled in the streets'.

Rocking to and fro in the morning light, the bare masts of the ships anchored in the harbour resembled a forest of leafless trees swaying in a winter wind. Mostly merchantmen, their crews had received a nasty shock when, instead of enjoying a few days' rest and recreation after their lengthy sea voyage, they were forced to take the King's shilling and recruited into the Army. After reluctantly receiving this unsolicited beneficence, a team of tough drill sergeants of the Light Division marched them brusquely off to the main square to put them through their paces, swiftly followed by weapons training. General Whitelocke needed every soldier he could lay his hands on for his coming invasion and these 400 merchant sailors would not only strengthen the 900 men he intended to leave behind to defend Montevideo, but their ships' carpenters could also help his sappers repair the town walls and shore up the breach.

Now that his Army was fully assembled, Whitelocke held

a general inspection and found to his dismay that it was a mass of uncoordinated regiments. In the hope of making it more flexible, he divided it into four brigades and, taking command of the first, placed Auchmuty, Craufurd and Lumley in charge of the other three. Once this reorganisation had been completed, the men boarded their ships ready to leave for Ensenada as soon as the wind and weather became more favourable.

It was now that Whitelocke showed his first failing as a General by ordering two companies of the 38th Regiment (The 1st Staffordshires) that were fit and in good shape to stay behind and garrison Montevideo, and instead chose the inexperienced 88th and 36th to take with him. Both of these regiments were suffering from their lengthy sea voyage, and the General made this stupid rearrangement purely to spite Lord Muskerry, Colonel of the 38th who, knowing the country well, publicly announced 'No one but a madman would attempt to land an Army at Ensenada in the middle of winter.' Not surprisingly, this remark upset the General, who out of pettiness left Lord Muskerry and his two companies of fit men behind, and elected to take the exhausted 88th and 36th with him.

Next, it was the turn of Major General Leveson-Gower to antagonise the Army, which he successfully achieved by snubbing Sir Samuel Auchmuty in peremptorily taking over his command without giving him any explanation. He quickly followed it up by upsetting Brigadier Lord William Lumley (younger son of the Earl of Scarborough, commanding the cavalry) by refusing to allow him to pay six dollars a horse to mount his troops. As this was only two dollars more than the Spaniards were paying, it resulted in the Army being sold some very inferior animals.

He further infuriated Lumley by ordering the cavalry to

leave their spare saddlery, clothes and equipment behind in Montevideo to be destroyed or sold, announcing that, 'The English Dragoons were always too heavily laden, particularly in this open country where they had to act against such an enemy'.

Furious at this outrageous order, Lord Lumley remonstrated with the Major General, pointing out that should any man lose his equipment in the coming conflict, it would be impossible for him to replace it. Many of his officers would be faced with serious financial embarrassment should they be asked to do so later and anyhow, the 5th Dragoons were expected to arrive from England at any moment who could use the saddlery and harness. He demanded Leveson-Gower rescind the order, or at least put it in writing, but the Major General stubbornly refused to do either. Tempers began to rise, the language became heated, and Leveson-Gower shouted at Lumley, 'We are then at issue!' Carefully choosing his words, His Lordship replied, 'I am too old a soldier to disobey a peremptory order but I feel it my duty as an officer to make a formal remonstrance.' Adding that, in his opinion, the order was totally contrary to King's regulations to which Leveson-Gower angrily retorted, 'He couldn't care less about King's regulations' and then made the extraordinary statement that, 'These could have no effect in this country, as we have come here to establish a new era!'

Lumley's officers were equally distraught, and demanded the Brigadier issue the order in writing, which Lumley was reluctant to do without first receiving the same from the Major General. Now thoroughly annoyed, Leveson-Gower indignantly complained of His Lordship's behaviour to General Whitelocke who, sending for Lumley, commanded him to obey the Major General's order, observing, 'He could not possibly have such a quantity of baggage following the

Army about the countryside, and he himself had no intention of turning storekeeper.' This ended the argument; Lumley was forced to obey Whitelocke's command and, to their disgust, the Carabineers were issued with muskets and dressed in white leather breeches with heavy cavalry boots and ordered to fight as infantry, a mode of warfare still an anathema to a cavalryman of today.

Montevideo now became a scene of hectic activity as worried staff officers, millboards in hand, hurried along the wharfs allocating ships to the different regiments, while the agents of the Commissariat rushed to issue the men with provisions and ammunition for the coming invasion. Hundreds of soldiers returning from the countryside jammed the narrow streets and, in the middle of this hubbub and confusion, a Spanish officer arrived at the city gates to offer an exchange of prisoners.

Overlong at sea, and starved of the fairer sex, three young officers stationed at St Lucia had fallen for the flashing eyes and curvaceous figures of the local señoritas, so when these seductive young ladies invited them to a rendezvous outside the town they eagerly accepted. It was a serious error, as this promising invitation turned out to be a well-laid honey trap for, as soon as they entered the house, a platoon of heavily armed enemy soldiers surrounded them and carried them off in a highly frustrated state to Colonel Elio's camp at San Pedro. A brother officer, describing this unfortunate incident, rather poetically writes, 'Falling into iron fetters, instead of the silken bands of love.'

The Spanish envoy also had three naval officers on offer: Thomas Blainey, Samuel Teacher, and George Stewart, who they had caught participating in the rather more mundane sport of duck shooting on the marshes. All these unfortunate sportsmen the Spaniard offered in exchange for the

Governor Ruiz Huidobro and two other senior officers. As it was well known that these gentlemen were already halfway across the Atlantic on a ship to England, it was reckoned his offer was merely an excuse to gain entrance into the town to spy out its defences.

These were not the only prisoners hoping to be exchanged, as the Spaniards languishing in Montevideo's jail were also becoming restless and began bombarding the Buenos Aires *Cabildo* with letters begging them to arrange for their release in exchange for Beresford's soldiers. The members of the *Cabildo* were far from keen on the swap, considering it a poor deal as Beresford's soldiers were experienced fighting men whereas most of their own were untrained militia. Instead of freedom, the unhappy prisoners received a courteous but disappointing reply from the *Cabildo* in the form of a long dissertation on the fortunes of war, which did little to alleviate their situation and even less in raising their morale. Their request, however, had one beneficial result, as the *Cabildo* magnanimously offered to pay the married prisoners' wives half their husbands' wages, but offered nothing to the wretched bachelors.

Once the ships were fully loaded, the fleet got underway on 17 June but, owing to poor weather and the wind blowing contrary all day, anchored for the night only seven miles away from Montevideo. For the next four days, the fickle wind continued to blow from every direction but the right one, and the convoy floundered helplessly around in the mouth of the River Plate. To counteract this boring lull, Lt Colonel Sir Lancelot Holland and Major Campbell occupied themselves by making pies and puddings that 'Did not quite succeed to our wishes.' In the evening of the 25th, the weather eventually cleared and next day the fleet reached Colonia, where Admiral Stirling took on board the remainder of Colonel Pack's garrison that had been left behind to spike the guns and two nights later, the entire invasion force assembled off the coast of Ensenada de Barragan. In the evening, General Whitelocke gave orders for every man to be issued with three days' rations before disembarking the following morning but, as he failed to put the order in writing, many of the officers and men never received them and, next morning, the Light Division landed with no provisions at all.

As dawn broke on 28 June, sixteen gunboats loaded with the advance party valiantly struggled through the turbulent water towards the empty shore. No sign could be seen of any enemy, and the only opposition came from a sand bar forcing those first ashore to wade chest high through the seething surf. To combat this irritating obstacle, a gunbrig was quickly moored at the mouth of the channel with a flag flying from its mast, which altered as the tide rose up and down to register the depth of water underneath. A channel was eventually found despite a thick fog suddenly descending, and the remainder of the Army reached the beach with their clothes and equipment relatively dry.

First to land were Auchmuty and Craufurd's brigades who straightaway headed for the ridge on the other side of the swamp. Describing their disembarkment, Lt Colonel Fletcher Wilkie writes,

'Here we were thrown ashore onto a strip of sand, bag, baggage, & etc. Just in front of us was an immense swamp, the depth of which no one knew anything about and its extent could only be guessed by looking at the distant hills. The caution with which some people traversed its unknown depths was quite amusing particularly those of about five foot two and after checking their equipment, the men plunged into the inky black water and waddled or skated as best they could along a submerged track to make camp on the other side.'

Successfully overcoming this aquatic struggle, the Light Brigade reached the ridge and to their relief found the ground firm, and covered in rich clover. Craufurd ordered the 87th to take up a position on the right flank and the 38th on the left and having checked that their pickets and sentries were correctly posted, Sir Lancelot Holland and Major Campbell bedded down for the night in the largest of three dilapidated farmhouses.

The *estancia* belonged to a certain Señor Duval, who luckily spoke a little French, and whose wife and children, according to Sir Lancelot seemed,

'Very unconcerned but laughed and talked a great deal. Our canteens soon arrived, and we immediately opened them up and ate largely of the sea pie that we had prepared aboard the *Chesterfield*. Colonel Pack who partook of it with us had also brought with him wine and at about ten o'clock, we spread our cloaks upon the bricks and went to sleep without having seen a Spanish soldier all day.'

By nightfall, all the Army had landed but the weather remained stormy, and the wind became so strong that the men were unable to erect their tents on the marshy ground. Major Nicholls of the 45th bitterly complains, 'Due to a dearth of blankets, only 380 could be issued and the majority of our 800 men spent the night lying in the open.' A few lucky ones found shelter among the deserted huts and cattle byres around the village, including Sergeant Morley of the 40th who cheerfully declares,

'We piled our rifles for the night, and our first exploit was the capture of an immense pig! This ill-fated prisoner was brought into a spacious area, killed, roasted, and quickly devoured.'

In the afternoon, General Whitelocke and his staff came ashore to establish Army Headquarters in the centre of the village and, as soon as it was dark, they were joined by an Anglo-American whose name Whitelocke carefully omits to mention in his report to the War Office. There can be little doubt that this was Guillermo White who, for obvious reasons, preferred his presence to remain anonymous in case something untoward should happen to the expedition.

Early next morning, some horses were found on the outskirts of the village. Hearing this good news, the Carabineers' spirits soared, only to drop again when they discovered that the staff officers had grabbed every one of them, not just for themselves but for their servants as well. Major Nicholls, a happy recipient, declares,

'One of the men procured me a horse, bridle, and saddle this morning not very honestly I believe but I was not by any means inclined to be particular on such an occasion!'

At around nine o'clock, the sea mist slowly lifted to reveal a great marsh covered in sea birds and isolated islands, marooned on which were a number of lonely sheep vainly searching for something to eat. Whitelocke could now see Auchmuty and his men patiently waiting for him on the other side of the swamp. Realising it would be dangerous to wait for the water to subside with his Army divided, he gave orders for the advance to begin and collecting up their equipment, the soldiers set off across the unwelcoming swamp.

The going was hazardous and, under two feet of water, the so-called road was almost invisible. Lacking any form of stone foundation, its condition steadily deteriorated as the Army advanced, and Major General Leveson-Gower, searching for a better route, nearly drowned when his horse began to sink in the grasping mud. Help arrived only just in time to pull him out but many of the men lost their shoes in the evil-smelling morass, and Thomas Howell was forced to continue the march barefooted all the way to Reducción.

Despite these vicissitudes, the six thousand men remained relatively in good humour, happily splashing each other and cracking jokes as they waded chest high through the swamp. But their high spirits abruptly vanished when they discovered that the water had ruined most of the food and they now had nothing to eat.

John Bullock Esq, the Commissary-General, had in fact landed with three days' rations, and the packhorses to carry them off the beach. But as soon as his men attempted to load the heavy packs onto the horses' backs, the untrained animals went berserk. Many broke away never to be seen again, while others galloped around in frenzied circles frantically bucking and kicking off their loads. Out of the eight tons of biscuits successfully landed only one ton remained edible and, to make matters worse, the camp kettles were found to be far too heavy for the mule carts to carry and had to be left on the beach. Nevertheless, the greatest calamity of all occurred when it was discovered that the rum casks were too bulky to fit on the carts, which left the Quartermaster-General no option but to stave in the barrelheads with a rifle butt. The soldiers watched in horror as the precious liquid vanished into the muddy waters of the thirsty swamp. One by one, the heavy field guns began to sink and, owing to the lack of horses, the soldiers had to manually pull them out. Many remained there for several days, including five captured Spanish cannons, which after carefully being spiked slowly disappeared beneath the muddy water.

The Army's progress was literally grinding to a halt and, in an attempt to speed things up, Whitelocke once again changed the formation of his troops. Dividing them into three groups, he put himself in command of the main Army and placed Craufurd and Lumley under the overall command of Major General Leveson-Gower in charge of the other two brigades, leaving Colonel Mahon behind with the non-existent cavalry and rear regiments to pull the cannons out of the swamp, and to act as a reserve.

TWENTY-SEVEN

THE ADVANCE ON BUENOS AIRES

Once the new formations were completed Whitelocke ordered Craufurd and his men to march on ahead, and Lumley to follow, leaving a three-mile gap between the two brigades. By advancing in this fashion, the General hoped to alleviate the problem of shelter and make it easier for his men to find food and lodgings along the way. It proved a disastrous innovation as, due to the dearth of horses, there were few mounted messengers and, as the advancing Brigades grew further apart, communications with Army Headquarters rapidly began to break down.

Lack of food was another serious problem. Many of the men had not eaten for over two days but fortune smiled on the morning of the 30th, when a flock of 4,000 sheep were rounded up, and a delighted Col Nugent declared, 'I think more than I ever saw before in my life.'

Owing to this providential windfall, much to the Army's relief Whitelocke postponed the next day's march to allow the soldiers time to consume this heaven-sent gift, and a sheep was allotted to every twelve men. But even this ended in disaster as, due to the lengthy delays and confusion in distribution, the men were given either a sheep and no fuel to cook it on, or fuel and no sheep. In the end, the only advantage of this delay was to give the Commissariat time to issue the men half a ration of biscuit out of the small amount salvaged from the swamp.

The Army was literally bogged down and, marching widely strung apart, the Brigades now faced a new danger with the arrival of a horde of ferocious gauchos who shadowed every move the soldiers made, and cut the throat of any man found lagging behind. They quickly lassoed two soldiers and a Corporal caught plundering a barn and, although one soldier managed to escape, they cut off the Corporal's head and, sticking it on the end of a pole, triumphantly paraded it up and down in front of the British lines. They soon became over-confident, and Sergeant Lawrence writes,

'As we marched along on our next day's journey, about two hundred Indians kept following us. The foremost of them wearing our dead corporal's jacket, and carrying his head. I do not exactly know for what reason, but perhaps they thought a good deal more of a dead man's head than we should feel disposed to do.

'We went on for some distance through a great many orange-gardens, until we came to a lane thickly hedged in on both sides which we entered by a gate. After the body of our Army had passed through, some few men including myself waited there in ambush for the Indians, after having first placed a reserve a short distance down the lane in case of a combat. The Indians soon approached but seemed to have some misgivings, although we could not exactly understand what they said. There being only a few of us not quite twenty in all, I rather shook in my shoes on seeing their number but we soon found there was very little occasion for this. For on our firing directly after the front party had passed the gate, we killed two of them and wounding and capturing their chief, the one that was so proud of his head. The rest fled for their lives not liking the smell and much less the taste of our gunpowder. We then picked up the wounded Indian and left him more dead than alive in a neighbouring village.'

The lasso proved a deadly weapon but the mounted

officers soon discovered a way of countering it. Instead of pulling away and slashing at the rope with their swords, they found it better to advance towards the thrower, making it difficult for him to pull it tight. By using this method, Lt Lloyd of the 17th Dragoons with the noose around his neck managed to escape but Lt Robert Cross of the 38th was even luckier. Despite a shot removing his hat and the lasso nearly carrying away his sword, he charged straight at the Indian and, cutting him severely on the head, managed to get away before the gaucho could pull him out of the saddle.

Leveson-Gower's criticism of the British cavalry now proved correct. Under the excessive weight of their equipment, the heavy Dragoons were incapable of defending the column as their native horses simply collapsed to the ground, making pursuit out of the question. But despite all these hazards, General Whitelocke and the main Army struggled on and, on the evening of the 30th, eventually caught up with Leveson-Gower's division. Seeing them about to strike camp, Whitelocke immediately ordered the Major General to press on to Reducción to make contact with Admiral Stirling and the fleet, now anchored off Point Quilmes. The division was very unhappy with the order and Lt Colonel Sir Lancelot Holland declares,

'After marching about three miles, General Whitelocke came to us full of doubts and difficulties, and appeared not to know what to do. After halting the column above an hour. and taking away our only guide (Senor Duval) and the lasso man who killed our bullocks, he determined we should advance to Reducción where the enemy was in force. I believe, though nobody knew very well, he intended to follow us and we were delighted to get quit of him'.

Whitelocke's order to embark on a night march was the straw that broke the camel's back. For after covering less than three miles, Lumley's brigade simply collapsed to the ground and despite every encouragement and threat, the men were incapable of marching another yard. Seeing their pitiful condition, Leveson-Gower sent a message back to Whitelocke informing him that if he wished his division to advance any further he would have to leave behind the 36th and 88th, as both Regiments were incapable of moving another yard.

For the first and almost only time in the whole campaign, Leveson-Gower was right. Riding up the following morning to review the situation, Whitelocke was shocked to find the men lying on the ground dying of exhaustion, hypothermia or starvation. Horrified by their condition, he immediately commanded them to abandon their blankets and greatcoats to lighten the weight of their equipment but, ignoring their desperate state, still ordered them to continue the march to Reducción.

From now on the advance on Buenos Aires became a continuous saga of disasters, not from any action by the enemy but by a complete breakdown of supplies and communications. The following year, at Whitelocke's court martial, General Craufurd bitterly complains about the state of the men and blames the shortage of food on the lack of lasso men. 'I mean persons who are in the habit of catching the cattle, the consequence of which was that, although surrounded by an abundance of cattle, we had no means of catching them.'

The situation was rapidly deteriorating and the men were not only exhausted but also becoming rebellious. In an attempt to raise their spirits, Whitelocke at times would dismount from his horse and march along beside them exchanging barrack room slang and cracking coarse jokes. His clumsy efforts to raise their morale failed to impress the men who wanted food not banter from their General.

At last light on the evening of 1 July, the Light Brigade finally reached Reducción. Quickly dispersing a small body of enemy cavalry with a sharp volley of grapeshot, they easily took possession of the village but it proved a disappointment, as it consisted of little more than a few dilapidated hovels and a small church. It did, however, have one redeeming feature as from here the soldiers caught their first glimpse of the lights of Buenos Aires shimmering in the distance. This raised their spirits, and made them forget the agonies of the march to replace them with the happy thought of plunder, alcohol, and what is politely called the spoils of war.

Suddenly, the sky blackened; the heavens opened, and the *palos borrachos* (drunken trees) began to twirl and dance like demented dervishes in the howling wind. The men desperately struggled to keep their balance, and the weather became so ferocious that Whitelocke decided the main Army should spend the night at Reducción. Following their orders, the Light Brigade bravely pushed on and, striking camp two miles on beyond the village, passed a sleepless night tormented by the enemy. Although not actually launching an attack, Linares's men kept them awake all night by blowing bugles, firing shots and stampeding their lines with cattle, in an early form of psychological warfare.

Thunder began to rumble overhead, sheet lightning flickered across the sky, and, in the glow of the ships set on fire in the river to prevent them falling into British hands, combined with the fires of the Spanish Army burning in front of the walls, the town resembled the background to a Goya painting depicting the 'Horrors of War.'

Ignoring these sinister omens, General Whitelocke spent a damp and uncomfortable night in a miserable shanty. At least he had the luxury of a roof over his head, unlike his men who were forced to spend another night sleeping in the open. Although relatively pleased at having accomplished his objective of reaching Reducción, the campaign was progressing not nearly as smoothly as the General would have liked. Establishing communications with the fleet, and transporting the provisions across the two miles of marshy ground between Punta Quilmes and Reducción was proving harder than expected, and the sea was so rough that disembarking the containers from the ships was proving dangerous. Captain Cobb, in charge of the operation, fought a desperate battle to save the boats from capsizing in the surf but, in spite of his strenuous efforts, much of the food supply was lost in the thundering surf.

Due to these circumstances, the General decided the Army should stay the whole of the next day at Reducción to wait for the supplies of bread and rum to arrive from Quilmes, and reconnoitre the fords across the Riachuelo.

It was welcome news, as the continual stops and starts of the vanguard searching for a way through the marsh had not only fuelled the men's bad temper, but also increased their doubts over their General's competence. Their good humour, however, was short lived as, at two o'clock in the morning, Whitelocke suddenly changed his mind and ordered the Light Brigade to cross the Riachuelo and take up a position in the northern suburbs of Buenos Aires.

Horrified by this sudden change of plan, Colonel Bourke, the Quartermaster General, insisted on personally carrying the order to Major General Leveson-Gower's command in the hope of persuading him to change Whitelocke's mind. His mission proved a failure as despite the 36th being in poor shape and the 88th dangerously unsteady, the Major General firmly declared he was not prepared to question the General's orders. In desperation, Bourke begged him to return to Headquarters and state his objections to Whitelocke in person, but Leveson-Gower stubbornly refused to do so, declaring 'I have received my orders and as a soldier, it is my duty to obey them'.

Equally alarmed, Sir Samuel Auchmuty warned Whitelocke that, although his own Brigade was in a parlous state judging by the number of stragglers he could see, Lumley's was in an even worse one. As usual, Whitelocke dithered and announced that he would make his final decision when he received Leveson-Gower's reply, which when it arrived proved of little help, as the Major General merely informed him that he intended to cross the river further up, where he had been (incorrected) informed that the waters narrowed. Whitelocke ordered the march to continue.

It was an inappropriate moment to say the least, as a large number of cattle had just been slaughtered, and the meat was in the process of being distributed among the starving soldiers when, to their fury, the men were ordered to leave all they had been given, and were not even allowed to put any pieces in their haversacks.

It seemed a senseless order, and Auchmuty desperately pleaded for his men to be given time to consume this providential windfall, but Whitelocke petulantly replied, 'Can't you see it is about to rain' and, at ten o'clock, the starving Army reluctantly moved off, leaving the precious meat scattered on the ground.

Whitelocke's remark may have sounded fatuous, but there was a reason behind it. For, according to a local inhabitant, the already bad weather was about to turn worse, and his men urgently needed shelter. This could be found only in the suburbs of Buenos Aires, and should the rain continue the Riachuelo might easily become impassable, forcing his men to spend another night in the open, and leave the heavily defended bridge at the Puente Galvez as their only possible crossing point. Even worse, the river might easily rise while his divisions were crossing it, dividing his Army in two, and leaving half of his troops to face the full weight of an Argentine attack.

Following Whitelocke's orders, a reluctant Leveson-Gower and disgruntled Light Division set off for Buenos Aires at first light the next morning and were soon four miles ahead, and out of touch with the main Army. The division's numbers by now were greatly diminished and had fallen to little more than a thousand bayonets. While the cavalry, whose number had never exceeded more than sixty owing to their horses breaking down, had shrunk to a mere handful and, much to his annoyance, Leveson-Gower was forced to mount two of his orderlies on his own expensive chargers brought all the way from England. The Division's morale was sinking fast, as they ploughed their weary way along the rapidly deteriorating road to Buenos Aires.

TWENTY-EIGHT

THE RIACHUELO AND PUNTA GALVEZ

Craufurd and the Light Division pushed on, and warned by his scouts that the bridge at the Punta Galvez was heavily defended swung left. Following the river upstream for less than a mile, they rounded a bend and came face to face with six hundred enemy cavalry. It could be seen by their yellow jackets and uniforms that these were trained soldiers, and not the unruly gauchos that up to now had been troubling them. Furthermore, their position was a strong one as the marshy ground running along the riverbank protected their left flank and a dense wood guarded their right.

With no time to deliberate, Craufurd quickly made an appreciation of the situation. Ordering the Light Brigade to form line, he sent two companies into the wood to clear it of any enemy, which was quickly achieved and, from the shelter of the trees, the riflemen opened fire on the enemy's flank. Confronted by this accurate fusillade, the enemy cavalry hurriedly retreated and, vanishing from sight, reappeared several minutes later on the other side of the river.

The 95th hurried after them and found to their surprise that they had crossed the river at the Paso Chico, which according to Leveson-Gower's report should have been impassable. But on close inspection, the river appeared to be only four feet deep with no current and a firm gravel bottom, and leaping in the men waded across to the other side. Standing on the bank watching them cross, Lt Colonel Sir Lancelot Holland proudly declares,

'We forded the river Chuelo at the Paso Chico. The men dashed through the water, which came about to their hips. Great was our joy at having gained this important pass, and every individual was animated. The men cheered and could hardly be restrained from boisterous expressions of delight.'

Leveson-Gower, following behind with Lumley's Brigade, reached the Paso Chico at around three o'clock in the afternoon, just as Craufurd and his division were leaving it. Weak from lack of food, his men were incapable of keeping together and were now scattered in little groups across the ground. Ignoring their desperate condition, Leveson-Gower with his customary lack of judgement ordered them to transport four heavy field guns across the river without giving them any time to rest or recuperate. The operation took several hours to accomplish as each gun had to be dismantled and carried across the river in separate parts on the exhausted men's shoulders or above their heads, along with the heavy ammunition boxes to keep them clear of the water, and be reassembled on the other side.

Once back on high ground, Craufurd took stock of his position and looking to his right saw a large column of enemy infantry advancing on the ford, obviously intent on stopping Lumley's brigade from crossing. To his front the road to Buenos Aires lay open, and never one to miss an opportunity, he immediately set off for the city and, seeing this, the Spanish column immediately abandoned their advance and returned to the Punta Galvez.

With Craufurd rapidly disappearing in front of him and no sign of Whitelocke behind him, Leveson-Gower panicked and twice sent orders to Craufurd to halt. But not for the first or last time in his military career, 'Black Bob' paid no attention to his Commanding Officer's order and, sending a messenger back to Leveson-Gower, assured him that in his opinion, 'it was very desirable to proceed' and firmly did so. On reaching the outskirts of the town, he ordered his riflemen to halt, as to advance any further without knowing the enemy's strength or the city's defences would be tantamount to lunacy.

Leveson-Gower and his men hurried after Craufurd and the rapidly disappearing 95th and eventually caught them up at Guillermo White's house, situated about half a mile outside the town and now, for the first time since leaving Reducción, the two Brigades came together again.

By now the countryside had changed from bare open land to orange groves and orchards and among them stood a number of small houses with pretty gardens surrounded by hedges and high fences. Continuing down a narrow lane, the two Brigades arrived at the Corral de la Miserere (the town's slaughterhouse) where Linares had mustered his troops the night before attacking Beresford.

It was midday; the weather hot, and after their lengthy march the men were resting against the Corral's whitewashed walls waiting for the field guns to catch them up, when suddenly there was a violent explosion and black smoke enveloped the yard. Grapeshot ricocheted off the walls and, deafened by the noise for a second, the men hesitated. Then Leveson-Gower shouted to Craufurd, 'We must turn their left and right flanks' and, leaping to his feet, Black Bob with the 95th behind him charged the enemy.

In seconds, the hidden gun, four eight pounders, a heavy five-and-a-half-inch howitzer, and their gun crews had been captured and a large number of enemy infantry who had been hiding in the hedgerows broke cover and ran for the safety of the city, with the 95th hard on their heels behind them.

Now that his blood was up, nothing was going to stop Craufurd and he and the 95th pursued the routed enemy through the suburbs of the city, until reaching La Calle de las Tunas (today the avenue Callao and Entre Rios) they stopped to allow Leverson-Gower and Lumley's Brigade to catch them up. Yet again the Major General lost his nerve and, sending for Captain Squires, instructed him to catch Craufurd up, and order him to return immediately to the Corral.

Strongly disagreeing with the message, Black Bob sent Brigade Major Campbell back to beg Leveson-Gower to allow the advance to continue, but the Major General insisted that he should return immediately, declaring that the wounded, who numbered only six officers and thirty men, could be cut off and killed by straggling parties of the enemy.

Forced to obey his superior's orders, Craufurd reluctantly pulled his men back and the chance to take Buenos Aires was lost. It was by far the greatest error of the whole campaign, for had Leveson-Gower allowed Craufurd to continue the city would undoubtedly have fallen as it was practically undefended, except for the small detachment of troops guarding the *Cabildo*.

Spotting Lumley's division about to cross the Paso Chico from his position at the Puente Galvez, Linares immediately ordered General Velasco and his men to advance along the riverbank and cut them off. Then, mustering every man he could lay his hands on, he set off to stop Craufurd from entering the town, and it was his men who laid the ambush at the Corral de la Miserere.

Despite a long and active military career, Linares was no Napoleon and his lack of military skill now became apparent. Having positioned all his men on the enemy's side of the Puente Galvez with their backs to the river, when the British veered west and began crossing it further up the Argentines found it impossible to get their cannons and men back over the narrow bridge in time to cut them off. Six thousand militia now lay stranded on the wrong side of the river, desperately struggling to cross the narrow bridge and return to the city, which now lay almost defenceless.

The situation was critical but, luckily for the *Porteños*, the British were also disorganised. Whitelocke was just leaving Reducción ; Leveson-Gower engaged in recalling Craufurd from his charge, and Mahon still at Ensenada with the Reserve struggling to pull the cannons out of the marsh.

TWENTY-NINE

CROSSING THE RIACHUELO

Lumbering along four miles behind Lumley's brigade, General Whitelocke with the main Army was completely oblivious to what was happening to his forward division. Confident that they were now within striking distance of the city he sent a message to Admiral Stirling stationed with the fleet off Quilmes, ordering him to sail immediately to the northern side of the city and make contact with Craufurd. At the same time, he dispatched another to Colonel Mahon at Ensenada ordering him to join him the next day with every cannon he could lay his hands on and after this set off in search of Leveson-Gower, Lumley, and the Light Division.

Whitelocke's guide, believing Leveson-Gower's information that the Paso Chico was impassable, advised him that there was another ford six miles on called the Paso de Zamora, which would certainly be passable. Instead of following Leveson-Gower's route, Whitelocke therefore continued his march along the high ground where the going was better and around noon spotted Leveson-Gower's column three miles away marching parallel to him along the riverbank. Both parties were obviously aiming for the same ford so Whitelocke continued his march and at around three o'clock in the afternoon arrived at a group of farmhouses and ordered the Army to halt.

Leveson-Gower's division was now out of sight, but the General was not unduly worried as he was convinced they were either level or ahead of him. As it was too late to start crossing the river, he informed Colonel Bourke that he intended to spend the night here, and continue the march the following morning.

Once again Bourke was unhappy with the order and pointed out that, unless Craufurd was informed, he might easily press on into the suburbs of Buenos Aires and lose touch with the rest of the Army. As usual, Whitelocke dithered and asked Auchmuty for his advice who, seeing the farm abounding with sheep and firewood and knowing his men to be starving, unhesitatingly agreed they should stop here for the night. Whitelocke therefore sent a messenger to Mahon cancelling his previous instructions, and ordered him to remain at Reducción until further notice and if necessary act as a reserve. Far away in the distance, the soldiers could hear the continuous rumble of gunfire but, determined to enjoy their first proper meal in four days, firmly turned a deaf ear to it.

Meanwhile Craufurd, still on the outskirts of the city, posted his pickets at the mouths of the main streets, and following Leveson-Gower's orders reluctantly returned to the discomfort of the Corral. This turned out to be a most unhygienic establishment and, describing it in his memoirs, Colonel Sir Lancelot Holland declares, 'Being the place where the cattle for the whole town of Buenos Aires are slaughtered the ground is covered with putrid offal and the stench sent forth horrible!'

'Black Bob' was not the only one to be annoyed as, robbed of success and drenched to the skin, the pickets were equally nonplussed. Adding further to their disenchantment, groups of inebriated townsfolk were continually harassing them, suddenly appearing from behind a house to fire a shot and disappear again. Only two things kept their spirits up: the ease with which they had put the enemy to flight and the plunder they could now see lying within their grasp.

By nightfall the battle had reached an impasse; Whitelocke had vanished, Linares was lost somewhere in the suburbs and devoid of leaders both sides had little idea of what to do next.

Linares in fact spent the night behind British lines, hiding with some of his men in a house next to the Chacarita de los Colegiales and convinced that the city had fallen; he was astonished on leaving the building early next morning to find the British still occupying only the outskirts of the town. Carefully weaving his way through the British pickets he reached the Fort at around midday to receive a rapturous welcome from the citizens, and a greatly relieved *Cabildo*.

General Whitelocke and the main Army camped for the night at the Paso de Zamora and next morning, as soon as it was light, began crossing the narrow ford. Due to unceasing rain during the night, this was now almost impassable and the water now came up to the men's armpits. A worried Sergeant Morley writes,

'The water was so high that the men with difficulty got their ammunition safely over but how a young gentleman, Ensign Hopkins got over, I never learnt as he was a mere boy and very short.' Private George Bee, writing home to his brother in his broad Lincolnshire accent and non-existent spelling, gloomily declares, 'On the 3 of July we ingages the Enimeney and Drove them into the Town that night and we had a Rever to Cros and ide was OBlight (obliged) to go up to the Nek in water, and sum of the men that was left behind, the Spanums cut thar ears off and thar hands by the rist and left them in thar Misery.'

Waking early the next morning, Major Nicholls of the 45th (The Sherwood Foresters) declares his Commander in Chief was in a foul temper and disparagingly writes,

'It soon became apparent that General Whitelocke was rather bilious this morning, and found much at fault. Amongst other things he called us "a Regiment of tailors," but we pushed on fast which fell very heavily on the rear notwithstanding that we repeated the signal of our being over pressed, no alteration was made to the pace and we were compelled to run uphill through ankle deep mud and clay. One regiment left twenty or thirty soldiers on the road; the 5th many more, and every Corps a few.'

It was well past one o'clock by the time the last man reached the far bank and another half an hour went by before an officer arrived to escort them to Leveson-Gower's Headquarters at the Corral and, for the first time since leaving the heights of Ensenada, the Army came together again.

THIRTY

THE CORRAL DE LA MISERERE

Situated on a rise, the ground sloped gently down from the Corral to the river and, stretching out below him, General Whitelocke could see the great city of Buenos Aires. Measuring roughly a mile from east to west and two miles inland from north to south, its numerous squares were set at right angles to each other to form streets that were roughly one hundred and thirty yards apart so, looking down from above, the city resembled a giant chequerboard.

Mostly one-storey high, the houses had gardens at the back enclosed by hedges of sloes, prickly pear or orange groves; built of chalk, brick or stone, every house had a balcony with sunshades and latticework. More significantly, all of them had parapets about four feet high running around the roofs that were soon to play a deadly role in the coming battle.

On the eastern side of the city flowed the river, and along the water's edge stood most of the principal houses, including the Fort, a large square building flanked on either side by small bastions, which served as Government House, military headquarters, armoury and home to the *Real Audiencia*. From the level of the interior to the top of the parapet, its walls rose to about fifteen feet, and running along the ramparts were a large number of field guns mounted on carriages so that they could be re-located at a moment's notice. A number of high houses overlooked the Fort from whose rooftops an enemy could bring down deadly fire on the defenders below, as Beresford had found to his cost the previous year.

A deep ditch ran along the side of the Fort facing the town, and beyond it stretched the Plaza Mayor that was cut in half by the Recoba, a long building embellished with arcades and a parapetted roof. This was the city's market place where the retailers carried out their daily business and behind it stood the Cathedral, and next to that the *Cabildo*, a colonial building with impressive columns.

Further to the north of the Plaza Mayor and separated from the town by a small ravine was a large park called the Retiro in which were situated the barracks, arsenal, and Plaza de Toros. South-west of the great square was a smaller one called the Plaza Chica, and beyond it soared the towers of the Convent of Santo Domingo, the largest ecclesiastical building after the Cathedral in Buenos Aires. To the south and almost on the outskirts of the city, Whitelocke could see the Residencia, a large white building which had once been the Royal Hospital.

Having explained the town's layout, Leveson-Gower brought Whitelocke up to date on all that had taken place in the town during the previous twelve hours. After establishing his Headquarters at the Corral he had sent Major Roache, who spoke Spanish fluently and had successfully negotiated the capitulation of Montevideo, into the city to summon Linares to surrender.

The Major set off at daybreak the next morning with a trumpeter and a captured Spanish officer to show him the shortest route to the Argentine headquarters, and close behind him marched a Corporal of the 17th Dragoons continuously waving a large white flag over the Major's head. Successfully negotiating their way through the narrow streets, they arrived at a British picket on the outskirts of the town where the officer in charge strongly advised Roache to take a platoon of his riflemen with him, 'As the town was in a state of total confusion led by an armed mob all of whom are drunk.'

Roache sensibly accepted his offer and an ensign and twelve men joined the little party, which was just as well as the drunken mob showed little respect for the white flag, and continually fired on them as they struggled through the narrow streets in search of Linares's headquarters.

These were eventually found but, as there was no sign of Linares, the Major was forced to deal with Colonel Elio, who true to form made the most of the occasion. Drawing himself up to his full height, the Colonel announced in a loud voice for his men to hear, 'We possess sufficient strength and courage to defend the town. Never shall we surrender.' Then stalling for time in the hope that Linares might yet appear he firmly announced that he could do nothing, unless the summons was put into writing. This forced Roache to fight his way back through the drunken mob to the Corral where the necessary document was hurriedly drawn up. Returning to the Fort at around midday, he presented it to Elio who firmly rejected it, as there was still no sign of Linares.

After listening to Leveson-Gower's report Whitelocke ordered the Army to rest, which was another serious blunder as this allowed the Argentines more time to withdraw their troops from the Punta Galvez, where the scene was one of utter confusion as shouting officers and swearing men feverishly struggled to manhandle the cannons back over the narrow bridge. Only to discover the road to Buenos Aires blocked by men, carts, and oxen, all desperately searching for a way through the deepening mud.

Whitelocke next asked Leveson-Gower whether he had

any thoughts on how to take the town and, delighted to air his view, the Major General promptly presented him with his plan of attack. After only a short perusal, this Whitelocke surprisingly accepted, discarding his own, which had been to take up a position on the northern side of the city and link up with the fleet before launching his attack. It had been a sensible plan as it not only ensured the Army's line of supply was kept intact but could also be a useful line of retreat in the event of the attack failing.

At nine o'clock the next morning, Leveson-Gower summoned the officers to a conference in Guillermo White's house to explain to them his plan of action. To say the least, this was elementary and totally devoid of any form of military strategy. Thirteen columns would simultaneously advance down the same number of adjoining streets, and on reaching the Plaza Mayor or river take up a position on the rooftops surrounding the Fort and demand its surrender. The four central streets, where the defence was expected to be strongest, should be left free except for the one running directly from Army headquarters down to the Fort in which Colonel Kington and his Carabineers would take up a position with two cannons, and mount a false attack.

It was disastrous plan that had three major faults. First, it divided the Army into thirteen uncoordinated groups, secondly it failed to offer any suggestion on how communication or contact could be kept between the battalions advancing down their adjoining streets and lastly, no back up or rendezvous was organised in the event of encountering strong resistance. The order of battle would be as follows:

1) Sir Samuel Auchmuty with the 5th, 87th, and 38th Regiments on the left flank would attack the Plaza de Toros, at the same time as Major Guard and Major Nicholls with the 45th on the right stormed the Residencia. Both buildings

were prime objectives as standing on high ground; a battery of artillery sited on top of them could quickly bombard the town into submission.

2) General Craufurd and Lt-Colonel Pack with the 71st, 88th, and 36th under the overall command of Brigadier Lord Lumley would muster on Major Guard's left and attack the centre.

3) The attack would start at noon and in the event of the columns encountering strong resistance, the men should veer outwards to avoid the cannonade in the centre.

4) No Quarter should be given.

Fortunately, General Whitelocke on Colonel Bourke's advice vetoed the last order and, after this, the officers were dismissed except for Craufurd, Lumley and Colonel Pack whose advice could be useful after being held a prisoner in the city for a year.

Owing to Leveson-Gower's ADC being captured on his way to summon him to the meeting, Sir Samuel Auchmuty arrived late at Headquarters. Hearing the plan he pleaded for his officers to be given more time to reconnoitre the ground, adding that in his opinion noon was an unsuitable time to launch an attack on a hostile populated city. Surprisingly, Leveson-Gower accepted his criticism and postponed the attack until daybreak the following morning, once again giving the Argentines more time to fortify the town.

Asked for his opinion Colonel Pack declared that, in his view, the assault should concentrate on first capturing the Bullring and the Residencia and, once these two vantage points had been taken, he was confident the town could be bombarded into submission. But warned, 'From the turrets of Buenos Aires the enemy would distinctly perceive every movement that we make, and if such an attack determined on it would be better to attempt it before daybreak, when we might have better means furnished us.'

Whitelocke and the other officers agreed but Leveson-Gower ignored his suggestion and Pack said no more, but a year later at General Whitelocke's trial observed, 'At the time, I noted that General Whitelocke had the air of a man acting against his better judgement.'

It was true as, only a month earlier, Whitelocke on his arrival in Montevideo had pointed out to Craufurd the peculiar construction of the Spanish houses, whose flat roofs and parapets made them ideally suited to defend. At the time, he assured Craufurd that under no circumstances would he ever expose his men to fight in such narrow streets, surrounded by similarly constructed buildings.

Sir Samuel Auchmuty agreed with everything Pack had said, adding only that they should blockade the town and starve the inhabitants into submission. Whitelocke firmly dismissed his suggestion, declaring that his orders had been to win over the goodwill of the people, which was unlikely to be achieved by cutting off their food supply!

Guillermo White was then called into the room and questioned on the state of the city. He pessimistically declared that there was no question of the enemy surrendering, as his spies informed him that all the main streets and avenues were in the process of being heavily barricaded with deep trenches dug across them.

This ended the meeting, and despite the plan's failings few officers raised any objections, although it was reckoned that the number of casualties would be high. However, the concept of failure was never entertained as up to now the opposition had been unimpressive and confronted by a British Army drawn up in full battle array, the officers were convinced that any Spanish resistance would swiftly vanish.

By the afternoon it became obvious that General

Whitelocke was having second thoughts about the campaign, as he rather naively asked Leveson-Gower whether he would agree that so far his plans had been correct and the Major General arrogantly replied, 'It is not for an inferior officer to judge the acts of his superior.' Furious at this unhelpful answer, Whitelocke shouted 'From now on he considered him to be his enemy, and would relieve him of his post.' By evening tempers had cooled, and Leveson-Gower's disastrous plan was left unchanged.

Colonel Bourke spent the afternoon struggling to point out to the Colonels the streets that their regiments should advance down. It proved a hopeless task as Leveson-Gower had drawn his plans up using a Spanish map that was not only out of date, but probably inaccurate in the first place. Many of the street names and their formation had been changed, and Bourke found it impossible to draw up the battalions in the manner the Major General ordered. He also added with a degree of logic that if the troops advanced down the streets from west to east as planned, an enemy positioned in those running from north to south could easily cut them off or enfilade them with cannon fire. Leveson-Gower arrogantly dismissed his criticism as being trivial and the plan remained unchanged.

In the afternoon the few crowbars and siege tools brought from Ensenada were distributed among the Regiments and, in a last attempt to avert a confrontation, the General sent his ADC Captain Whittingham to offer Linares a last chance to surrender. He ordered him to offer the Argentine General at least half an hour to consider his answer, which proved unnecessary as Linares rejected the offer out of hand. On receiving his reply, Whitelocke gave his final order, 'The attack should start at first light the following morning and the men advance with their rifles unloaded.'

In the end the majority of officers had little idea of their orders as only a few Commanding Officers had the time or inclination to put them in writing. Having given his final orders, General Whitelocke retired to his quarters in Guillermo White's house and passed a peaceful night convinced that, by the following evening, Buenos Aires would be safely back in British hands.

THIRTY-ONE

THE STORMING OF THE CITY

PART 1: THE RIGHT FLANK

Pandemonium reigned inside the city as panic-stricken citizens ran from house to house, desperately searching for a suitable place to hide their valuables, while others sought safety in numbers and those of a nervous disposition prepared to flee to the country, preferring to save their own lives rather than their worldly possessions.

Faced with the increasing chaos, Martin Alzaga and the *Cabildo* rose to the occasion and began organising the citizens into separate groups, who they quickly put to work digging trenches and throwing up barriers. Men, women and children rushed to barricade the church doors, or convert the ground floors of the government buildings into powder magazines and hospitals. To ensure the work continued throughout the night, the *Cabildo* delegated a special group of citizens to keep the streetlights permanently lit, some of whom could be heard sarcastically chanting 'Who needs soldiers' as they laboured.

Gun emplacements were quickly sited at strategic points along the avenues, and teams of oxen rounded up to tow the heavy cannons to their positions. By midnight some order had been restored but supplying the Army with provisions proved a problem. The meat situation was easily sorted out by driving eight hundred animals into the city; owing to the English occupying the town's slaughterhouse, they were herded into the ditch in front of the Fort which from now on would be used as an abattoir. Bread was another problem and the bakers struggled to keep up with the constant and unending demand from the hungry soldiers entrenched at the Punta Galvez.

Slowly throughout the following days, a steady stream of exhausted militia began to drift back across the Puente Galvez, bringing with them the urgently needed cannons. These were quickly mounted at strategic points around the city and a forward observation post established in the Plaza Nueva (now the central block of Carlos Pellegrini, Suipacha, Rivadavia and Bartolemé Mitre), which was hurriedly stocked with rockets and the soldiers manning given strict instructions to light the fuses as soon as they saw the enemy advancing down the street, and return to the Fort as quickly as possible.

Owing to the split between Linares and Alzaga a year after the battle, the Argentine position is difficult to identify as chroniclers differ on who actually organised the line of defence, and where the defending troops were precisely situated. The main line of defence was definitely centred round the Fort and stretched from the Convent of La Merced along the Calle Defensa past the Convent of Santo Domingo to the Residencia, while the frontline ran roughly along the present day Calle Suipacha.

Linares positioned his troops roughly as follows: a battalion of *Arribeños*, a company of *Correntinos*, and the 3rd *Patricios* surrounded the Church of La Merced, and the *Andaluces* with another company of *Patricios* covered the Church of San Miguel. Colonel Saavedra with a company of *Patricios* guarded the Collegio de San Carlos which stood next to La Casa de la Viuda Vicereina (the late Viceroy del Pino's family house) where the fighting would be heaviest.

Argentina: The British Invasion of Buenos Aires, 1806

On the extreme right flank in the Parque del Retiro, Gutierrez de la Concha with roughly a thousand men consisting of a regiment of Artillery, two companies of *Patricios*, a company of *Galicians*, the *Cantabrians* and his marines occupied the Plaza de Toros, and Captain Murgiondo and his sturdy *Montaneses* defended the Calle de Santo Domingo. Linares stationed all his remaining troops either on the rooftops of the houses in between, or held them in the Fort to act as a reserve.

As darkness fell on the night of 5 July 1807, the city was silent. No light shone, as an hour before dawn the British troops silently took up their positions at the mouths of their allotted streets and, quietly disencumbering their heavy knapsacks, waited patiently for the signal for the attack to begin.

The Army was considerably smaller than when it landed at Ensenada, and by now could barely muster 5,000 bayonets. Many soldiers had been killed, captured or wounded during the previous day's fighting, and hundreds more lay suffering from exhaustion, exposure or hypothermia with Mahon and the Reserve at Reducción.

At precisely half past six, a thunderous cannonade shattered the silence to signal the attack to begin and, due to the guns being set at maximum range, several cannonballs reached the Plaza Mayor. One crashed through the eastern window of the Sala Capitular causing a considerable amount of structural damage but luckily harming no one.

Swords drawn, bayonets fixed, the grim-faced British soldiers advanced determinedly down their allotted streets, expecting at any moment to encounter heavy opposition. Instead, they were greeted by an ominous silence broken only by the whoosh of rockets rising into the sky from somewhere in front of them. A few faint whispers could be heard coming from the rooftops, but these were barely audible above the squelch of the soldiers' boots marching through the mud. Mystified by the eerie silence, Colonel Pack with four companies of the 95th and the newly arrived recruits of the 71st pushed on down their allotted street.

All remained silent until the leading files came in sight of the river, when suddenly the entire street erupted into an inferno of gunfire. Bullets poured down from the surrounding rooftops and stretched out along the narrow thoroughfare, the six hundred riflemen fell like wafers in a shooting gallery.

Men ran in every direction to avoid this lethal fusillade but could find no cover as every door was firmly barricaded and those attempting to shelter in the doorways were burnt to death by the cascades of boiling pitch that teams of women and children hiding behind the parapets poured down on them from above. The heat of this liquid was so intense that one body was still found burning half an hour after the battle was over. These women proved formidable adversaries and one fearsome virago, dressed in a man's uniform, was later killed wielding a sword in one hand and brandishing a pistol in the other. Grapeshot spewed from the mouths of the cannons sited at the end of the street mowing down the leading files and, due to Whitelocke's order to advance with their rifles unloaded, Pack's soldiers were unable to retaliate.

Grown men caught in the middle of this lethal crossfire gagged from the acrid smell of burning flesh, and young recruits barely fifteen urinated in fear. But now was the time the battle-hardened veterans turned their thoughts to more serious matters and began looting. Thomas Howell, advancing with the 71st, describes what followed,

'With their rifles unloaded and bayonets useless, the cry "We are betrayed" spread through the British ranks.

"Mind your duty lads, Onwards, Onwards," roared Captain Brookman but these were the last words he uttered before falling to the ground, shot through the head. Many of our men now made sallies into the houses to search for plunder, and one sergeant had made a longish hole in his wooden canteen into which he slipped all the money he could lay his hands on. As he came out of a house that he had been ransacking he was shot through the head and in his fall the canteen burst, and a great many doubloons ran in all directions down the street. Then began a scramble for the money and about eighteen men were shot grasping at the gold they were never to enjoy. They even snatched it from their dying companions although they themselves were to be in the same situation the next moment.'

In an attempt to avoid this deadly fire, Colonel Pack divided his column in two and sent Lt Colonel Cadogan with half his men and a three-pounder down a street to his left to attack the Jesuits' College. After half an hour of bloody fighting, Colonel Saavedra and his Regiment of *Patricios* successfully managed to drive them off and Cadogan with his few remaining men returned to find Colonel Pack and his men pinned down in front of the Convent of Santo Domingo. A year later, describing their encounter at General Whitelocke's court martial, Colonel Pack declared,

'I learned the failure of the other column for going into the street I found the men retiring and soon met Lt Colonel Cadogan who was excessively agitated. He assured me that he and all his men had done their duty but possessed not the means of succeeding as every man and horse accompanying his column had been killed or wounded and the gun itself was lost. I could readily believe his statement, and directing the men to form in line with mine I went myself to reconnoitre from the bottom of a building forming the square in which the Jesuits' College is situated, but found it impossible to get an entrance there.'

It was obvious that the enemy's position was far too strong so Pack ordered Cadogan to retire to the Residencia, but the Colonel flatly refused to give up ground gained by the loss of so many of his men. Taking possession of a large house belonging to the dowager Vicereine, he and his men put up a desperate defence for the next three hours but with a sergeant and fourteen men killed and five officers and eighty-two men wounded he eventually surrendered. Martin Rodriguez, a witness to this brutal struggle, declares,

'The blood from the dead and wounded British soldiers pouring down the outside walls from the gutters of the building flooded the street below, making it almost impassable.'

Advancing down the adjacent street, Craufurd and the other battalion of the 95th reached the beach without encountering any serious opposition and, sending a messenger to Major Guard proceeding down the street to his right, ordered him to join him as quickly as possible. Then, swinging left towards the Fort, he found Colonel Pack and his men pinned down in front of the Convent of Santo Domingo.

The dense smoke enveloping the street made visibility almost nil, and missiles and shot poured down from every rooftop. Caught out in the open with no available cover, Colonel Pack with five musket balls in his uniform was now in serious trouble and had already lost a great number of officers and men.

The situation was desperate, so Craufurd sent for the Light Brigade's field gun and ordered the gunners to blow down the Convent's wooden doors. One shot was enough; the heavy doors disintegrated into a shower of splinters and, storming into the Church, the 71st were astonished to see hanging above the altar their regimental colours, which the previous year Santiago Linares had presented to the Church in a moving ceremony to thank the Almighty for his help in defeating General Beresford.

Pack immediately ordered them to be taken down and re-flown from the rooftop to signal their position, and show the Convent was now in British hands. Their sudden appearance on the Convent's roof caused consternation in the Fort, and the Argentine officer in charge of the artillery immediately ordered two guns to bombard the building, but this the superstitious gun crews flatly refused to do, declaring it would be sacrilege to fire on such a holy building. It was not until Martin Alzaga assured them that 'The Almighty would understand they must first save the city and his temple afterwards' that they reluctantly fired two shots.

The Mayor's assurance proved of little benefit as both shots fell well short of their target. The first landed in the middle of the Plaza Chica, and the other blew a hole in the roof of Don Francisco Tellechea's house, causing a considerable amount of damage to the building and even more to the owner's nervous system.

It was not the last of poor Don Tellechea's worries as, a few minutes later, Jose Fornaguera, now in command of *Las Patriotas de la Unión*, arrived with his men and began mounting two cannons in his garden. Once sited these began bombarding the Convent, which resulted in heavy retaliatory fire from the British marksmen on the Convent's roof, shattering all the windows of the house and causing Don Tellechea even more anguish and a considerable sum of money, glass being a scarce luxury.

Following hard on Pack's heels, Craufurd and his men

swarmed into the Cathedral and Sir Lancelot Holland writes,

'On entering the Cathedral we expected to find it full of enemy soldiers but there were very few. Two monks were badly wounded, one of whom had lost his arm, and the other shot in the breast. So we collected all the frightened monks and friars of whom there were many and protected them and their altar plate with sentries, but it was difficult to prevent plunder as the Cathedral was rich and magnificent'.

Seeing the situation rapidly deteriorating, Craufurd sent a messenger to the Corral urgently asking General Whitelocke for reinforcements and further orders. Neither were forthcoming but at around noon a Spanish officer arrived under a flag of truce with a message from General Linares and, believing it to be an offer from the Argentines to surrender, Craufurd was mortified to discover that it demanded his own.

Linares assured Craufurd that the Convent was surrounded; Major Vandeleur and the 88th had surrendered and, to avoid further bloodshed, he strongly advised Craufurd to do the same. Outraged at his suggestion, Black Bob unhesitatingly rejected it and instructed his men to lower the colours, and prepare to retreat to the Residencia which they could see from the Convent's roof was now in the hands of Major Nicholls and the 45th.

The order was in the process of being carried out when the Argentines suddenly rushed the field gun that had been left outside the Convent walls, owing to its axle being too wide to pass through the narrow gateway. Seeing the attack, Major Guard and his Grenadiers on their way to join up with Craufurd attempted to beat it off but, in less than three minutes, forty of his men were dead and, with three musket balls through his sword, the Major with his few remaining men hastily took refuge inside the Convent.

Craufurd, Guard, Pack and the 71st were now surrounded; death greeted anyone trying to leave the building; attempting to mount a sally, Major Trotter was shot through the head the moment his foot touched the pavement outside the building. Inside the Convent, the carnage was terrible, as wounded soldiers crawled or pulled their way across the blood-soaked flagstones desperately seeking refuge in the crypt and Colonel Pack, propped up against a wall wounded in one leg, watched helplessly as his men fell dead around him.

In a desperate attempt to save the gun and deter the enemy from repeatedly attacking the gateway, Riflemen Plunkett and Fisher, two marksmen of the 95th, were hoisted onto the roof of an outhouse commanding the approaches to the Convent. Although exposed to heavy fire for several hours they managed to kill or wound every Argentine venturing within range, including Captain Don Jose Pasos carrying a white flag who had been sent by Colonel Elio to negotiate a surrender. Remarking on this incident in his memoirs, Colonel Sir Lancelot Holland writes:

'Seeing a figure waving something white at the corner of the street and ignorant of the customs of war, Plunkett shouted to Fisher, "I'll have a slap at the fellow with the white handkerchief" and shot the Captain through the thighs.'

Tom Plunkett was a popular character who for many hours could keep the men of the 95th entertained with his tricks and funny stories. Not only renowned as a fierce fighter and heavy drinker he was also a celebrated dancer, who could perform a merry jig balancing on top of a water butt even in the roughest seas. Tom would make his name two years later in the Peninsular War, when he shot and killed a dashing young French Cavalry officer, General Auguste-Marie Francois Colbert, and his ADC coming to his rescue at the remarkable range of over 600 yards.

It was an enormous distance for a rifle at the time and the shot became famous throughout the Army. Delighted by his performance, his Commanding Officer paraded Tom in front of the regiment and proudly announced, 'Here men stands a pattern for the battalion,' and presented him with a purse of money and his corporal's stripes.

Promotion came fast and Tom soon reached the rank of sergeant, but his meteoric rise lasted for only a short time before drink brought about his downfall. Over-indulging on the local *aguardiente* (Spanish spirit) after a hard day's training, Tom became fighting drunk and started laying about him. Unable to restrain him, his messmates hurriedly sent for an officer to deal with the situation and, hearing this, Tom promptly seized a rifle and running into a nearby hut firmly barricaded himself in.

The officer arrived a short time later and, nervously approaching the building, heard Tom swearing inside he would shoot anyone that tried to arrest him. Coming from a man acknowledged to be the finest shot in the British Army, this was a threat not to be taken lightly, but luckily the alcohol soon began to wear off and, becoming maudlin, Tom after much coaxing was persuaded to come out and hastily clapped in irons.

His offence was serious and, if arraigned before a court martial, he would certainly have been shot, but realising this would damage the regiment's reputation, Colonel Beckwith and his Company Commander decided to deal with the case themselves. Finding Tom guilty, they sentenced him to 300 lashes and reduced him to the ranks.

A few days later the now Rifleman Plunkett, stripped to the waist, was paraded in front of the battalion and tied to a tree. Two buglers then stepped forward with their cat o'nine tails ready in their hands and waited for Colonel Beckwith to give the order for the punishment to begin. This was duly given, but after only a few lashes the Colonel, suspecting the buglers were laying it on lightly because of Tom's popularity, barked, 'Do your duty fairly Sirs.' Nevertheless, after only a further thirty-five strokes, even he could stand it no longer and, ordering Tom to be cut down, shouted loudly at the bleeding Plunkett for the regiment to hear, 'You now see Sir! How very easy it is to commit a blackguard's crime but how difficult it is to take the punishment.' Many years later, an officer in the 95th ran into Tom down and out selling matches in a London street and, discussing old times, asked him how many Argentines he had shot that day in the gateway of the Convent of Santo Domingo. 'I think I killed about twenty Sir,' Tom replied adding, 'I also shot a gentleman carrying a flag of truce.' Despite every effort to help him, Tom died a few years later unrepentant and in penury. Any money given to him he spent on gin, and the current saying 'Drunk for a penny, blind drunk for two pence' had no finer exponent than ex-Sergeant Plunkett, late of the 95th.

Lack of respect for the white flag at the time was not uncommon and General Sir Harry Smith, then an ensign in the 95th also trapped inside the Convent, encountered the same difficulty seven years later in 1814 at the siege of New Orleans. Approaching General Jackson's troops under the protection of a white flag to request a truce to bury the dead and retrieve the wounded, Sir Harry writes,

'The Americans like our old associates the French were not accustomed to the civility of war, and it was a long time before I could induce them to receive me. They fired on me with cannon and musketry that excited my choler somewhat for a round shot tore away the ground under my right foot, which would have been a bore indeed to have lost under such circumstances.'

With no sound of fighting on either side of him and no news or sign of reinforcements from Whitelocke, Craufurd realised his position was untenable. Summoning his officers to a meeting at around half past three, except for his brother-in-law Lt Colonel Holland which 'motives of delicacy prevented me from doing,' he asked them for their opinion of the situation. All agreed that they should surrender, except for Major Macleod of the 95th who hesitatingly remarked, he thought they might be able to extricate themselves. Face black with fury Craufurd icily replied,

'Major Macleod do you think we can get out of this although I do not, I will this moment place myself with you at the head of the column and we will be the first to lead it out'.

Faced with this, Major Macleod quickly changed his mind and a white flag was hurriedly raised and, minutes later, Colonel Elio arrived at the door of the Convent to discuss terms of surrender. His appearance failed to impress Sir Lancelot Holland, who rudely describes him and his troops. 'As a dirty ill-dressed man surrounded by a riotous armed rabble hooting and screeching, who every moment we expected to fire on us, ordered us to march out without arms. It was a bitter task; everyone felt it, and the men were all in tears as we marched through the town to the Fort. Nothing could be more mortifying than our passage through the streets amidst the rabble that had conquered us. They were very dark skinned people, short and ill made, covered with rags and armed with long muskets and some swords. There was neither order nor uniformity amongst them.'

Argentina: The British Invasion of Buenos Aires, 1806

As the shattered Rifle Corps were in the process of being escorted out of the Convent, an excited Argentine Lieutenant of Hussars, Antonio Leiva, dashed into the church and to the cheers of the watching crowd began climbing up the highest tower to haul down the 71st colours. After successfully completing his mission he was about to descend, when his foot slipped and he hurtled into space clutching the colours between his hands. To the amazement of the spectators, these opened up like a parachute, slowing down his fall and miraculously saving his life. His action was not forgotten, for fifty-two years later on 25 May 1859 (Argentina's national day), the Municipality of Buenos Aires presented Don Antonio, now an old man, with an award in honour of this remarkable event.

Meanwhile on the extreme right flank beyond the Convent, the battle was progressing better and Major Nicholls and the 45th were now occupying the Residencia. Being out of range of the cannons of the Fort and higher than the surrounding buildings, this was relatively easy to defend as the men could bring down gunfire on the neighbouring rooftops. After withstanding several enemy charges, they seized the surrounding houses and, for the rest of the battle, the Residencia stayed in British hands.

THIRTY-TWO

THE STORMING OF THE CITY PART 2

Sir Samuel Auchmuty, on the right flank with a battalion of the 87th on the other side of town, was meeting stiff opposition. Like the 71st they had advanced unopposed down their street for more than a mile, when suddenly a cannon opened fire in front of them, swiftly followed by a howitzer firing grapeshot, and the leading files disintegrated into a shower of arms, legs, and headless torsos.

Undeterred by this flying debris, the 87th bravely charged the enemy and, abandoning their guns, the gun crews ran for the safety of the barracks. As the gun smoke slowly thinned, out of the haze and dust at the corner of the street appeared a heavily barricaded house with a flat roof covered in enemy soldiers watching their movements.

The street was obviously too heavily defended to proceed down any further, so Auchmuty ordered his men to break down a garden fence on their left and search for a detour around the enemy's position. This was quickly found and reaching the adjacent street, they discovered a deep ditch running down its centre and quickly jumping into it, the high sides gave them cover all the way to the river. Reaching the end, Auchmuty surreptitiously poked his head out over the top and saw a large white house in front of him. Ordering the doors to be forced, he quickly took refuge inside and began reassembling his troops.

Advancing down the adjoining street, heavy musket fire brought the Regiment's other battalion to a halt. This was so intense that the men panicked and, loading their rifles, began firing wildly in every direction and, for a minute, the battalion wavered. Then, breaking ranks, the men careered back down the street hotly pursued by their Colonel, Sir Edward Butler, and his officers, who waving their swords furiously above their heads shouted at the men to 'Standfast.' After a short chase, they managed to halt them and rallying his men to the colours, Sir Edward and his battalion once again set off down the street to join Auchmuty in his building. Apart from this unfortunate incident, the 87th had done well and had taken over a hundred prisoners and captured three guns, though in the process suffering many casualties.

Taking stock of his position, Auchmuty found to his surprise that the musket fire checking his advance was coming from the Plaza de Toros, which according to Leveson-Gower's map should have been three streets further to his left. A new plan of attack was therefore needed which was difficult to make without knowing the position of the battalions on either side of him.

The battalion of the 5th Foot, commanded by Lt Colonel Davie on his right, had encountered little resistance, and successfully seizing the Church of Santa Catalina ran their colours up on the roof to signal position. Advancing down the adjacent street, Major King with the regiment's other battalion were not so lucky, and immediately came under heavy fire the moment they crossed the start line. Nevertheless they bravely charged the guns and, after shooting their horses and spiking their cannons, the enemy gun crews ran up a side street to vanish among the houses. Describing this action in his Lincolnshire accent and shaky handwriting, Private George Bee, a member of this Battalion declares,

'When we got in the town we took no prisoners, kill all before us. The dead Bodies lies in tha streets as thik as tha cod lie. Bunosayris was a strong place. The Houes was strang Belt for we cod not Break into them and was o'Blight to fier in the dors tow or three tims before tha wold fli hopen and a nubber of women and childtrn was killed that Day.'

After this success, the 5th continued their advance but immediately came under heavy fire from the rooftop of a nearby house. Breaking down the door with a heavy entrenching tool, they charged up the stairs and drove the enemy off the roof but the incoming fire from the surrounding rooftops proved too fierce so Major King ordered the men to kneel down behind the parapet. It proved too low to give them cover, and the enemy snipers began picking them off one by one, forcing them to return to the street. Spilling out of the door in an undisciplined group, they now saw advancing on them, at the trot, a troop of cavalry wearing yellow jackets. One of the men was carrying a white flag and the cry went up 'They want to surrender.' Sergeant Morley writes:

'A man named Redmond O'Connell, a powerful rawboned lad of the Emerald Isle and as kindly a being as ever existed, observing the enemy remarked, "To surrender is it, then I'll be just after giving them an airy touch". He had no sooner spoken than they were upon us demanding our surrender and our Major looked what he felt a proud defiance. He was a tall man and a ponderous sabre gleamed in his powerful hand. In the mêlée that followed Redmond fired as did the rest of us and many of the men and horses came down together. The resistance was feeble and short, and those that were able turned round bowed their heads close down upon their horse's necks and galloped off. When order was restored, we found our Major in possession of one of their sabres.'

After this skirmish, the battalion reassembled in a nearby yard and under heavy fire set off again down a narrow alleyway towards the Bullring but the opposition proved too strong. Many died; others including Major King were wounded, and they were forced to return to their previous rendezvous and, taking refuge in the house, hoisted up their colours, and waited for reenforcements to arrive.

Auchmuty from his position was greatly relieved to see their colours billowing in the breeze and now knew that his right flank was covered. Flying the colours nevertheless had a major drawback for, although registering a regiment's position to its own side, it also disclosed it to the other, and Major King's house now came under heavy fire from the guns in front of the Plaza de Toros. This abruptly stopped at around ten o'clock, thanks to the arrival of Colonel Nugent and the 38th.

Starting on the extreme left flank this battalion, after a twenty-minute silent march, arrived in a narrow alleyway approaching the Plaza de Toros. Owing to the street being deep in mud, the going was slow and many men and officers, including Colonel Fletcher Wilkie, lost their boots in the sticky sludge. Despite this handicap the men stalwartly pressed on barefooted but soon came under heavy fire from the cannons lined up in front of the Plaza de Toros. These they promptly charged, but heavy rifle fire from the surrounding buildings drove them back, and after suffering severe casualties they hurriedly took refuge in a nearby house called 'La Casa del Azquenega'.

Climbing onto the roof to take stock of his position, Colonel Nugent spotted a prominent building to the right of the Plaza de Toros from where it might be possible to turn the enemy's flank and immediately dispatched two companies of his men to seize it.

A grenadier with the worst reputation in the regiment was the first to reach it. Smashing down the door with one blow of his rifle butt, he dashed up the stairs and single-handedly attacked the fifteen men stationed on the roof. Two he quickly bayoneted but the others hurriedly feigned death, except for four who, regrouping in a corner, prepared to rush him. The Grenadier gave them no chance. Charging straight at them he killed one and the others in terror leapt off the roof into the street below, and by the time his comrades arrived he had taken the remainder prisoner.

Now in position on either side of the Plaza de Toros, Nugent's men opened fire on the guns lined up in front of it. Caught in this withering crossfire, the gun crews hastily spiked their guns and retreated into the building. One battery bravely stood its ground and kept on firing, but this ended a few minutes later when, slipping unseen out of the back of their house, a party of the 38th took them by surprise and, abandoning their gun the crew ran for the safety of the Bullring. They had left it too late, for just as they reached its entrance the doors closed and, taking refuge in the nearby barracks, the pursuing riflemen hunted them down like a fox that has gone to ground. Finding the gun unspiked, Nugent's men quickly swung it round and began bombarding the Bullring's gate at close range. Colonel Fletcher Wilkie, standing to one side watching his men pursue the enemy through the barracks, was delighted to see returning from the chase,

'Corporal MacKay, a regular built Highlander of his company with a well stained sword in one hand and a pair of boots in the other. Knowing that I had lost mine in the muddy lane, he had shot dead Spanish Officer for the sake of his Captain and the property however doubtfully acquired was very acceptable, as the Spanish boots fitted me very well.'

Inside the Plaza de Toros, the situation was rapidly deteriorating as the defenders were running out of powder and shot. Although the ammunition park was less than a hundred yards away from the building, Gutierrez de la Concha made no attempt to reach it as, in the excitement of the battle, he had mislaid the keys. Despite their rapidly diminishing ammunition, his men staunchly continued to defend their position and Captain Jacob Varela, realising the situation to be hopeless, urged Gutierrez to abandon the Bullring, and return with him to the Fort. Gutierrez de la Concha flatly refused to do so, declaring he would defend his position to the last man and reckoning this was fast approaching, Varela left him to his fate and, escaping with his sixty men, joined the battle waging in front of the Convent of Santo Domingo.

He was lucky to escape for, seconds later, the 87th captured the houses surrounding the Plaza de Toros and began bringing heavy fire down on the defenders below. Out of ammunition and with over 200 men dead Gutierrez de la Concha, badly wounded with a bullet hole through his hat, ordered his men to lay down their arms and a white flag was hurriedly displayed from the Bullring's balcony and, like a bursting dam, Auchmuty's men came charging through the broken gates and triumphantly took possession of the building.

Despite capturing their objective and thirty-seven guns, the 87th had suffered severe casualties. Out of less than seven hundred men of all ranks, they had lost fourteen officers and over a hundred and seventy men dead or wounded. On the plus side, the two most important buildings, the Residencia and the Plaza de Toros, were now in British hands. On the minus side: Craufurd, Pack and the Light Division were in captivity, and Lumley's brigade left of centre was now in serious trouble.

Accompanying the right half of the 36th, Lord Lumley from the start had found the going slow. Every hundred yards deep ditches yawned across the muddy road and, unlike Colonel Pack and Craufurd, the battalion had come under heavy and remorseless fire the moment it entered the town. Nevertheless, the men bravely pressed on and reaching the Calle de Santo ran their colours up on a high building overlooking the beach belonging to the widow Sotoca.

Flying their colours proved a serious error as their sudden appearance alerted the enemy gunners to their position, who immediately brought down on them a thundering cannonade even heavier than the one that had greeted Major King and the 5th. Not only the seven guns on this side of the Fort opened fire on their house but the cannons mounted in front of the Plaza Mayor also swept the street with grapeshot. Although able to hold the position, Lumley and his men found it impossible to leave the building and, from now on, took virtually no further part in the battle.

Major Vandaleur with the 88th on Lumley's right was faring worse for, successfully reaching a third of the way to the beach, they suddenly came under heavy fire from the surrounding rooftops. Shouting at his men to advance at the double, Vandaleur and his men careered down the street under a hail of bullets, hand grenades, stink bombs and every other kind of missile, but had not gone far when two guns suddenly opened fire in front of them and two more followed suit with enfilading fire from the Plaza Mayor. Bravely ignoring this deadly barrage, they plunged on down the street and, reaching the end, scrambled over a barricade into a ditch and into a trap.

The ditch had only one exit that ran along a narrow ramp in full view and range of the Fort's guns and, realising that any attempt to take this route would lead to certain death, Vandaleur ordered his men to break down the doors of a nearby house with the aid of an entrenching tool. This was swiftly achieved and, mounting the stairs, his men gained the roof, which turned out to be lower than those on either side, so that anyone stepping onto it was instantly killed by the enemy snipers hiding on the rooftops above, forcing them to abandon their position. After several attempts, they managed to seize the house next door but, this time, heavy cannon fire from the Fort drove them off the roof. Having lost most of his men and with no sign of help, Vandaleur realised his position was hopeless, and hoisting up the white flag surrendered.

When the 88th's other battalion paraded at the start it was so weak that Colonel Duff, its Commanding Officer, took one look at the state of the men and ordered the colours to be left behind. After this pessimistic beginning he sent a messenger to Leveson-Gower requesting him to release his other two companies, which had been delegated to guard Army Headquarters. Surprisingly, the Major General granted him his request, but when Major Ironmonger and his men arrived it was discovered that their muskets were useless, as on the Major General's orders they had removed all the flints. This entailed a further delay, while a hunt began to collect as many spare flints as possible from the other soldiers.

Once this had been completed the battalion set off for the Church of La Merced, which they reached without encountering any opposition. However, the moment they attempted to force the gates, the street came alive with rifle fire and all their efforts to break down the heavily barricaded doors proved futile. Caught out in the open with no available cover, Duff and his men plunged on down the street under a hail of bullets towards the Fort. It was an alleyway of death; over half his battalion fell dead or wounded, and any hope of reaching the beach was out of the question, so Duff ordered his men to break down the doors of three adjacent houses, and manning the roof with what remained of his men he valiantly held the position for several hours. In the end his casualties became too great, and at quarter to twelve he reluctantly surrendered. This battalion had gone into battle five hundred strong but by now had lost fifteen officers, over a hundred and eighty-three men killed or wounded, and had achieved nothing.

Still holed up in their house, Lord Lumley and his men began to suffer from Duff's surrender, as all the guns on that side of the Fort now swung onto their position and began bombarding it. Twice he was summoned to surrender, twice he refused and, irritated by his stubbornness, the Argentines now made a serious error. Led by the ever impetuous Colonel Elio, they began pulling two cannons along the beach to blow the house at close range to pieces; spotting this manoeuvre, Colonel Burne dashed out of his house with fifty men of the 36th and taking Elio and his men by surprise drove them back into the Fort. Quickly spiking the guns they sprinted for cover, and jumping over a wall vanished from sight before the cannons of the Fort could bear down on them.

Despite this success, Lumley realised his position was rapidly becoming untenable and with no sign of support he sent an officer to the Plaza de Toros to ask Auchmuty for help. But Sir Samuel was fully involved in his own battle, and the best he could do was to advise Lumley to join him in the Plaza de Toros as quickly as possible. Taking his advice, Lumley and his men, with some soldiers of the 5th who had managed to escape over the rooftops, set off at two o'clock in the afternoon along the beach towards the Plaza de Toros. Weathering a storm of gunfire from the Fort, they reached the Bullring an hour later to join up with Auchmuty and his men. In retrospect Lumley and his brigade had been of little use, suffered severe casualties, and in the end been sacrificed for no good purpose at all.

THIRTY-THREE

THE STORMING OF THE CITY
PART 3: ARMY HEADQUARTERS

General Whitelocke remained all day at his Headquarters in the Corral de La Miserere; out of touch with the Army, the battle and the Reserve who, only a mile away to the East, sat listening to the gunfire, impatiently waiting for orders to join the attack. Owing to the General stubbornly rejecting any suggestion of moving his Headquarters closer to the action, throughout the day no messenger from any battalion reached the Corral de la Miserere. But by the incessant roar of cannons and increasing crescendo of musket fire it soon became obvious to the watchers at the Corral that a fierce battle was in progress in the city and, at around nine o'clock in the morning, Army Headquarters came in for its share of the excitement.

A troop of enemy cavalry was spotted approaching from the rear and, hurriedly sending for his Military Secretary, Lt Colonel Henry Torrens, a nervous General Whitelocke ordered him to take 16 mounted Dragoons of the 17th and 33 dismounted troopers of the 9th to drive them off. Cautiously approaching the enemy, the Colonel received a nasty shock when, instead of the thirty enemy horsemen reported, he found an entire cavalry regiment of over three hundred men confronting him. Undeterred by this disparity in numbers he sent a messenger back to Captain Blake, the Assistant Quartermaster General, informing him that he was about to engage them and, after a brisk skirmish, successfully drove them off.

The enemy's number seems rather large to be routed by only 49 men, but the following year at General Whitelocke's court martial Torrens related the encounter under oath and, as no one questioned it, one must assume that at the time enemy numbers for senior officers were permitted to increase in size like a fish that gets away.

All over the city, British colours began to sprout above the rooftops, and first to show were the colours of the 71st fluttering over the Convent of Santo Domingo, which were swiftly followed by the 45th above the Residencia and the 5th's above a building close to the Plaza de Toros and, finally, the battle-scarred colours of the 38th rose triumphantly over the Bullring.

A large French flag was also spotted flying in front of a house in the centre of the town that caused a considerable amount of alarm, as no French troops were believed to be stationed in the Rio de la Plata area. Major King, holed up in the house next door, was equally surprised and, reckoning it belonged to someone important, twice attacked the building. Each time heavy rifle-fire drove him back and only after the battle was over was it discovered that the house belonged to Anita Perichon, and that Santiago Linares had personally placed the flag outside the door either from patriotic pride or in the hope that the British troops would treat her with respect should the city fall.

At one o'clock the sensational news reached Headquarters that the Spanish fort had struck its colours, and Captain Frazer of the Artillery, spyglass in hand, hurried forward to verify this splendid piece of news only to return five minutes later and disappointingly report, 'They were in fact wrapped around the flagstaff but, owing to the wind having dropped and the density of gun smoke, they were difficult to see'.

General Whitelocke and Leveson-Gower spent all the morning at the Corral, nervously pacing up and down waiting for reports from the advancing columns. None arrived and, at around two o'clock in the afternoon, General Whitelocke, seeing Colonel Torrens, Captain Whittingham and a group of officers strolling across the malodorous yard, approached them and declared, 'I do not like to order any person but I would feel much obliged to any officer that would go to the left flank and bring me back information of Sir Samuel Auchmuty's situation.'

Captain Whittingham promptly volunteered and, taking a sergeant, 10 mounted Dragoons, and 30 infantrymen, immediately set off towards the town. The route was one continual skirmish so, dividing his infantry into two separate bodies, he sent one group to act as flankers on either side of the road, and ordered a corporal and two mounted Dragoons to ride in front of him to act as an advanced guard and two to guard his rear.

Due to the barricades, ditches, and smoke, the going was slow, and the little party soon got lost. Whittingham therefore ordered his flankers not to fire on the next armed group, and instead attempt to take them prisoner. Three citizens were successfully captured and under threat of being strung up from the nearest lamppost, nervously showed them the way to the Plaza de Toros where they found Auchmuty busily engaged in beating off a counter-attack.

Sir Samuel reported he had suffered many casualties and begged Whittingham to ask General Whitelocke to send him more reinforcements, and especially men to work the captured guns, and join him as soon as possible in the Plaza de Toros. Leaving his infantry behind to assist Auchmuty, Whittingham and his Dragoons galloped back under heavy fire to the Corral and delivered Sir Samuel's message to the General.

His mission proved a waste of time, as apart from dispatching Sergeant Hamilton of 17th Dragoons with 18 artillerymen to assist Auchmuty with the captured guns, Whitelocke ignored his other two requests. The first because he had no reinforcements at Headquarters; the second because he was out of touch with Colonel Mahon and the Reserve. As for shifting his headquarters to the Bullring, the General firmly declared it was far too late an hour to embark on such a complicated action.

By now it was five o'clock, getting dark, and the battle was slowly drawing to a close. Driven into isolated pockets around the city and unable to make contact with either their Commander-in-Chief or those on either side of them, the British soldiers slowly began to surrender and, as night fell, the only soldier at liberty to leave his position was General Whitelocke. Surrounded by his staff and cavalry escort, he left the Corral and rode to his sleeping quarters in Guillermo White's house where, after posting sentries on the roof, his ADCs took it in turns to stay on duty throughout the night to ensure that nothing unimportant disturbed the General from his slumbers.

THIRTY-FOUR

A DEFEATED ARMY

Early next morning Captain Whittingham set off in search of Colonel Mahon and the Reserve, who he eventually found at the Puente Galvez impatiently waiting to join the battle. The General's orders to join him at the Corral had failed to reach them and, using his initiative, Colonel Mahon had advanced his men to the bridge to be closer to the action.

Having informed the Colonel that General Whitelocke urgently needed him and his men at Army Headquarters, Whittingham left 30 of his men behind to show them the way to the Corral, and set off with Captain Giles and a hundred men of the 40th in search of General Craufurd.

Successfully fighting their way to the Residencia, they found it in the hands of Major Nicholls and Major Tolley, who informed Whittingham that they also had received no news from General Whitelocke. While the last they had seen of Craufurd were his colours flying from the roof of the Convent of Santo Domingo about 800 yards away which had been struck at around three o'clock in the afternoon.

As they stood on the roof of the Residencia discussing their next move, a cannon ball suddenly whistled over their heads, which made them hurriedly dive for cover below the parapet and, gingerly raising his head, Major Tolley peered over the edge and saw advancing down the street towards them a large number of enemy troops. Shouting at his men to follow him, he dashed out of the building and returned five minutes later with his men, pulling a large enemy howitzer behind them. After satisfactorily dealing with this irritating interruption, the three officers held a hasty discussion and agreed that to take a small force in search of Craufurd would be far too dangerous, while a larger one could put the Residencia at risk.

Whittingham therefore returned to the Corral to find Colonel Mahon and the reserve but no sign of General Whitelocke or Leveson-Gower. Enquiring as to their whereabouts, he was informed that while away searching for the reserve, Sergeant Harrison of the Light Dragoons had arrived from the Plaza de Toros with a message from Linares informing Whitelocke that Craufurd, King, Cadogan, Duff, and Vandeleur with all their men had surrendered and he was now holding over a thousand prisoners in the Fort. All these he offered to release, along with Beresford and his men, if Whitelocke agreed to surrender and abandon Buenos Aires, Montevideo and the River Plate forever. To put further pressure on the General to accept his demands, Linares added the ominous postscript to his letter, 'Should this offer be refused, I can take no responsibility for the safety of the prisoners. Feelings in the city are running high, and in no way can I guarantee being able to keep the citizens under control for very much longer.'

Not only was this true, but it was also one of General Whitelocke's greatest worries. Bands of drunken citizens were roaming the streets crying for revenge who at any moment might gain entrance to the Fort and slit the throats of the imprisoned British soldiers.

In his original terms of surrender, Linares had made no mention of the return of Montevideo but Martin Alzaga insisted that this should be included. Much against his will Linares agreed, as he was convinced the English would never accept this and it could easily jeopardise the offer. Despite his reluctance Alzaga remained adamant and the Mayor proved right as, in the end, the British agreed to all their demands.

On receiving Linares's offer Whitelocke as usual dithered, and begged for more time to consider the terms of surrender. In the meantime, he suggested there should be a short term of truce for both sides to collect their dead and wounded. Linares agreed and as soon as the firing ceased, Whitelocke and Leveson-Gower, escorted by a troop of cavalry, rode despondently through the corpse-strewn streets to discuss their next plan of action with Auchmuty, now firmly entrenched in the Plaza de Toros.

The situation was serious. For although Whitelocke reckoned he had lost two and a half thousand men, it was way short of the mark as four hundred lay dead; six hundred and forty-nine wounded, and nineteen hundred and twenty-four were now prisoners of war. Many of the latter were seriously wounded and the total came to nearly three thousand casualties or almost a third of his Army. On the plus side, Mahon and the reserve were intact; two strong positions were now in British hands and, at any moment, Colonel Acland was expected to arrive with reinforcements from Montevideo. In spite of this, the minus side far exceeded the plus as Whitelocke had lost the most important thing of all: the confidence of his officers and men.

After a lengthy discussion, the three Generals unanimously agreed that even if they succeeded in capturing the city, they would never be able to hold it without further reinforcements arriving from England. As these were unlikely to reach them in time, they had no alternative but to surrender.

At two o'clock in the afternoon, Whitelocke therefore sent Leveson-Gower to the Fort to negotiate a truce, and gave him specific instructions to demand a suitable length of time for the British merchants to dispose of their cargoes in Montevideo.

The route to the Fort proved difficult but, successfully weaving his way through the numerous barricades and ditches, the Major General arrived there several hours later to find Craufurd dining with Santiago Linares and his officers. Describing their meeting a year later at General Whitelocke's court martial, Craufurd declares,

'I had no opportunity of saying a word to him that would not be heard by everyone at the table but afterwards, I went with Major General Leveson-Gower and General Liniers into the latter's apartment. Before they entered upon business, I thought it my duty to take the Major General to one side and told him that from what I had observed I was quite convinced that if the Army attacked again in the same way as they had done on the 5th, they would be completely defeated.'

After receiving this unhelpful piece of advice, Leveson-Gower and Linares began a lengthy discussion and a treaty was eventually drawn up, in which it was agreed that Whitelocke and his troops would abandon Buenos Aires inside ten days but Montevideo should remain in British hands for a further two months, and then be handed back with all its guns intact.

Whitelocke's optimistic proposal that the British merchants should be allowed four months to dispose of their wares in Montevideo, Alzaga and the *Cabildo* firmly rejected and both sides agreed that two hostages should be exchanged to ensure the handover ran smoothly. Captain Carrol and Captain Hamilton of the 5th were chosen to act for the British and Colonel Fletcher-Wilkie, commenting on their selection declares,

'Hamilton's Spanish was decidedly shaky but he was a

fine strapping handsome fellow with no great critic in the Spanish lingo. Arriving at the castle his appearance drew the attention of a group of Spanish ladies who were watching him, and the closest of these said to the other, "*Que hombre! muy hermoso y fuerte*," (What a man! very good-looking and strong) to which Hamilton indignantly retorted, "You Lie Señora! I was only five and thirty on my last birthday."'

The treaty was very unpopular and the British soldiers considered it not only an outrageous betrayal but also a shameful surrender. Colonel Fletcher Wilkie ruefully writes:

'Nothing could exceed the disgust of the men, who had hitherto withstood all temptations of deserting but now went over to the Spaniards in considerable numbers and had we not very speedily embarked, our losses in that way would have been very heavy.'

Graffiti began to spring up all over the town, and painted signs covered the walls of the houses declaring 'General Whitelocke is a coward, a traitor, or both!' and, in one of his famous rages, General Craufurd reportedly announced, 'Any man under my command has permission to shoot General Whitelocke on sight'.

As for the jubilant citizens, all feelings of elation vanished when they surveyed the carnage in their streets. On every corner the piles of corpses steadily grew higher, and shadowy figures methodically stripped them of uniforms and boots. Wild dogs roamed the ill-lit alleys, fiercely fighting over the festering remains of human arms and legs clenched firmly between their teeth, and the sharp tang of cordite combined with the sickly stench of coagulating blood blocking the gutters discouraged the citizens from leaving their houses.

Teams of exhausted doctors, aided by an army of women volunteers, worked unceasingly over the following days tending the wounded, and hundreds of stretcher-bearers were quickly organised to carry the seriously wounded to the Convent of San Francisco, which had hurriedly been converted into a hospital. While those with only minor wounds were nursed in private houses, or cared for by the Bethlehemite friars.

Safely locked in the Sala de Acuerdos, the *Cabildo* remained in session, while underneath, the Quartermaster Don Marcos Cordores and his men were hard at work removing the rifles and swords from the captured English prisoners to exchange them for biscuits, cheese and a shot of *aguardiente* (spirits) for the wounded.

The *Cabildo* was now confronted by a serious problem as, despite a truce being signed, the Argentines were finding it hard to persuade Whitelocke's troops to surrender, as many of the British officers refused to abandon positions that had cost so many of their men's lives. Major Nicholls flatly refused to leave the Residencia until General Craufurd arrived with Colonel Elio and ordered him to lay down his arms and, even then, the Major demanded to have a private conversation with Craufurd, which 'Black Bob' refused, declaring it would be discourteous to Elio. In the end, the Major was forced to obey his superior officer's orders but Captain Davenport in charge of the 6th Dragoons (owing to Colonel Kington and Captain Burrell being seriously wounded) stubbornly defended his house for the next two days, until a captured English officer arrived and persuaded him to lay down his arms.

Once they had surrendered, the British officers were escorted to the Fort where General Linares and General Balbiani politely received them. Reaching the Fort, however, proved a hazardous affair, and the Argentine officers escorting the prisoners found it difficult to protect them from the insults of the drunken crowd who, brandishing their rifles and knives above their heads, spat viciously in the prisoners' faces and threatened to slit the throats of every redcoat they could lay their hands on.

Once they had signed their paroles the officers were offered refreshments and ushered into two large rooms overlooking the beach to use as their quarters but, after Beresford's escape, Linares was taking no chances for, despite the officers having given their word of parole, he ordered a platoon of smartly dressed grenadiers to guard them night and day on the pretext of protecting them from the fury of the crowd.

Craufurd firmly maintained this courteous behaviour was entirely due to his resourceful action as, hearing of Leveson-Gower's orders to give no quarter, it was rumoured that the Argentines intended to treat them harshly. Fumbling through his overcoat's pockets, Craufurd discovered a copy of Whitelocke's order of attack which showed that, far from giving no quarter, the General had been anxious to prevent any unnecessary spilling of blood and had strictly forbidden any act of violence against anyone not carrying arms. Craufurd firmly maintained that, thanks to his discovery of this crumpled piece of paper, the Argentines had changed their attitude and it was entirely due to him that they were treating the officers so courteously.

The other ranks were quartered in their former barracks in the Fort and treated fairly, although Tom Plunkett declares the conditions were far from pleasant,

'We were then marched into the Citadel where a hundred and five of us were crammed into two rooms leading into each other. A motley group sure enough, and we certainly looked monstrous queer. The first day we had little or nothing to eat but a little tub of water that was placed in the outer compartment. The object of which was not exactly understood by all, and some went to drink, some went to p---, and some went to drink again. The inner room was made the sleeping one where each occupied as many bricks as his body covered and we lay down not quite sure whether our throats would be cut during the night.'

Meanwhile Admiral Stirling with the Navy, anchored off Buenos Aires, was feeling frustrated, forgotten and abandoned. He had received no news from Whitelocke since leaving Quilmes, and had little idea how the campaign was progressing. This changed on the morning of the 5th, when hearing heavy gunfire in the city, through his glass he spotted British colours flying over the Bullring, and immediately dispatched his transport vessels ashore to provide the occupiers with ammunition and supplies.

The Captains returned in the evening to report that a major battle was in progress in the city. Determined not to be left out of the action, next morning the Admiral sent a flotilla of gunboats to take up a position under the pier and bombard the Fort into submission. A fierce barrage began that continued for an hour but did little damage to either side, as only four British shells actually hit the Fort, though one scored a bull's eye when it landed in Linares's room, which happened to be empty at the time.

The British officers imprisoned in the Fort were mystified by the bombardment suddenly ceasing and only afterwards discovered that this was due to Whitelocke receiving Linares's warning letter concerning their safety. This in fact was never in doubt, as at no time did the prisoners feel under any threat and were constantly chatting to senior Argentine officers and Linares's ADCs who assured them that, whatever the outcome of the battle, their personal safety would be respected. One British officer even goes so far as to declare,

'If the character of the lower classes is savage and fierce, it is strongly contrasted by that of the higher classes whose conduct towards the British that fell into their hands exhibited the highest civilisation and humanity. Those officers of the 71st that had the opportunity of becoming thoroughly acquainted with them spoke of their hospitality in high terms. Not the least injury was offered to our wounded that fell in the streets who were taken up and carried into the houses, where the females dressed their wounds. Instead of heaping insults and reproaches on those that had entered their peaceable abodes with hostile views, they showed them as much attention as they could have done to their own friends.'

This was in contrast to the treatment the Argentine prisoners were receiving from the British in the Retiro where, contrary to military etiquette, the officers and men had indiscriminately been thrown together. After receiving no food for forty-eight hours, the officers forcibly complained to General Whitelocke that this was a breach of the Rules of War but, with his customary bluntness, Whitelocke ordered the English interpreter to tell them, 'They were damned rascals, and he would send them on board the ships if they continued to make so much fuss.' Fortunately, the interpreter was a British prisoner of war who had been especially released from the Fort to arrange the truce and had the good sense not to repeat the General's language and diplomatically fudged the translation. Their complaint, however, had some success for at eight o'clock the following morning, Whitelocke sent an officer to the Fort to request the *Cabildo* send the prisoners four cauldrons of stew which soon arrived and were instantly devoured.

Two days later, the British officers held captive in the Fort were escorted to the Retiro to be exchanged for the Spanish prisoners of war. What should have been a cheerful occasion

ARGENTINA: THE BRITISH INVASION OF BUENOS AIRES, 1806

quickly turned to one of gloom when, marching along the waterfront, they saw the corpses of their comrades stripped of all their clothing lying naked on the beach.

THIRTY-FIVE

PEACE AT LAST

Now the fighting was over, the apprehensive *Cabildo* officially thanked the slaves for their zealous actions and hastily removed their weapons. Many over the following months were offered their freedom, and to hurry up the handover of their arms the *Cabildo* generously offered to pay the bearer two pesos a rifle, and eight *reales* for every sword, bayonet, or knife as soon as it was handed over.

In dribs and drabs, groups of dispirited English soldiers slowly began to arrive at the Retiro. Including Colonel Mahon and the reserve, who were bitterly disappointed at being made to surrender without having fired a shot. Each soldier was thoroughly searched on his arrival and any hidden arms or plunder instantly removed.

Despite this meticulous examination, a large number of valuable items were reported missing, including a golden crucifix stolen from the Church of Santo Domingo. First to come under suspicion were naturally the 71st, who were immediately ordered to assemble on the parade ground, where they were quickly surrounded by a crowd of angry Spaniards, Indians, and half-breeds. Waving their knives in the soldiers' faces they threatened to cut every Highlander's throat unless this holy relic was instantly returned. Luckily, in the middle of this furore the crucifix miraculously appeared on the ground between the ranks. As no one could explain this fortuitous appearance, it was firmly ascribed to the powers of St Anthony, for every soldier solemnly swore on his mother's life that he had never even seen, let alone touched, such a holy relic.

Loot was everywhere, and all day long dubious characters could be seen skulking in the shady corners of the Retiro, surreptitiously buying stolen objects from the British soldiers for a tenth of their proper value. Incensed by this disgraceful trade, the owners bitterly complained to the *Cabildo*, and the Bishop of Buenos Aires sternly announced from his pulpit on Sunday that anyone involved in this criminal behaviour who did not return these objects to the authorities or their rightful owners within fourteen days would be summarily excommunicated.

Little was found despite the sporadic search of their belongings, as the prisoners were experts in the art of concealing their plunder. One wily soldier kept his stolen doubloons hidden under a vast hunk of beef in the bottom of a pot of permanently boiling water and as the days went by, his puzzled companions grew increasingly annoyed when their so-called comrade-in-arms stubbornly refused to share with them this slowly disintegrating piece of meat.

Once order was restored Whitelocke began embarking his men onto a fleet of shallow barges to ferry them out to Admiral Stirling's ships, now lying at anchor five miles out in the middle of the estuary. It was a complicated operation, as many of the soldiers had not only lost their regiments, officers or NCOs in the battle, but almost all of them were drunk. Accidents were frequent and Sergeant Morley aboard the *Lady Delaville* declares, 'Corporal Hutchins of the Quarter-Master General's Department came on board in a sad state of inebriation which being noticed, the unfortunate man was made prisoner and being sent forward missed his footing and falling overboard drowned, as the ship at the time was going at a rapid rate.'

Loading the wounded onto the boats was another problem. The sea was rough and the swell dangerous so, to make the operation easier, stretchers were laid out on the pier and the wounded were gently loaded onto them and by a system of ship's cradles carefully lowered into the rocking boats. Lockjaw soon began to take its toll, and despite being nursed in the comfort of Anita Perichon's house and therefore visited every evening by General Linares, Colonel Kington the Commanding Officer of the 6th Dragoons succumbed to this devastating disease.

After the carnage of Buenos Aires, the familiar streets of Montevideo seemed a haven of peace. However, not everyone was happy and Samuel Whittingham writes,

'All the English merchants are in an uproar. They say their losses will be immense as upwards of three million pounds worth of property is on its way to this country and if this is given up, half the merchants in England will be ruined. God knows what will be the result of this most unfortunate affair! It appears to me to be one of the most severe blows that England has ever received.'

The officers were comfortably lodged in the houses in which they had been billeted before embarking for Buenos Aires, and Harry Smith having miraculously survived unscathed from the holocaust in the Convent of Santo Domingo was housed with the same family who had nursed him back to health from dysentery after the siege of Montevideo. Describing his hosts' hospitality in his memoirs, the future General generously writes,

'I confess I parted from the kind Spanish family who during my illness had treated me with such paternal kindness with feelings of the deepest sorrow, and most lively gratitude. The old lady offered me her daughter in marriage and $20,000 with as many thousand oxen as I wished, saying she would build me a house in the country upon any plan I chose to devise.'

Harry resisted this tempting offer and, being the perfect English gentleman, refrains from referring to the daughter's age or looks. But five years later he would make a romantic marriage to another Spanish girl who this time had no dowry or any future prospects. Their meeting took place at the siege of Badajoz where, out of control and drunk, the victorious British Army was in the process of sacking the city. Harry Smith and his friend Captain Kincaid were vainly attempting to stop the riot when out of the fire and smoke emerged two heavily cloaked female figures who, throwing themselves on the officers' mercy, begged them for protection from the drunk and rapacious soldiers. Streams of blood trickled down their necks from where the impatient looters had wrenched their earrings through the flesh of their earlobes, and the hems of their skirts smouldered from the fires lit by the drunken soldiers.

Dona Juana Dolores de Leon, the youngest of these ladies, was a raging beauty, and Harry fell madly in love with her at first sight and they were married a few days later. The love match would last a lifetime as Juanita followed the future General on all his campaigns, and soon became the toast of the Army. Her popularity was such that, forty years later during the South African campaign, the town of Ladysmith was named in her honour.

Despite their efforts to hurry it along, the evacuation was progressing slowly and the vexing problem of desertion now confronted the *Cabildo*. Many of the British soldiers were daily disappearing from the Retiro and, although Linares managed to round up and return thirty, the flow was hard to stem and the *Cabildo* became seriously worried as a large part of the British Army were very unhappy with General

Whitelocke's surrender. A failure on their part to return the deserters could well give the disgruntled officers an excuse to renew hostilities on the pretext that the treaty had been broken. Adding further to their worries, the news reached them at the same time of the arrival of a troopship in Montevideo with Colonel Acland and over 1,600 British reinforcements on board, and they had little wish for the battle to begin again.

In spite all the *Cabildo*'s threats, the townsfolk refused to hand over the deserters as many had not only become friends but also helped with their training and fought alongside them in the defence of the city. In no way were they now prepared to see them flogged to death or hung.

One deserter, Charles Dixon, a drummer in the East India Company, was lucky to escape with his life. Caught fighting with the enemy in the Retiro and duly sentenced to death by a court martial, a platoon of soldiers surrounded by a bevy of chanting priests escorted him to the gallows in the centre of Montevideo's main square. The drums began to roll; silence fell; the trap door opened; the noose broke and Dixon fell to the ground bruised but relatively unharmed. After this stroke of luck he was duly pardoned, but the authorities were most upset by the unseemly scene that followed as, insisting that this miracle had been in answer to their prayers, the priests loudly began to praise the Almighty. The soldiers, who had probably sabotaged the gallows in the first place due to Dixon's popularity, strongly refuted it and the two parties came to blows in the middle of the square, enthusiastically cheered on by the delighted spectators. Despite his miraculous escape, Dixon's luck soon ran out as, in a rough sea on the passage home, he fell into the hold and broke his neck.

Another deserter, Francis Smith, a bugler by profession,

also came to an unhappy end. Stationed the previous year at Shorncliffe, Sir John Moore had carefully trained the Rifle Brigade in Coote Manningham's new theory of using bugle calls instead of verbal commands in battle and, throughout the engagement, Smith caused havoc by using his musical talents to confuse his ex-comrades-in-arms by blowing his entire musical repertoire from the reveille to the charge. Although successful to begin with, the incessant sound of his bugle soon disclosed his position and, shot through the shoulder, he died a few days later.

In spite of all their efforts, the desertions continued to increase and, in an attempt to show their willingness to stop them, the *Cabildo* announced that anyone found harbouring a deserter would be fined 500 pesos. The ruling had little effect as every citizen knew that once the English had departed any deserter he was harbouring could safely come out of hiding and start a new life in some distant province.

Most of the deserters were Roman Catholics, whom the priests persistently urged to leave this predominantly Protestant Army and thereby secure a certain place in heaven. Thomas Howell declares that his best friend Donald MacDonald, a Roman Catholic, was quite at home during the whole of his stay in South America.

'He was a good Catholic, and much caressed by the Spaniards. He attended mass regularly, bowed to all the processions, and in their eyes was everything a good Catholic ought to be. He often thought of remaining in Buenos Aires under the protection of a worthy priest and had actually agreed to do so, when the order arrived for our release and we were to join General Whitelocke. After fourteen days confinement, Donald was still wavering yet most inclined to stay, so I sang to him "Lochaber no more" and the tears started into his eyes. He dashed them off, "Ah, Na!" he cried

"I canna stay, I'd maybe return to *Lochaber nay muir.*" The good priest was hurt at his retracting his promise but was not offended and said it is natural, "I once loved Spain above all other parts of the world" but here he checked himself gave us his blessing and ten doubloons apiece and left us.'

Santiago Linares was also unhappy with the British troops' rebellious mood and, equally keen to get rid of them, hastily dispatched a convoy of carts to the provinces to bring back Beresford's Army. The task proved harder than expected as many of the prisoners had already married, and having settled down to rural life had little inclination or incentive to return to Europe. Most of the prisoners that Linares's soldiers managed to round up simply disappeared on the journey back to Buenos Aires to resurface a few months later in some faraway province.

The campaign officially ended on 11 July 1807, when Santiago Linares gave a great banquet in the Fort in honour of General Whitelocke and his officers. It was a magnificent affair: wine flowed, toasts were drunk, and at the end of the dinner Linares presented General Whitelocke with a golden engraved sabre. In return, the General presented Linares with a Toledo steel sword given to him by the Prince Regent and his travelling coach, brought all the way from London and still sitting in Montevideo.

After this solemn ceremony, the assembled officers stood to attention as the band played 'God save the King' followed by the Spanish national anthem, bringing the curtain down on one of the most disastrous campaigns in the history of the British Army.

THIRTY-SIX

THE ENGLISH AFTERMATH

SIR DAVID BAIRD

On 26 July 1806, a startled British Government received Sir David Baird's letter advising them of Popham's departure for South America, dispatched three months earlier from the Cape of Good Hope. They then received Beresford's report of his capture of Buenos Aires. Furious with Baird for allowing Popham to set off on his unauthorised venture, Windham, Secretary of State for War and the Colonies, immediately ordered him to return to England, forbidding him even to wait for the arrival of his successor Lord Caledon. It proved a fortunate decision, for just as His Lordship was about to leave England a serious domestic crisis delayed his departure.

Surprised by his sudden appointment as Governor of the Cape, and urged by the Government to leave as soon as possible, Lord Caledon decided to take the sensible precaution of stocking his ship with a suitable amount of refreshment to sustain him on his lengthy voyage to South Africa. Sending for his Swiss valet, Jean Louis Baptiste Barnelet, he ordered him to dispatch thirty dozen bottles of his best claret, madeira and champagne to his ship anchored in Portsmouth Harbour.

Arriving there a few days later he was surprised to find only twenty-one cases waiting for him. To begin with he was not unduly worried, as freight was frequently delayed by the wagons breaking down on the rough country roads, but this changed when, out of the blue, he received an urgent letter from his brother Colonel Alexander containing some startling news.

Returning the previous evening from a convivial dinner at his London club, a female of very doubtful virtue barred his progress and, drawing him to one side, announced in furtive tones that she had some vitally important information that would be greatly to his, and His Lordship's, interest. She then disclosed that His Lordship's personal valet, Jean Luis Baptiste Barnelet, had not only stolen the missing nine cases of wine but also purchased an extremely expensive necklace from that fashionable London jewellers Messers Runcorn and Briggs, and charged it to His Lordship's account. This fabulous piece of jewellery he promised to give to her as soon his master left the country, when they would set up home in Lord Caledon's house in marital bliss and enjoy the wine.

With tearful eyes and melodramatic sobs, she declared that this romantic idyll had abruptly ended when an impudent young doxy had caught the rogue's roving eye and he reneged on his offer. This blatant act of betrayal had naturally stirred her conscience and, knowing the Colonel to be a true gentleman well known for his generosity, she realised it was her duty to inform him of his valet's criminal behaviour.

This unfortunate misdemeanour forced Lord Caledon to delay his departure, leaving Cape Town for several months without a Governor, and appear as principal witness at the Old Bailey where Jean Louis Bapiste Barnelet was found guilty of robbery and sentenced to be deported to Botany Bay.

Already on the high seas, Sir David Baird learnt of this unfortunate event on his arrival in London and, at the same time, discovered that 'The Ministry of all the Talents' had fallen, and the Tories were back in power. This was bad news but, with the help of Lord Castlereagh who had replaced Windham as Foreign Secretary, and the support of Frederick, Duke of York, a court martial was skilfully avoided and, dismissing the whole unsavoury affair, he returned to the front to fight alongside his old rival General Sir Arthur Wellesley at the siege of Copenhagen.

Baird's attitude towards the future Duke of Wellington had by now distinctly mellowed and towards the end of his days, he was even heard to remark, 'It is the highest pride of my life that anybody should have ever dreamed of my being put in balance with him… I know him and myself now.'

At the end of the Danish campaign, Sir David joined Sir John Moore in Spain. While defending the walls of Corunna in January 1809, a volley of grapeshot shattered his left arm, which immediately needed to be amputated at the shoulder. Minutes later, Moore was mortally wounded, and Sir David with typical gallantry ordered the doctor to leave his side, and attend his senior officer. Despite being in severe pain, on Moore's death he oversaw the Army's evacuation, with the help of Lt General Sir John Hope, and returned to England.

Corunna was to be his last campaign and, while convalescing in Scotland, he met and married Miss Campbell-Preston, a great heiress and formidable wife and, in later years, the General would plaintively remark, 'Only to think! I could easily command 10,000 men but not a woman!' Nevertheless, she was undoubtedly fond of him, as on his death in August 1829 she erected an obelisk to his memory in a moving tribute to the service he had given his country.

The monument is an exact copy of Cleopatra's Needle and stands on a picturesque hilltop halfway between the Scottish country towns of Crieff and Comrie. Inscribed on three sides of the obelisk are Sir David's battle honours and, on the fourth, Lady Baird's memorial to his unselfish service. While under the plinth, according to his biographer Theodore Hook, are buried various documents, money and masonic items.

No mention is recorded on the obelisk of his South American campaign, which did little harm to the General's reputation and greatly benefited his finances. For the following year, as overall commander of the invasion, he received £24,000 in prize money as his share of the captured Spanish treasure. This was an enormous sum of money, worth well over £1,400,000 today, and far larger a share of the booty than received by either Popham or Beresford. This seems ironic, for as well as being reluctant to authorise the expedition in the first place, Sir David never saw — let alone set foot in — South America.

ADMIRAL SIR HOME RIGGS POPHAM

On his return from Montevideo, the Lords of the Admiralty placed Sir Home Riggs under open arrest and, being still a Member of Parliament, the House of Commons was duly informed. Scheduled to be held on 16 September 1807, his court martial had all the makings of a 'cause celebre' and therefore was keenly awaited by the general public.

Politicians when necessary have notoriously short memories, and Thomas Grenville was no exception. Having acclaimed Popham's success only a year earlier he wrote a long letter on 16 September 1807 to his elder brother the Marquis of Buckingham over the handling of the trial.

'I have made no such charge as you allude to against Popham because there is much to question in his whole conduct. It seemed most prudent to confirm the charge to one simple and undeniable proposition viz: that being ordered to carry out a force to the Cape and India he had no justification for going a-buccaneering in South America.

'Young (The President of the Court) is so correct and well versed in Admiralty orders that I am persuaded he will not let the Court run loose upon private conversations of which no valid traces can be found. Our counsel and solicitor are well instructed in the case, and being on the spot to act as prosecutors I trust the case will have fair play and if it has, there can be but one result of more or less condemnation.'

On the day of the trial, a noisy crowd of supporters greeted Sir Home's arrival at Portsmouth Harbour, loudly cheering him as he descended from his carriage. Waving their hats in the air, they enthusiastically shouted words of encouragement, as he walked along the quay to board his personal barge and be rowed out to HMS *Gladiator* where the court had assembled. Accompanying him in the boat were his counsel Harrison and agent Lawes, along with various other friends, and last to embark was John Cricket Esq., Marshal of the High Court, carefully carrying in his hands Sir Home Rigg's ceremonial sword.

Sitting at the head of a long table waiting for his arrival was Admiral Sir William Young, the President of the Court, (no friend of Popham) and on either side of him in order of precedence sat four Vice-Admirals: Sir E. Gower, Holloway, Rowley and Stanhope; two Rear Admirals: Vashon, Sir Richard Strachan; and five Captains: Graves, Scott, Linzee, Irwin, and Boyle. Judge Advocate Moses Greatham Esq. represented the Crown; Mr Jervis conducted the prosecution, and on the advocacy and judgment of these two lawyers rested the Commodore's reputation and future career.

Sir Home faced two charges. 'Relinquishing his duty by leaving the Cape of Good Hope in a defenceless state and undertaking, an expedition for which he had no direction or authority whatsoever'. His guilt was taken for granted and only the severity of the sentence was awaited with interest.

The trial lasted for five days and, with his customary eloquence, Sir Home ably represented himself. His defence ran to over 18,000 words: 50 pages of foolscap that produced a wide range of reasons for his attack on Buenos Aires, some of them decidedly dubious.

Lord Melville – called as a witness to verify Popham's discussions with Pitt and Miranda – although sympathetic to Sir Home Rigg's cause, emphatically declared at no time had Popham ever been given any authorisation to attack Buenos Aires. In the end, the issue centred on how much discretion an officer on a distant station was entitled to use in forming his actions when out of touch with his superiors at the Admiralty.

It was not the first case of a Commander taking decisions with impunity, as Admiral Rooke had captured Gibraltar without orders and Nelson had disobeyed his, when swinging out of line at the battle of St Vincent and boarding the *San Nicolas* with the stirring cry, 'Westminster Abbey or Victory'. Even Popham's mentor, Ned Thompson, was accused of contravening his orders to remain in the West Indies when submitting to the pleas of the Barbados planters and escorting a convoy back to England; he faced a court martial by which he was honourably exonerated.

The Court took four hours to reach the verdict, which was guilty on both counts and his conduct deemed 'Highly Reprehensible.' A long silence followed this pronouncement; the spectators waited in suspense for the sentence to be read and a roar of approval greeted the verdict when it was announced that Sir Home was to be 'Severely Reprimanded'. This was tantamount to an acquittal, and the proceedings ended with the following solemn ceremony taking place:

'The Provost Marshal proceeded to the President and

presented Sir Home Riggs Popham's sword to him, which he was ordered to return to the Commodore. The Provost Marshal then returned to the bottom of the table and with respectful salutation presented the sword back to Sir Home Riggs, and the Court was then dissolved.'

The press had a field day, and *The Courier* enthusiastically reported, 'Upon Sir Home getting out of the ship and into the boat, he was acclaimed from a vast number of boats and an immense multitude assembled upon the beach that waited the issue of the trial. As soon as Sir Home had landed the acclamation was repeated, and the horses taken from his carriage that waited to convey him to his lodgings but perceiving this Sir Home declined to enter the carriage. After thanking the people for their attention, he exhorted them to disperse but the people continued to follow him, until he reached Captain Madden's house expressing as they went along the strongest interest in his fate. Sir Home seemed to feel his spirits renewed by their enthusiasm; he smiled and frequently pulled off his hat, and as it were instinctively waved it in the air, when the people cheered him'.

Outside Portsmouth, the verdict was not so avidly acclaimed; but opinion in the London press and public was definitely divided. The *Morning Post* welcomed the result but that old thunderer *The Times* professed to be shocked. While Henry Brougham, later Lord Chancellor and founder of the *Edinburgh Review*, indignantly declared, 'Sir Home should have been shot!' In contrast, the City of London as might be expected expressed its delight at the outcome of the trial.

Some critics condemned Popham for not aiding Beresford in his defence of Buenos Aires but this was an unfair accusation, as the sea had been rough, the water shallow, and the weather atrocious. Only one small sloop, the *Justina*, managed to reach the shore; she promptly became grounded and, seeing her predicament, Pueyrredon's cavalry quickly galloped across the sand and seizing her performed that rare and unusual feat of winning a naval engagement on horseback.

All agreed that Popham had been more interested in the financial rewards from the expedition than in any patriotic motives, and Colonel Fletcher Wilkie even goes so far as to accuse him of holding back from taking Rat Island during the siege of Montevideo, 'As the engagement would bring him no financial gain.' He further asserts that Sir Home was most distressed at being sent home from Montevideo, thereby missing a considerable amount of prize money and truthfully adds that the Argentines loathed him,

'One old lady with whom I was on terms of intimacy talked to me often of our invasion, which she spoke of in terms not very feminine. She said she forgave all of us who were merely the instruments of others but old as she was and a woman, she would have the greatest delight in driving a dagger into the heart of that avaricious merchant Popham! Indeed, I found that name in exceedingly bad odour among all classes.'

After surviving the court martial Sir Home returned to service and, after taking part in the attack on Copenhagen, the Admiralty sent him to the Peninsula where he found himself in a tricky position. Stationed off the north coast of Spain, he was forced to deal with General Mendizabal and his Spanish officers, who not surprisingly were most reluctant to cooperate with a man who had not only attacked their city of Buenos Aires, but also criminally removed its treasure. Despite Sir Home proffering the standard British excuse that he had only taken the treasure to stop it falling into the hands of Joseph Bonaparte, the hated King of Spain, relations were decidedly sticky. However, at the end of 1812 the Admiralty recalled the *Venerable* home to England to escort Lord Moira to India, and a serious confrontation was avoided.

After a year away, he returned from India and was put in charge of organising England's defences against Napoleon's expected invasion and he successfully established an effective signalling system between London, Deal, and Dover, and when peace was declared in 1815, he joined most of London society on a visit to France to relish the delights of Paris.

Three years later, the Admiralty promoted Sir Home to Rear Admiral and sent him as Commander-in-Chief to the West Indies where, in 1820, he caught a fever and returning to England died seven weeks later. His funeral was well attended and he was buried with his sword by his side in St Michael and All Angels Church, Sunninghill. His handsome memorial stone recording his achievements still stands in the graveyard but, over the years, the wind and rain have erased much of the letters, so perhaps the thousand British soldiers who two hundred years ago lost their lives in the streets of Buenos Aires due to his greed have finally taken their revenge.

Sir Home Riggs's share of the treasure came to only £7,000, a far smaller amount than that allotted to the two other leaders. This seems ungenerous, as it was solely due to his audacity that Buenos Aires was captured and the Spanish treasure fell into the welcoming hands of the British Treasury. Nevertheless, those soldiers and sailors lucky enough to survive the campaign were grateful to Sir Home, as even the lowest ranks received the princely sum of £18 and six shillings, or the equivalent of nearly two years' pay.

GENERAL SIR WILLIAM CARR
1ˢᵗ MARQUESS OF BERESFORD

There was no question of Beresford facing a court martial on his return to England as, unlike Baird and Popham, he had merely been carrying out his superior officer's orders. Promoted to Major General in 1807, the Government appointed him Governor of Madeira where he not only became popular with the Portuguese but more importantly fluent in their language. At the start of the Peninsular War, the Generals at Horse Guards recalled him to England and dispatched him to Portugal where he took part in the disastrous retreat to Corunna. Successfully surviving this bloody campaign, he returned to Lisbon in 1809 and Wellington promoted him to the rank of Marshal, and seconded him to the Portuguese Army. The appointment proved a great success and, at the end of the campaign, the Regent Dom Joao granted him the title of Marqués de Campo Maior in gratitude for his actions.

When the war ended, Portugal under Beresford's rule had become almost a British military protectorate, but the Marshal found his position difficult, as he was constantly receiving contrary orders from London and Rio where Dom Joao had moved with his entire court in 1807 on the arrival of the French Army at the gates of Lisbon.

Over the following years, the Council of Governors left behind by the Regent in Lisbon steadily became more mutinous and uncooperative. They considered the British a colonial presence and felt humiliated by England continuing to control the Portuguese Army and bitterly complained to Dom Joao of the size of Beresford's budget, which they declared was consuming three-quarters of Portugal's annual revenue, and ruining any attempt at post-war reconstruction.

They strongly implied that the money was being squandered, and Beresford in turn complained to London of the corruption and unhelpful behaviour of the Portuguese Council.

The increasing attacks by Artigas and his gaucho hordes on the Banda Oriental brought matters to a head and, determined to stop their raids on land he considered Brazilian territory, Dom Joao in 1816 ordered Beresford to dispatch 5,000 troops to Rio to deal with the situation.

It seemed an opportune moment to explain the worsening state of affairs in Portugal, so Sir William decided to accompany them and personally discuss the problem with Dom Joao. After an uneventful journey, the fleet safely reached Rio; a grand parade was held to welcome their arrival and Dom Joao and the Marshal, with suitable pomp and ceremony, personally inspected the four battalions of Light Infantry.

Over the following days, Dom Joao and Beresford held a number of private meetings during which Sir William successfully renegotiated his position and, a few weeks later, he returned to Lisbon with his powers greatly increased. Not only had Dom Joao promoted him to Marshal-General of all his soldiers but also given him the right to recruit fresh troops, something that up to then the Council of Governors had firmly prohibited him from doing.

Over the next four years, unrest continued to spread across the Iberian Peninsula and, on Fernando VII ceding power to the newly elected 'Cortes' in 1820, a serious revolt broke out in Spain. Alarmed by this and the current situation in Portugal, Beresford hurriedly boarded a ship and returned to Rio, hoping to persuade at least one member of the Royal family to return to Lisbon to combat the threatening rise in Republicanism and stave off the rising dissatisfaction against a distant monarchy residing in Brazil.

The Marshal on his arrival in Rio found Dom Joao evasive, and completely unconcerned by the seriousness of the situation in Europe. Instead of discussing the crisis in Portugal, the Regent sent him off on a lengthy tour around the countryside to inspect the Brazilian Army depots and hospitals, and seemed completely uninterested in the rising unrest in Lisbon. As this grew worse, the British Government became increasingly annoyed at Beresford's lengthy delay in Rio and sent frantic messages ordering him to return at once to Portugal. Eventually, they succeeded in getting him recalled and Beresford set sail for Lisbon in August but failed to persuade any member of the Royal family to accompany him.

During the voyage home, a revolution broke out in Oporto and, as his ship approached Lisbon Harbour, a member of the newly formed Republican Government came on board to inform Sir William that his presence was no longer welcome and forbade him to land. This ended the Marshal's rule in Portugal and, returning to England, the King made him Master of the Royal Ordinance and the Government gave him various senior appointments in the administration.

Beresford may not have been a battlefield genius like Wellington, but he was undoubtedly an expert in training and organising troops. Under his guidance, the Portuguese Army became a formidable fighting force and played a significant role in Wellington's success in the Peninsula. Undoubtedly, his most famous success was the battle of Albuera where, greatly outnumbered, he successfully defeated Marshal Soult. Although after the battle it was claimed the casualties would have been considerably less if Wellington had been in command, that was an unfair accusation, as many of his troops came from different nations and the battle had been difficult to control, as orders had to be given in different languages, which were frequently misinterpreted. However, his personal bravery was never in doubt, as taken by surprise in the battle by a troop of Polish cavalry and without time to draw his sword, the Marshal bare-handedly thrust the charging Uhlan's lance to one side and, pulled him out of the saddle and hurled him to the ground.

Beresford's name soon became internationally famous and towns all over the world were named in his honour – including Beresford Town, Quebec, although he never returned to Canada after losing his eye there in 1786. In 1832 the Marshal married his first cousin, the Hon Louisa Hope, an old girlfriend who was said to be very rich and who, on her death, left him her large fortune. When the Marshal died in 1854 at the ripe old age of eighty-four, having no children his titles became extinct and he left his considerable fortune to his nephew, Colonel Pack's son and his favourite godchild.

Beresford's share of the Spanish treasure came to only £12,000 and although £5,000 more than Popham's, it was still only half the sum received by Baird, which once again seems unfair, as not only had he captured Buenos Aires almost single-handedly but also suffered the humiliation of being held for almost a year a prisoner of war in Argentina.

GENERAL JOHN WHITELOCKE

As already mentioned, politicians when necessary have short memories, and Thomas Grenville, writing to his brother the Marquis of Buckingham from the Admiralty on 16 September 1807, conveniently forgets his previous letter praising Popham's venture and overlooks the Government's specific orders to Whitelocke not to upset the Argentine citizens.

'I have just received a letter from Admiral Murray from Buenos Aires with the disastrous news of Whitelocke's expedition. I confess I am not much surprised by the account and although I know no details, I think I can see in Murray's letter enough to convince me that there was a total want of military conduct in the attack that was made. The capitulation is endeavoured to be justified upon two grounds: the loss we incurred in killed and wounded from the houses in the town, and the number of prisoners taken with Craufurd who were menaced with death if we refused to capitulate.

'Now considering the knowledge we had of their town, it is manifest that Whitelocke should have given early notice that in case of any such defence being adopted at the very first shot fired from a church or house; the town would be set fire to. Secondly, with regard to the prisoners and the menace of killing them, such a menace is only to be resisted by a threat of retaliation and not submission. The unpardonable part of the failure in my eyes is to have made the attack without almost a certainty of success. With Montevideo in our hands, and the river at the command of our ships, what need had we to go and knock our brains out against the narrow streets of Buenos Aires? The thing speaks for itself, and shows a total want of common prudence on the part of our military officers.

'Murray writes that Whitelocke told him he could destroy the town but that he should not be so enabled to conquer the country, and that this consideration together with his fear for the prisoners made it necessary for him to sign the capitulation. But why then did he make the attack? Why did he not keep the fortress and the river, and send home to say that he could destroy Buenos Aires but could neither force it to surrender or find friends to our interest? How came Craufurd and all his brigade to be made prisoners at once by a tumultuous multitude? The whole history seems to me to be disgraceful beyond measure to our officers' gallantry. After all, this is a precious result of Sir Home Popham's plundering and privateering expedition and contributes not a little to lower our military character in Europe in the very moment in which it is essential for us to establish it.'

Grenville and the politicians were not the only ones in search of a scapegoat, as many citizens were also deeply ashamed of this embarrassing defeat. Thomas Hall on 30 September, writing to Lord Castlereagh from his house in Bloomsbury, heatedly declares,

'There is no one I know that can calmly tolerate, or hear of this capitulation. All consider it a national disgrace and nothing can repair this mistake without sending at the very least, a fleet and troops to retake Montevideo.'

He was not the only one to plead for action, as the entire City demanded vengeance but, owing to the 'Ministry of all the Talents' resigning in March 1807, this left only General Whitelocke on whom to lay the blame.

The General's court martial was held on 28 January 1808 in Chelsea College (now the Royal Hospital) and all the surviving senior officers at the siege were summoned to give evidence. An angry crowd of bankrupt merchants and investors assembled at the entrance to vent their fury on the General. Not to be outdone, the weather also showed its displeasure as the torrential rain and high wind on the morning of the trial was so strong that it forced the carriage drivers to drop their passengers off at the back entrance of the College, so their occupants could alight in safety, and in some degree of sartorial elegance. Indeed it was an impressive sight, as six full Generals and thirteen Lt Generals in full dress uniform, accompanied by their ADCs, descended from their carriages to assemble in the Great Hall.

The President of the Court, General Sir William Meadows, was a popular officer who was much admired for his bravery and wit. One famous story demonstrating these attributes relates that, on a reconnoitring party in the Mysore country, Sir William spotting a twenty-four-pound shot hurtling along the ground towards him, dextrously pulled his horse to one side and gracefully doffing his hat as it passed good-humouredly remarked, 'I beg you to proceed Sir! I never dispute precedence with a member of your family.'

Many other eminent Generals were present to pass judgment on the General's actions, including Field Marshal Sir Samuel Hulse (personal friend and advisor to the Prince Regent), Lord Cathcart, Viscount Lake, and the redoubtable Sir John Moore, who never ceased to ask the witnesses searching questions on the planning and execution of the siege. In the two full reports of the court martial (Gurney and Blanchard, and Ramsay), it is noticeable that during the trial Sir John is particularly polite to Sir Samuel Auchmuty, whom he obviously admired, and conversely aggressive to Major General Leveson-Gower whom he clearly didn't. One exchange goes as follows:

'Was the country from Ensenada so little frequented that a perfect knowledge of it might not have been obtained in Montevideo, as well as men found who might have been forced to lead the army?' Leveson-Gower meekly answered: 'For my own private information, I tried to collect what I could but could not find anybody that could speak very exactly on the subject in Montevideo'.

This answer was not good enough for Sir John who would have held little regard for today's Geneva Convention or Human Rights Act. He thundered at the witness:

'We all know that there may be found a thousand persons who know the road from London to Windsor perfectly well, yet would not be inclined to point it out to an enemy but might be made to do so by putting a halter round their neck and threatening to hang them. What is meant by the question, "Was there nobody to be found whom you could force to guide the army?"' Leveson-Gower made no reply.

The trial lasted for thirty-one days and, owing to the large number of German stoves failing to give off sufficient heat, the Great Hall was icy cold and Lord Lake not Whitelocke was the first victim of the trial. On Tuesday 16 February, *The Times* reported, 'His Lordship was observed to rise from his seat twice to warm himself'; on Thursday, 'he had to be helped to his carriage,' and on Sunday night, the hero of Farrukhabad and late Viceroy of India died from inflammation of the lungs.

The press warned its readers that only officers in uniform would be admitted to the courtroom and no reports allowed to be published during the trial. Both statements were later overruled and, every morning, *The Times* printed a paragraph headed, 'The Trial of General Whitelocke.' This reported on the opening day,

'The General dressed in the uniform of a General Officer, the sword excepted, was in the custody of Colonel Burnet (ADC to the King), General Calvert, and General Hope whose arm was in a sling. These officers took up their positions beside the President's chair and General Whitelocke who looked less corpulent than usual assumed a dignified composure, and when arraigned pleaded in an audible voice, "Not Guilty".'

Celebrities and onlookers packed the hall and so great was the crush, that several onlookers had their clothes torn by the jostling crowd. Every morning a gin-fuelled crowd of hecklers waited outside the building to hurl insults at the General, as he descended from his carriage. This quickly became a popular pastime and all over London in taverns and pothouses, sarcastic toasts were drunk such as, 'Health to all Grey locks and down with all White locks.' A witticism that much appealed to the Regency's rather heavy sense of humour that was gleefully reported in all the broadsheets of the day. The General faced the following charges,

'Having received instructions from his Majesty's principal Secretary of State to proceed for the reduction of the Province of Buenos Aires, Lt General Whitelocke pursued measures ill-calculated to facilitate that conquest.

'1) That; when the Spanish commander had shown such symptoms of a disposition to treat and express a desire to communicate with Major General Leveson-Gower, the second in command, upon the subject of terms. The said Lieutenant General Whitelocke did return a message in which he demanded amongst other articles the surrender of persons holding civil offices in the government of Buenos Aires as prisoners of war:

'2) The said General Whitelocke in making such an offensive and unusual demand tended to exasperate the inhabitants of Buenos Aires to produce, and encourage a spirit of resistance to His Majesty's arms. Exclude the hope of amicable accommodation thereby increasing the difficulties of the service with which he was entrusted; acted in a manner unbecoming his duty as an officer prejudicial to military discipline, and contrary to the articles of war.

'3) The accused ... showed great professional incapacity and lessened the confidence of the troops in the conduct of their officers by ordering them to enter the town with rifles unloaded; insufficient siege tools; and by dividing the army into parts.

'4) The General showed incompetence and cowardice by remaining at the Corral de la Miserere out of contact with the army; failed to support those fighting in the town, and surrendered prematurely, while still holding dominating positions in the town and with sufficient troops to continue the attack on Buenos Aires. Relinquished Montevideo, which was not under blockade, and sufficiently garrisoned and provisioned to repulse an attack.'

Whitelocke denied all the charges. The first he declared to be ridiculous as in no way were the citizens of Buenos Aires ever going to welcome the English invaders, and certainly not without being guaranteed protection from the Spaniards should a peace treaty later be signed with Spain. The second charge was more serious but Sir Samuel Auchmuty, like Whitelocke, believed the use of loaded rifles in confined areas could be dangerous, and reloading them would certainly have slowed down the impetus of the attack. As for the shortage of crowbars and siege tools, Whitelocke rightly blamed this on the lack of space aboard the ships, and the scarcity of carts to carry them from Ensenada to Buenos Aires.

The last charge of staying in the same place throughout the battle, the General dismissed outright and insisted that, by remaining at the Corral de la Miserere, the Army knew his exact location and, had he moved his headquarters into the town, they would have been impossible to find among the numerous houses and narrow streets. As for continuing the attack, this would have been impossible without bombarding the city from the Plaza de Toros or Residencia, thereby antagonising the citizens, which his orders specifically forbade him to do. Furthermore, contrary to what the Government had informed him before leaving England, the inhabitants of the Provincia del Rio de la Plata were totally hostile to British rule, and had emphatically refused to release Beresford's men or accept a treaty without

Montevideo being relinquished. Failure on his part to have agreed to their terms might well have resulted in the prisoners of war being massacred by the hostile crowd.

After a lengthy deliberation, the Court exonerated Whitelocke of the second charge but found him guilty of the others, and sentenced him to be cashiered and declared, 'Unfit, and unworthy to serve his Majesty in any military capacity again'.

The general public considered the verdict lenient, and believed him lucky not to have suffered the same fate as Admiral Byng. General Sir Charles Napier vehemently declared, 'He should be put up against a wall and shot, a shocking thing for his family but the blood of hundreds lies on his head.' Summing up the trial, Sergeant Morley more sombrely writes, 'I think his sentence such, as to the truly brave must be worse than death'. His judgement may have been correct as far as other officers were concerned but Whitelocke was no hero. Retiring to his house at Clifton, near Cheltenham, he lived happily for another twenty-five years until his death in 1833, and was buried in Bristol Cathedral. His tomb lies in the western aisle and is modestly marked, 'John Whitelocke Esq, resident of Clifton.'

The Government, merchants, and public had obtained their revenge but in fairness to Whitelocke, his orders had placed him in an impossible position. Officer Cadets at the Royal Military Academy, Sandhurst, today are still taught 'The Ten Principles of War,' which have remained unchanged since the days of Julius Caesar and Alexander the Great.

Whitelocke successfully broke every one of them except the first, 'The Aim', which the Government expertly did for him. Considered the most important rule of all, this should be short, succinct and to the point, using as few words as possible so that in no way can it be misinterpreted. The Government's orders to Whitelocke were totally to the contrary. First, he was to seize Buenos Aires but when doing so not to antagonise the population. Next, he was to place the inhabitants under British rule but not to guarantee them protection should a peace treaty later be signed with Spain, and lastly he was recruit a local army of malcontents but spend as little money as possible on training and equipping them.

Whitelocke may have been an incompetent, weak leader dominated by the vindictive Leveson-Gower, but he was not the villain of the piece. Those guilty were Sir Home Riggs Popham, who started the whole affair, and the 'Ministry of all the Talents', who gave the General such contradictory orders.

In the end, the General's capitulation had a happy outcome, as had Whitelocke successfully captured Buenos Aires he would never have been able to control it and the whole province of the Rio de la Plata with so few men. While an Argentina that was struggling under an Army of occupation would not have entered into the profitable trading bond, formed only three years later, that would last for the next hundred and fifty years and vastly benefit both countries.

SIR SAMUEL AUCHMUTY

Sir Samuel attended General Whitelocke's trial and as a witness gave his opinion that the General was right in ordering the troops to enter the town with their rifles unloaded, but wrong in the way he handled the campaign. Returning from Buenos Aires, he was promoted to Major General, and two years later the Government sent him to India as Commander-in-Chief of the Indian Army. Arriving in Madras, he found Lord Minto, the Governor-General, determinedly planning to capture all the French and Dutch possessions in Asia. Setting off with His Lordship in August 1811, they successfully captured Java, Batavia and, a month later, defeated General Janssens at Samara, which ended the expedition. He returned to England in 1815 to be created a Knight of the Bath and receive the thanks of Parliament for his services.

Bonaparte's defeat at Waterloo ended Sir Samuel's active service and, for the next five years, he remained unemployed until he was made a member of the Irish Privy Council and Commander-in-Chief of the British forces in Ireland in 1821. The position lasted for only a short time, as on 11 August 1822 he dropped dead out riding in Phoenix Park, and was buried with full military honours in Christchurch Cathedral, Dublin. Owing to neither fighting in the European campaign, or at Waterloo, Sir Samuel's career is less well known than many other Generals of the period, but it was no small achievement for an impecunious young American boy to be knighted and reach the highest echelons of the British establishment.

GENERAL ROBERT CRAUFURD

After the débâcle in South America, Craufurd's career went from strength to strength, and he soon gained the reputation of being the finest commander of light troops in the British Army. The Duke of Wellington openly declared him to be one of his ablest officers but, despite this satisfying accolade, 'Black Bob' could frequently irritate the noble Duke. This happened before the battle of Fuentes d' Oñoro when, heavily outnumbered by Massena's Army, Wellington waited anxiously for the arrival of the Light Division. 'Black Bob' failed to make the night march; Wellington was extremely cross and on Craufurd's arrival the following morning the Duke sarcastically remarked, 'I am glad to see you're safe!' Falling into the trap, Craufurd cheerfully replied, 'Oh! I can assure you Sir; I was never in any danger.' 'Maybe!' thundered the Duke 'but I was!' Distinctly nonplussed, Craufurd was heard muttering under his breath, 'By God! He's damned crusty today.'

Wellington was not always the winner of these encounters, as Craufurd could hold his own, and was not in the least afraid of answering back. Some weeks later, Wellington was in the process of reviewing the Light Division when Craufurd arrived on horseback looking rather flustered, and the Duke shouted, 'Craufurd, you're late!' Carefully restraining his famous temper, 'Black Bob' replied with fervour, 'No my Lord, it is you who are before your time. My watch is to be relied on.'

Craufurd remained a strict disciplinarian throughout his career, and insisted that 'Standing Orders' should be followed at all times. These stated that under no circumstances should military formations be broken unless vitally necessary and 'Any man for the sake of avoiding water or any other bad places, or for any other reason presume to step aside and quit his proper place in the ranks must be confined,' which in essence meant flogging. Streams should be forded in column and leaving the ranks to search for a convenient bridge to cross over was strictly forbidden. Likewise, officers were banned from being carried across rivers on their men's shoulders. Spotting a soldier halfway across a river carrying an officer on his back during the retreat to Corunna, Craufurd shouted furiously at him, 'Put him down Sir! PUT HIM DOWN!' and to the delight of the watching troops the soldier jettisoned his offending load straight into the middle of the icy water.

Craufurd was killed by a French sniper at the siege of Ciudad Rodrigo while directing an attack on the lesser breach, and he was buried with full military honours in a niche cut out of the wall below it. Over a thousand men of the 5th Division lined the route to salute the coffin as it passed carried on the shoulders of a sergeant major from each battalion of the Light Division. An impressive cortege came behind the bearers led by Adjutant General Sir Charles Stewart, and followed by Lord Wellington and a long line of Generals and friends. As the haunting notes of the bugler's final salute echoed across the city's walls, the riflemen slowly reversed their arms and, bowing their heads in unison, gently lowered the coffin into the open grave. After the funeral, the Light Division paid their General a unique and unpremeditated tribute for, coming to a marshy pool about 50 yards wide on their way back to their camp, instead of following the road around it, the leading files marched straight into the thigh-deep icy water. Every officer and man followed in silence, in a sombre and moving farewell to their dead Commander.

'Black Bob' remained a stern disciplinarian and an advocate of the lash for the whole of his life, which made him unpopular with the men and many officers considered him an ambitious intriguer. In spite of this valid-or-otherwise criticism, all ranks recognised him as a brilliant fighting soldier; an innovating General who at all times kept the welfare of his men at heart and not just a martinet with a terrifying temper.

PRIVATE THOMAS HOWELL
After the disaster at Buenos Aires, Thomas Howell returned with his regiment to Ireland and landed at the Cove of Cork on Christmas Day 1807. After a short stay in Middleton

Barracks, the regiment embarked again and sailed for Portugal to take part in the battle of Vimeiro, where Thomas witnessed a scene as macabre as that after the siege of Montevideo.

'The Spanish peasants prowled about more ferocious than the beasts or birds of prey finishing the work of death, and carrying away whatever they thought worthy of their grasp. Avarice and revenge were the causes of these horrors, and no fallen Frenchman that showed the least sign of life was spared. They even seemed pleased in mangling the dead bodies and when light failed them, they kindled a great fire and remained around it all night shouting like as many savages. My sickened fancy felt the same, as if it were witnessing a feast of cannibals'. He goes on to describe the horrors of the retreat to Corunna.

'The road was one line of bloody footmarks from the sore feet of the men. Orders were issued warning and exhorting us to keep order, and march together but alas! How could men observe order amidst such suffering, or men whose feet were naked and sore keep up with men who being more fortunate had better shoes and constitutions? I have seen officers of the Guards and others worth thousands of pounds with pieces of old blankets wrapped round their feet and legs, the men pointing at them with malicious satisfaction saying, "There goes three thousand pounds a year."'

Thomas survived the retreat and returned with his regiment to England in 1809, and in a matter of weeks was back again aboard a ship on the way to capture Walcheren Island in the River Scheldt. The aim of this controversial campaign was to destroy the dockyards of Antwerp, and sink any French ship found at anchor in the river. It proved to be a disastrous campaign, and instigated the famous duel between Canning and Lord Castlereagh who, as the

Minister of War, had authorised the expedition, and placed the incompetent Earl of Chatham in command.

Strongly disagreeing with the war, and even more with the management of the military campaign, Canning challenged Castlereagh to a duel, and the two senior Cabinet ministers met at dawn on Wimbledon Common where Lord Castlereagh shot Canning, who hardly knew how to fire a pistol, in the hip. Both contestants resigned from the Government and the scandal kept London society entertained for several weeks, and the satirical cartoonists for even longer.

Although the Government considered the campaign a great success, the British casualties were horrific, chiefly due to the enemy opening up the sluices and flooding the trenches with polluted water. Cholera and typhoid spread like wildfire, and dysentery ran rampant through the Army. This was treated with that popular naval antidote gunpowder and brandy and, though the efficacy of this medication was never in doubt, the death rate soared and by the third week 1,564 men out of the 40,000 engaged went down with disease and, by the end, 60 officers and nearly 4,000 men died, and over 11,000 were sick.

Thomas Howell survived this disastrous campaign and, returning to Spain, in 1810 fought his way from the lines of Torres Vedras through Spain to France to take part in the battle of Waterloo. Although less well known than those of Rifleman Harris and other soldiers of the period, his memoirs paint a vivid picture of the hardship of a soldier's life during the Napoleonic wars.

COLONEL SIR DENIS PACK

Denis Pack was lucky to survive the South American campaign and, for this, he was indebted to Santiago Linares and the kindness of the Roman Catholic priests. Carried out unrecognised among the wounded from the Convent of Santo Domingo, the Colonel reached the safety of the Fort but rumours began to circulate in the bars and cafes that the infamous perjurer Pack, a man who had twice attacked their city, was sheltering within its walls and the mob demanded vengeance.

On the morning after the surrender, General Whitelocke was despondently eating his breakfast in the Retiro when his thoughts were rudely interrupted by the arrival of an Argentine officer bringing a message from Santiago Linares, which bitterly complained that during the night the British soldiers had shot two of his men. Clearly, the truce had been broken and Linares warned the General that, 'If these acts persist, I cannot be answerable for the lives of the prisoners in my care.'

This was true, as order in the city had completely broken down and drunken mobs were roaming the streets killing every redcoat they could lay their hands on and threatening to break into the Fort and massacre the imprisoned British soldiers. It was one of General Whitelocke's major fears and, hurriedly sending for his ADC Captain Foster, he ordered him to take an escort of troopers and return with the Argentine officer to the Fort, and assure Linares, 'That the circumstances of this regrettable incident were as yet unknown at his Headquarters, and must surely have arisen through an unfortunate misunderstanding.'

The Captain set off immediately but the mile journey to the Fort was a hazardous undertaking for, on reaching the Plaza Mayor, a drunken crowd of four thousand shouting ruffians brought the Captain and his little party to a standstill. Paying no attention to the white flag, the infuriated mob threatened to kill Foster and his escort, and only the arrival of two Argentine officers with a troop of Dragoons enabled the party to reach the Fort, where as soon as the gates opened the rabble dashed past Foster and his party and vanished into the interior.

Quickly dismounting from his horse Foster nervously followed after them, and entering a large room found the mob surrounding General Linares screaming, 'Pack! Señor Pack! Give us Señor Pack!' Linares was doing his best to calm them but, to Foster's horror, he saw Colonel Pack with a number of British officers sitting at a table only a few yards away from the Argentine General. The cloth and plates were still on the table so, obviously, they had just finished their dinner, and hovering behind Pack's chair were three priests clearly intent on protecting him should he be recognised.

The confrontation between Linares and the crowd rapidly began to grow more heated until, suddenly losing his temper, the General seized the most vociferous of the agitators by the scruff of the neck and shaking him like a dog threatened to have him shot. Taking advantage of the shocked silence that followed this outburst, the Captain hurriedly pressed Whitelocke's letter into Linares's hand who, after only a swift perusal, proceeded to read its contents to the crowd. To Foster's astonishment this appeared to have a calming effect and, having accomplished his mission, he was permitted to leave the room.

His journey back to the Retiro proved more dangerous than the arrival, as an even larger and more belligerent crowd now filled the square who, despite the Argentine escort's pleas, held the party stationary for over an hour. Night had fallen by the time the Captain reached the safety of the Retiro to report his meeting with Linares to General Whitelocke.

By now it was past midnight and, having finished

discussing the day's events, the British officers were about to go to bed when through the door strode Colonel Pack. Banishing all thoughts of sleep, they crowded round the Colonel and began bombarding him with questions on how he had managed to escape. Apparently this had been thanks to the priests who, with Linares's permission, had smuggled him out of the Fort after the mob had left. Disguising him in a cassock and cowl, they had then escorted him back through the unlit streets by a roundabout route to the safety of the British lines. After his lucky escape, the Colonel was taking no chances and, next day, he was smuggled off hidden in the hold of a small ship to the safety of Montevideo.

After the truce, the Colonel returned with the 71st to Ireland, and after a short stay in Cork sailed with his regiment to Portugal to take part in the disastrous retreat to Corunna. During which, according to Thomas Howell, he showed himself to be a brave officer and popular with his men. During the retreat food was short; rations non-existent, and many officers being inexperienced in foraging were forced to ask their men for scraps of food. The Colonel was no exception. One day, seeing his soldiers slaughtering a bullock, he sent his orderly to ask them for the heart, and the man returned a few minutes later not only with the heart but with the kidneys as well. This was no trifling gift, as the soldiers were starving and, discipline having almost vanished, it was every man for himself.

After fighting a bloody rear-guard action, the Colonel and his few remaining men finally reached Corunna, and boarding one of the ships waiting in the harbour they returned to England. But instead of being granted some well-deserved leave, they were immediately ordered to re-embark and join the expedition about to leave for Walcheren.

It was during this campaign that the Colonel won the

admiration of Thomas Howell for his prowess with the sword. Describing an attack on an enemy position, Thomas writes,

'Colonel Pack made a sally into one of the enemy's batteries. We crossed the cut in silence and the Colonel on entering, first struck off the sentinel's head with one blow of his sword!'

Although branded a liar and perjurer by the Argentines, Denis Pack was in fact a brave and distinguished officer who five times received the thanks of Parliament for his services. In 1810, he commanded a Portuguese brigade at Busaco and the following year took part in the battle for Almeida. Two years later, he was promoted to Major General and led a Portuguese division with great distinction at Quatre Bras, two days later at Waterloo.

Denis Pack and William Beresford remained close friends for the rest of their lives, and in 1816, when a Knight Commander of the Bath, Pack married the Marshal's half-sister Elizabeth, the youngest daughter of that prolific breeder the Earl of Tyrone. Beresford died in 1854 without an heir and left a large part of his fortune to Pack's second son Denis, on condition he added Beresford to his surname. In compliance with the old soldier's wishes, the young man assumed the name of Pack-Beresford and, with it, a major part of the Marshal's considerable fortune.

THE CITY OF LONDON

In the frantic rush to speculate in Popham's newly opened market, merchants, bankers and investors not only lost their own worldly wealth in this exciting new venture but also encouraged their neighbours to follow suit. Some of the less reputable merchants even went so far as to load their ships with tons of rubbishy merchandise, believing they could gull the supposedly ignorant colonists into purchasing them. After Whitelocke's surrender all these goods, whether valuable or worthless, were returned to their owners who found them impossible to sell.

Many of the great merchants faced severe losses as, convinced they were about to make a huge killing, practically none of them considered unloading their cargoes before reaching Buenos Aires, although, according to Colonel Fletcher Wilkie,

'A few of the smaller ones turned a quick penny by opening up shops in Montevideo to dispose of two or three cargoes, and quickly pocketing the cash in hard dollars were off again for England.'

Some of the lucky ones managed to sell their cargoes in Brazil, while those who could afford it anchored their ships off the coast of Montevideo, and opened up negotiations with the smugglers. These invested in a large number of European dresses, which at the time were popular with the fashion-conscience women of Montevideo. Their design caused quite a scandal, and one shocked clergyman complained that these ladies were not only almost naked from the waist up but the sleeves of the dresses were so scandalously short, that their arms and armpits were clearly visible. 'Such an exhibition of nudity,' he thundered from his pulpit on Sunday, 'will bring down the wrath of God on Montevideo.' It was not the dresses' only crime, as they also resurrected the feud between General Elio, the newly arrived Governor of Montevideo, and his ancient enemies the Catalans.

Walking one afternoon through the little square in front of the Citadel, four young ladies dressed in these fashionable habits were most upset at being greeted by loud catcalls and wolf whistles from the sentries guarding the gate. Well-bred and the daughters of Colonel Iriarte and

Captain Ballesteros, they were profoundly shocked at being called 'English brood mares' and other rude names by the common soldiers on duty at the gate. Matters turned worse when, finding a violin, the soldiers pursued them down the street singing lewd songs, elaborating on the physical and promiscuous habits of the women of Montevideo.

It was too much for the frightened and hysterical young girls who fled down the street in floods of tears and, reaching their destination, fell into the arms of an officer of marines. Deciphering through their sobs the reason for their present state, he rushed to inform General Elio of the men's shocking behaviour. Seizing a carbine from the rack, the General charged out of the Citadel in a towering rage and placed the soldiers, except the sentry guarding the gate, under arrest, but on discovering they were members of his old enemy the Catalan Regiment he promptly threw the lot of them into the stocks in the centre of Montevideo's town square.

Outraged at having his men treated in such a fashion, Olaguer Reynals, Colonel of the Catalan Regiment, wrote a long and indignant letter to Santiago Linares bitterly complaining of Elio's behaviour and firmly pointing out that, whereas Elio had lost every battle he had ever fought, his men in contrast had beaten the English in Buenos Aires. It was entirely thanks to their bravery that Montevideo had been liberated, and these young ladies had not only insulted his soldiers by flaunting their indecent English dresses in public but his men were also fed up at having their behaviour compared to that of the departed British. Instead of criticising his soldiers, the citizens should be complimenting them on their Spanish valour, and every honourable gentleman should regret the disgraceful levity of these young ladies who ought to be concentrating on their duty in becoming mothers, wives and good citizens, rather than promenading half-naked through the city streets. He ended the letter by demanding Linares recall his soldiers to Buenos Aires where, at least, they could receive a fair trial.

Although slow to begin, trade between Britain and Argentina steadily began to increase, and soon became extremely profitable for both countries. Only three years after hostilities had ended, the British Commercial Rooms opened in Buenos Aires in 1810, with a membership of 1,355 English merchants and, by 1834, this had tripled to 4,072.

The English merchants mostly exported textiles in exchange for hides and gold and silver bullion – while the Potosi mines lasted. Out of the five and a half million hides imported into Britain between 1810 and 1815, three million or 54% of the market came from Argentina. Both countries greatly benefited from the exchange, especially Argentina whose exports exceeded her imports by over 400 per cent.

This trading bond rapidly began to increase, and by the beginning of the twentieth century the British had not only built, but also owned, most of Argentina's railways. The track alone covered over 15,000 miles, and British companies were soon earning around four-fifths of the country's total railway revenues.

British banks, telephone companies and other major businesses began to open up offices or agencies in most of the cities and, in 1900, Harrod's B.A. (a sister company to the famous Knightsbridge store) flung wide its doors to a crowd of excited customers in the Calle Florida, then a street as elegant as Fifth Avenue, Bond Street or the Rue St Honoré.

English companies soon began to dominate the meat trade, and families like the Vesteys not only owned large numbers of cattle *estancias* but more importantly, the *frigoríficos* (freezing plants) that allowed the meat to be exported all over the world.

Many Englishmen or those of British descent owned, or were employed as managers on, *estancias* throughout the provinces. Particularly in the Provincia de Santa Cruz and Tierra del Fuego where, after Chile and Argentina had agreed on their territorial rights, the Argentine Government invited the inhabitants of the Falkland Islands to settle and bring their sheep with them.

British Clubs began to spring up all over the country and among the most famous of these is the Hurlingham Club, which is situated in the leafy suburbs of Buenos Aires and, along with the Palermo Club, is where the most important polo matches are played. The British introduced the game from India and, to begin with, played on their *estancias*. The teams would often consist of the owner and three gauchos, whose sole role was to ride off their opposite numbers and allow their *patron* to gallop unimpeded down the ground and score a goal.

Horseracing soon became fashionable. Many of the best British and French stallions were imported into the country from Europe and, in 1882, Carlos Pellegrini, future President of the Republic, founded the Buenos Aires Jockey Club. Racehorse breeding soon became important and in 1905 Ignacio Correas purchased the Prince of Wales's volatile Triple Crown winner Diamond Jubilee. Renowned as being very bad-tempered, Diamond Jubilee confirmed it by savaging the stud manager on his arrival at his future residence, Las Haras Ortigas. The beautiful paddocks of Chapadmalal (the Martinez de Hoz family's *estancia* near Mar del Plata) abounded with famous stallions and mares including 'Barham', the Aga Khan's Triple Crown winner whose progeny still win races in North and South America.

Golf became popular as, wherever the lines took them,

the Scots and English railway workers built courses, and naturally called the first San Andres. Golf courses began to be constructed in almost every province and Argentina soon began to produce famous international golfers, winners of the British Open and US Masters.

The most popular sport of all was undoubtedly introduced on 9 May 1867, when two English immigrants, Thomas and James Hogg, obtained permission from the Buenos Aires Cricket Club to organise a football match in the Parque Tres de Febrero (today the site of the Galileo Galilei Planetarium in Palermo), which gave birth to the Buenos Aires Football Club. The game spread like wildfire; clubs quickly began to spring up across the country, including the famous Club Atletico Newell's Old Boys, named by the ex-pupils of the English High School of Rosario in homage to their English director and football coach, Isaac Newell.

Commonly called Club Atletico, Rio de la Plate, its black and red colours are taken from the flags of England and Germany (Isaac Newell being English and his wife German) and its nickname, '*los leprosos*', from a charity match played in the 1920s to raise funds for a leprosy clinic. Among its past and present members are many famous international players including Lionel Messi, currently considered one of the best players in the world.

Farming became important and meat quickly became Argentina's most valuable export. The merits of the Aberdeen Angus over the Hereford and Charolais are hotly argued in the Rural, Argentina's great cattle show, but sadly the great swathes of *campo* that once held thousands of heads of cattle have greatly diminished owing to the recent rise of *sorga* (oil seed rape).

Not all the British enterprises were successful. Baring Bank's investment in the Buenos Aires Water Supply and

Drainage Company in 1890 not only nearly brought about their own collapse but also all the other banks. Only with the assistance of the Bank of England and the Rothschilds did they manage to survive, but it cost the family an enormous amount of paintings, furniture and real estate, although by 1894 the Argentine investments were making a profit. Their poor judgement in choosing Mr Sandford as an agent, who was thoroughly dishonest, was equalled by their lack of equine expertise. Talked into selecting and sending the Governor of Buenos Aires a racehorse stallion in 1882, the animal they sent him turned out to be ten years older than its proclaimed age, bandy legged and the first two foals it sired were both stillborn. (Philip Zeigler's *The Sixth Great Power*.)

English culture is visible throughout the country. Travellers visiting Buenos Aires for the first time are often startled to hear the familiar chimes of Big Ben ringing out across the Plaza San Martin, which come from the Torre de los Ingles, today called El Torre Monumental after the Falklands War. It is a replica of the famous clock constructed of Portland stone and bricks from Stonehouse, Gloucestershire that the British community presented to the city in 1911, to celebrate the centenary of Argentina's independence.

Forecast over two hundred years ago, Sir Home Riggs Popham's vision of a profitable future between the two countries has proved spectacularly correct. Only the bickering of ambitious politicians over the ownership of a small group of islands 500 miles away in the Atlantic Ocean have come between the two nations since, two hundred years ago, General Whitelocke and Santiago Linares stood to attention in the Fort, as the band played the British and Spanish national anthems.

THIRTY-SEVEN

THE ARGENTINE AFTERMATH

DON FRANCISCO SEBASTIAN MIRANDA
After his betrayal by the British Government, Miranda returned to the United States to seek the aid of President Jefferson and the American Government. Both were uncooperative but, in contrast, Alexander Hamilton proved more sympathetic to his cause, and introduced him to Samuel Ogden, a rich businessman, who along with Rufus King and Colonel Smith helped him to acquire three boats, the *Leander*, a 190-ton brig, and two smaller ones, the *Ambassador* and *Hindustan*, both very unseaworthy.

The timely arrival of £2,000 from London, acquired by putting his library of six thousand books up for surety, enabled Miranda to recruit two hundred volunteers, and the following year he set off from Boston to achieve his life's ambition of liberating Venezuela from the domination of Spain.

All the time, the Spanish Ambassador in Washington had been monitoring his movements and, getting wind of the expedition, angrily accused the American Government of aiding Spain's enemies, but Jefferson stoutly denied any involvement in assisting Miranda or his expedition. Frustrated by the Americans' lack of response, the Ambassador dispatched two strongly armed Spanish frigates to lie in wait for the revolutionary invaders off the coast of South America. Successfully intercepting Miranda's little fleet, they captured the two escort vessels and, hanging ten of the sixty volunteers on board, threw the remainder into jail. Those fortunate enough to survive their imprisonment were later ransomed and repatriated to the United States, and after being ceremoniously paraded through the streets of Caracas, Miranda's effigy was burnt and a $30,000 reward offered to anyone capturing him dead or alive.

Miranda, on board the *Leander* with the major part of the expedition, fled to Grenada and after replenishing the ship's stores sailed on to Barbados, hoping to obtain the support of the British Governor. Either unimpressed by the mission, or the aspect of the Liberator and his motley crew, General Bowyers firmly declined to give them any assistance. Disappointed by this cold reception, Miranda sailed south to Trinidad where he managed to raise five hundred volunteers and, purchasing fifteen small transport boats to carry them in, once again set off to liberate Venezuela.

On 1 August 1806, Miranda landed safely on an empty beach near Coro and encountering no opposition or for that matter any sign of support, he quickly overcame the town's small garrison, and hoisting up his standard proudly proclaimed the territory liberated.

Over the following weeks, emissaries were sent to all the local towns requesting their support but it soon became obvious that the inhabitants had no intention of joining his revolution. It was a severe blow to his morale; he was forced to accept it, and hearing that a large Spanish Army was approaching from the south, the self-proclaimed Liberator hurriedly embarked his troops and returned to Trinidad where once again the English refused to help him. This final setback ended the expedition and re-embarking his men he sailed back to Boston, sold the ship, and discharged the men. The whole affair had been a complete fiasco; and the disillusioned revolutionary returned to London, and taking up residence in Panton Street began re-organising his plans.

Argentina: The British Invasion of Buenos Aires, 1806

A major change had taken place in British foreign policy since leaving England, as thanks to his friend Popham's capture of Buenos Aires the Government was now heavily involved in South America, giving Miranda hope that the British might offer him some support. It proved wishful thinking but, two years later, the situation radically changed when an important delegation from Venezuela's newly formed Revolutionary Government arrived in London to seek assistance from the British Government.

Disappointingly, the delegation received a mixed reception, for although His Majesty's Government considered their revolution to be a setback for the French, it was equally anxious not to upset any allies in the Spanish Government with whom it was in the process of negotiating a secret peace treaty. Cautiously welcoming the Venezuelans, the Foreign Office offered them only 'benevolent neutrality,' and a promise to do everything in its power to promote commercial relations between the two countries.

After receiving this unsatisfactory response, the delegation set out to achieve its second objective: to persuade Miranda to return to Venezuela and take his place at the head of their new liberating movement. They assured him that his help would be invaluable in forming a new Constitution, and his well-known ideals could give a boost in popularity to the newly formed Government.

Now sixty years old, Miranda's enthusiasm remained undiminished and, flattered by their invitation, he graciously accepted the offer and a British Man-of-War transported him back to Venezuela where wild scenes of acclamation greeted his arrival in Caracas. A 'Patriotic Society' was immediately formed to demand independence and, a few days later, a General Congress assembled and solemnly announced, 'The moment had come to speak of absolute independence.' A fiery debate then took place that continued throughout the day and ended by the radicals just out-voting the conservatives; on 5 July 1811 independence was triumphantly proclaimed.

In reality this announcement was little more than words, as the country was hopelessly split into different factions. The upper and middle classes were equally divided between the royalists and federalists, but the centralists and lower classes that made up the greater part of the population were definitely against the new regime. While the mulattos, negroes, and *mestizos* at the bottom of the social ladder remained in awe of the sacred symbol of King and Church promoted by the old regime, and hated the rich Creoles who had always been their most persistent exploiters.

Faced with these adversaries, the newly elected Government proved incapable of preserving any semblance of order, and to make matters worse a powerful earthquake destroyed Caracas. Ten thousand victims were buried in the debris, and the military barracks collapsed into a pile of rubble, killing most of its occupants. It was a bad omen, and those of a superstitious nature noted that whereas the royalist Army strongholds of Valencia, Coro, Maracaibo and Guayana had been left untouched, Caracas, La Guaira, Merida, Barquisimeto, Trujillo and San Carlos – all of whom supported the revolution – had suffered severe damage.

Encouraged by the opportunist Archbishop of Caracas, Coll y Prat, the clergy preached that this was divine retribution against the revolutionaries, 'Who through their disavowal of Fernando VII, the anointed of the Lord had provoked the terrible wrath of heaven,' and urged the terrified poor to repent and beg forgiveness, 'from that most virtuous of monarchs.'

When the news reached Caracas that a victorious royalist

Army was advancing unimpeded on the capital, law and order completely collapsed and, in desperation, the Congress invited Miranda to become Generalissimo and Supreme Commander, 'Entrusting the salvation of the nation to his hands'. Miranda accepted this flattering offer but could do little to stop the rot.

His soldiers were disloyal and undisciplined; the Revolutionary Government's paper currency worthless; and treachery began to spread among his partisans. Fanned into flames by the royalists and clergy, an insurrection of the slaves and lower classes spread like wildfire, and resenting Miranda's appointment as Supreme Commander (a position he felt by right should have been his), Bolivar left Caracas in a huff to take command of the garrison at Puerto Cabello. Adding fuel to the worsening situation, Miranda now successfully alienated his Creole supporters by appointing French and English soldiers of fortune to hold senior positions on his staff, and among these was Sir Gregor MacGregor, a Highlander whom he appointed his Adjutant-General.

Styling himself, 'His Highness, Gregor Cacique of Poyais,' Gregor was neither a chieftain, a knight, or for that matter did a land of Poyais exist. He was in fact, one of the most notorious fraudsters of the nineteenth century but, due to the position given to him by Miranda, and the assistance he gave to Bolivar whose cousin he married, he is still honoured and revered in Venezuela as one of the heroes of their struggle for independence.

Owing to Bolivar's forces being betrayed, Puerto Cabello, the strongest fortified town in revolutionary hands, surrendered with hardly a shot being fired, bringing matters to a head. Realising that further resistance was out of the question, Miranda hurriedly sent agents to the Spanish General

Domingo de Monteverde, offering to lay down his arms in exchange for a general amnesty.

Misguidedly he attempted to flee the city before the agreement was signed, not from cowardice but to ensure he could continue his struggle for independence in another country and, hearing of what he considered an act of treachery, Bolivar immediately sent a posse of men to arrest him. Seizing the old man, they carried him off to captivity shouting contemptuously to all and sundry, 'Riots! Riots! Such men as you are only capable of riots.' Then, in an act of treachery that would remain a stain on his career for the rest of his life, Bolivar handed Miranda over to the royalist General Monteverde in exchange for a passport allowing him to leave the country.

Thrown into prison to await shipment to Spain, Miranda reached Cadiz a year later, and was incarcerated in La Carraca, the city's gruesome jail, where after numerous unsuccessful plans to escape, or obtain his release, he died four years later, to suffer the final indignity of being cremated and his ashes cast into an unmarked grave.

Another century would pass before Venezuela finally acknowledged Miranda as a national hero and his crusade for independence was acclaimed throughout the whole of South America. Today, an empty tomb lies open in the Pantheon in Caracas to commemorate his life; the Arc de Triomphe still bears his name, and a life-size statue proudly stands at the corner of Fitzroy Square, London, in recognition of his lifelong achievement.

THE MARQUESS OF SOBREMONTE

After his cowardly flight in the face of Beresford's little Army, Sobremonte never returned to his Viceregal throne, nor did the citizens of the Provincia del Rio de la Plata ever accept him as their ruler again. The Marquis firmly declared, in defence of his hasty retreat to Monte Castro, that he had only been following a contingency plan made many years earlier that stated, 'In the event of the city succumbing to a foreign invasion, the Viceroy should retire to the provinces and raise an Army to repel the intruders.' He assured the cynical citizens that this was the only reason he had left the city but they refused to accept his lame excuse, firmly pointing out that this plan was intended to be put into operation after and not before all resistance failed.

Vilified by the public, and forbidden by the *Cabildos* of both Buenos Aires and Montevideo to enter their gates again, the Viceroy roamed the countryside issuing a multitude of controversial edicts, to which no one paid much attention. Eventually, he was captured and placed under house arrest in the suburbs of San Fernando until directions as to his future arrived from the Spanish *Junta* now governing in Seville.

On his arrival in 1810, the new Viceroy Cisneros sent the Marquis back to Spain to be put on trial for his cowardly behaviour; astonishingly, he was absolved of any wrongdoing, a verdict that was undoubtedly due to the aid of his friends at court. Instead of disgrace, he was showered with honours, culminating in his promotion to the important Council of the Indies. Widowed at the age of seventy, he married again in 1817 and ten years later died peacefully in his bed.

In spite of being an arrant coward, incompetent soldier, and disastrous administrator, the Marquis was buried with full military honours, leaving history to condemn his cowardly behaviour.

SANTIAGO LINARES

After his victorious retaking of the city from Beresford and the defeat of Whitelocke's Army, Linares became the hero of Buenos Aires, and its grateful citizens appointed him Commander-in-Chief of the Army. His career and fortunes continued to flourish and reached a peak in 1808, when he was created the acting Viceroy. The *Real Audiencia* and *Cabildo's* first choice for the post had in fact been the fragrant Ruiz Huidobro, but as this gentleman was still in captivity in England, Linares was the obvious alternative.

Success went to the Frenchman's head; he soon became increasingly dictatorial, and realising the basis of his power lay in the loyalty of the Army he kept 8,000 troops permanently under his command to ensure his position was safe. These soon became a problem, as he needed to find money to pay them and, to remedy this difficult situation, he demanded the merchants pay the soldiers' wages out of the Patriotic Fund that had been created to finance the defeat of the British.

His demand outraged the *Cabildo* and worse antagonised Martin Alzaga, now the most important figure in Buenos Aires. The British were clearly no longer a threat, and they failed to see why the fund should give money to the soldiers just to bolster the Viceroy's ambitions. Moreover, the country's finances were in poor shape due to Linares permitting a large number of merchants to trade with the British in Montevideo, and cheap English goods were flooding the market. Under such circumstances, Alzaga and the old established merchants were in no way prepared to accept Linares's demand to subsidise his Army, and firmly refused to accept his suggestion.

Adding further to their discontent, the most barefaced and prolific *contrabandista* of all was Anita Perichon, now openly Linares's mistress, who had been well tutored in the smuggling profession by her husband, the disreputable O'Gorman. Along with her friends and son (now married to Linares's daughter), she was employing his lessons with spectacular success and accumulating a huge fortune by dealing in the trade herself, or encouraging others to do so by selling them expensive licences.

Nicknamed 'La Perichona,' Anita flaunted her new-found wealth for the world to see, and almost every night threw lavish parties festooned from head to toe in glittering jewellery. Diamonds sparkled from every part of her well-shaped anatomy, and this vulgar display upset the sensibilities of the respectable Buenos Aires matrons. They were also deeply shocked when, dressed in a Colonel's uniform with a dashing hat, she reviewed the Army at Linares's side mounted on a prancing grey charger.

This wanton behaviour outraged the staid merchants' wives and encouraged the street urchins to chant ribald anti-French songs outside the windows of her house, which was conveniently situated close to the Fort so that every evening, after finishing his work, the Viceroy could stroll up the street and join her for dinner.

This intimate arrangement was the cause of an unpleasant incident, for stepping early one morning out of Anita's front door, a stranger suddenly attacked Linares and grabbing him by the neck threw him to the ground. After a brief struggle, the Viceroy's orderly managed to overpower him and the *Guardia* carried the assassin off to jail ranting, 'That if the Viceroy continues to behave in this manner, the city is doomed.'

His assailant turned out to be a disgruntled soldier from the *Andaluz* battalion who the Viceroy insisted should be freed at once, and under no circumstances charges brought against him as at all costs, Madame Perichon's honour must be saved. Despite all his efforts, the scandal couldn't be hushed up and everyone agreed that the Viceroy was besotted with his mistress.

Like the tentacles of an octopus, Anita's influence wound its way into every aspect of the city's life, and Ignacio Nuñez writing in his memoirs declares, 'Madame Perichon's house was converted into a ship of State, which sailed under the captaincy of its owner. Everything that happened in Buenos Aires came under the influence of this Imperial woman just as everything in the world, now comes under the influence of the Emperor Napoleon'.

Linares and Anita followed a daily routine. All morning, the Viceroy worked in the Fort organising his new Army, while, gracefully reclining on a *chaise-longue*, Anita received homages in her house from a long line of hangers-on and delegations from the provinces. After lunching together, they would then ride or promenade through the streets, Anita dressed in a military uniform, and always escorted by two dashing young ADCs even if accompanied by the General and his entourage.

Almost every evening, Anita opened her house to a crowd of fawning admirers who she lavishly entertained with sumptuous food and expensive wine. Arriving in Buenos Aires in 1808, William Parish attended one of these glamorous affairs. Writing home to England he admiringly reports, 'Night after night, Madame Perichon gives the most wonderful parties in her house and these glittering assemblies would be the envy of any London hostess.' Less impressed, Martin Alzaga, writing to the *Junta* in Seville, scathingly declares, 'This woman with whom the Viceroy has an attachment is a disgrace!'

Owing to his dictatorial behaviour Santiago Linares's

popularity soon began to wane, and reached an all-time low when as a Frenchman he publicly supported Napoleon and his brother Joseph (the newly created King of Spain), as opposed to the exiled Fernando VII, now languishing in captivity in France. However, the arrival in 1810 of Baltazar Hildalgo de Cisneros as the newly appointed Viceroy forced Linares to retire to Cordoba, where he announced that, after putting his affairs in order, he would return to Europe. Anxious to soften the blow of his dismissal, the *Junta* in Seville generously granted him the title of Conde de Buenos Aires but, owing to there being no Spanish monarch to confer it, the title remained unsubstantiated. Several years later it would be offered to his son who, after the manner of his father's death, requested it to be changed to the Conde de la Lealtad.

After a lengthy struggle, the Independence party in 1811 finally gained power and formed a *Junta General* bringing matters to a head as, due to lack of funds from Spain, Cisneros was unable to pay his soldiers' wages to gain their support. In a desperate attempt to solve the problem and counteract this dangerous move, he allowed trade to be re-opened with the British merchants in Montevideo and, by heavily taxing the imports, managed to raise sufficient revenue to pay his Army.

Although this temporarily solved the problem, it also antagonised his chief supporters: the old established merchants and – worse – Martin Alzaga. Realising his position was in serious jeopardy, Cisneros secretly appealed to Linares for help.

The former Viceroy was still residing on his estate in Cordoba, having rightly decided that as a Frenchman it would be unwise to return to Spain – where the Peninsular War was raging – while to take up residence in France would give his enemies an excuse to brand him a traitor and confiscate his Argentine properties. Hearing of Cisneros's move, the *Junta* wasted no time in countering it and immediately dispatched a platoon of 40 soldiers (two of them British deserters) to seize Linares and his small band of supporters before they left Cordoba. This they successfully achieved and, without even the formality of a trial, Linares and his supporters were executed by firing squad on Monte de los Papagayos (the Mountain of Parrots) near Alta Cruz in the Provincia de Cordoba.

Santiago Linares did not deserve such a brutal ending, as he was a brave soldier who had twice saved the country from the English. However, his strong French accent and loyalty to France and Napoleon, rather than to Spain and Fernando, combined with *La Perichona*'s lavish lifestyle, made him unpopular with the people and brought about his downfall.

He would soon become the prototype of all future South American dictators, who from then on would rely on the support of their Army to keep them in power; a century later Evita Peron, following in Anita's lavish footsteps, would dazzle the nation with her fabulous jewels and Parisian gowns.

GENERAL FRANCISCO ELIO
Fortune favours the brave and, despite being bombastic, impulsive, and stubborn, General Elio was undoubtedly a born leader, but not always in the right direction.

Linares appointed him Governor of Montevideo after the British left the Rio de la Plata and he soon became popular with its citizens, but in contrast the *Porteños* would never forgive him for his defeat at San Pedro and his reckless behaviour during La Defensa.

Elio and Linares soon fell out, and the new Viceroy Cisneros, on his arrival in 1810, brought orders for Elio to immediately return to Spain. Furious at this treatment, the General left Montevideo in a huff without waiting for the arrival of his replacement, the Marques de Nieto, or even saying goodbye to his friends.

He was not away for long as a year later, the newly formed Argentine *Junta* expelled Cisneros from Buenos Aires and the Regency Council in Cadiz sent Elio back to the Rio de la Plata as its new Viceroy. It was a disastrous appointment, for after successfully alienating his own supporters and aggravating the situation beyond redemption, he was hurriedly recalled by the Council to Spain to fight against the French, alongside his old enemies Colonel Pack and Marshal Beresford, now in command of the Portuguese Army.

When the war ended, Fernando VII appointed him Captain General of Valencia, and as a loyal supporter of the King and monarchy he spent the next five years waging a ruthless battle against the liberals, who gaining power in 1820 condemned him to death by garrotting. Thus died the twelfth and last Viceroy of the Rio de la Plata: foolhardy, stubborn but loyal to his sovereign to the end.

DON MARTIN ALZAGA

Martin Alzaga remained staunchly loyal to Spain for the rest of his life and, along with the other traditional Spanish merchants, yearned to return to the old trading ties with the mother country that war in Europe and British supremacy at sea had almost ended. Many of the old established firms were going bankrupt but, in contrast, the younger merchants encouraged first by Linares and then Cisneros were adapting to the developing free trade, and appreciated the burgeoning market in Montevideo.

These two groups split the *Cabildo* in half but, as Linares's excesses grew, and his favour for French rule increased, the parties steadily drew closer; the traditionalists advocating self-rule under the auspices of Spain, the Creoles outright independence. One thing united them: a firm determination not to fall under the rule of France, England, or for that matter any other foreign power.

Aided by their common hate of Linares and his support of Napoleon, Martin Alzaga, now Mayor and President of the *Cabildo*, slowly began to bring the two sides together, and Linares's outrageous demand for the merchants to pay the Army's wages out of the Patriotic Fund brought matters to a head; the decision was made to depose him. Quickly getting wind of this, Linares secretly removed all the revenue from the Royal Treasury and distributed it among his soldiers to guarantee their loyalty.

Alzaga and the *Cabildo* searched high and low for some legal pretext to depose Linares, but hard as they tried they could find no precedent for such an action, except for an obscure law introduced three centuries earlier in the reign of Philip II that stated, 'The Viceroy's children are forbidden to marry within the territory governed by their father.' As Linares had just married off his daughter Carmen to Anita Perichon's son, this gave them a legal though flimsy excuse to demand his resignation. To embarrass him further, they unfairly vetoed Linares's candidate Bernardino Rivadavia for the position of Royal Officer to the *Cabildo*, as it was common knowledge that Linares had borrowed large sums of money from Bernadino's father to pay his soldiers, and finance Anita's expensive lifestyle. Lastly, they insisted Linares should sign a document accepting the creation of a *Junta General*, which would greatly reduce his viceregal powers; convinced he would never agree to these tough demands, they began making plans to mount a *coup d'état*.

On the morning of New Year's Day 1809, the weather was stifling hot, broken only by intermittent heavy rain and thunderstorms, as thousands of Alzaga's supporters thronged the Plaza Mayor shouting, 'Down with Linares', 'Death to the French,' and dubious comments on Anita's profession and the Viceroy's parentage. All morning delegations passed back and forth between the *Cabildo* and the Fort until, to the delight of the crowd and surprise of the *Cabildo*, the rumour spread that Linares had accepted their demands.

It was true, but Linares made one stipulation, 'Under no circumstances would he sign such an important document without the entire *Cabildo* being present to witness the ceremony.' Then, to show his peaceful intentions and calm the anxiety of his opponents, he ordered his troops to evacuate the Fort, and seeing the soldiers leave the building a great cheer went up from Alzaga's supporters. Convinced that the battle was over and the Viceroy had resigned, they left the square, congratulating each other on their great victory and hurried home to devour their midday meal.

In the afternoon, the *Cabildo*, dressed in their full regalia and led by Martin Alzaga, marched triumphantly through the main gate of the Fort to witness the signing of this vital document, unaware that Colonel Saavedra, still loyal to Linares, was secretly smuggling his troops from a nearby house through a rear entrance into the building.

Just as Linares raised his pen to sign the document, the Colonel and his soldiers burst into the room and, arresting Alzaga and the *Cabildo,* hurriedly bundled them onto a waiting ship, which immediately upped anchor and sailed to Carmen de Patagones. Linares's triumphant troops flooded the empty square shouting 'Viva Linares', and the coup was over.

When news of the kidnapping reached Montevideo, General Elio sprang into action and quickly dispatched a fleet of ships to rescue the *Cabildo*. Easily overpowering any resistance at Carmen de Patagones, they triumphantly brought Martin Alzaga and the *Cabildo* back to Montevideo. Here they remained until the arrival of Viceroy Cisneros, returned to their families and friends in Buenos Aires.

A leopard never changes his spots and, for the rest of his life, Don Martin remained a dyed-in-the wool conservative and found it impossible to accept the idea of independence now openly demanded by the citizens of Buenos Aires. In 1810, the newly formed *Junta* (three of whose members were old friends) accused him of plotting against them and, despite his eminent position, put him on trial for treason. Found guilty, he was for a short while imprisoned but it proved no deterrent, as on his release he continued to plot against the Government. Fed up with his continual scheming, the *Junta's* patience finally ran out and in 1812 he was tried, found guilty of treason and condemned to death.

On the day of his execution, Alzaga was led to a bench in front of the Fort and offered a handkerchief to blindfold his eyes, which he graciously accepted but, instead of tying this around his head, he carefully wiped the bench with it before sitting down to face the firing squad. A contemptuous gesture and unworthy end to a man who had devoted his entire life to the welfare of Buenos Aires and her citizens. After the execution his body was taken to Victory Square where it hung for the next three days, as a warning to all those who dared to oppose the Revolution.

GUILLERMO PIO WHITE

After Whitelocke's defeat, the wily Bostonian hurriedly

escaped to Montevideo where, desperate to get rid of their cargoes, the English Captains were offering their goods at rock-bottom prices. Times were good; fortunes were being made and merchants and entrepreneurs crammed the city, excitedly fighting over everything the British had to offer. Young Argentine merchants and prosperous smugglers packed the gambling saloons, rapidly disposing of their new-found wealth and happily entering into this free-for-all; Don Guillermo joined this rowdy band of entrepreneurs and quickly recouped his financial losses. The departure of the British sadly brought an end to this prosperous mêlée, and the arrival of Montevideo's new Governor, the now General Elio, in October 1807, gave Don Guillermo cause to worry.

Nicknamed 'Robespierre' by the citizens of Montevideo for his arrogant behaviour, Elio promptly threw the old smuggler into jail, and hearing of this splendid piece of news the Buenos Aires *Cabildo* immediately wrote a long letter imploring him, 'To keep the traitor White under strict supervision at all times, and under no circumstances let him out of the Fort.'

At the same time, Elio annoyingly received a message from Linares commanding him to return White immediately to Buenos Aires so he could be put on trial in the city where his crimes had been committed. Now at daggers drawn with Linares, Elio rejected his demand, firmly declaring that he had sufficient evidence to put White on trial in Montevideo and, after serving his sentence there, he could be sent back to Buenos Aires for Linares to do what he liked with him.

However, on Linares's appointment as Viceroy, Elio could no longer refuse his superior's orders and Guillermo White was escorted back to Buenos Aires to be put on trial for treason, which he successfully avoided thanks to Anita

Perichon, whose powerful position as the Viceroy's mistress gave her ample scope to help him. Under her protection, he was sheltered from the *Cabildo*'s wrath, allowing him to concentrate on his business and, in return, he helped Anita with her numerous ventures. They remained good friends and in correspondence with each other for the remainder of their lives.

Despite Anita's help, Don Guillermo was not yet out of the woods as the unwelcome arrival of Viceroy Cisneros in 1809 gave him cause to worry. Fortunately, his main enemies Alzaga and the Spanish party were now out of power and, with the advent of the *Junta* a year later, his worries were over. Questioned by the so-called Patriots over his collaboration with Beresford and Whitelocke, Don Guillermo blithely assured them that he had done this not out of self-interest, or from any traitorous intent, but purely to help them in their noble fight for independence. Events had proved him right, as thanks to his aiding the British the country had escaped from Spanish rule, and it was entirely due to his perspicacity that they had achieved their goal. This dubious explanation appeared to satisfy the *Junta* and, from then on, they left him in peace to continue his nefarious business.

Guillermo White continued to deal in some shady business or other for the rest of his life. Irregularities in payments were frequent, often leading to many trials, court cases, and bouts of imprisonment. To his credit he supplied the Government with arms in the War for Independence, and in March 1815 helped Almirante Guillermo Brown (ex-Lt William Brown RN, founder of the Argentine Navy) to obtain ships for his successful campaign in the struggle for independence.

Despite, or perhaps because of, all these ventures, William

Pios White died penniless on 3 January 1842, and President Bartolemé Mitre, finding his children living in extreme poverty, was forced to subsidise them. The story happily ends on a more cheerful note, as his grandson Alem William White recouped the family fortunes by becoming a skilled engineer, famous for constructing most of Argentina's railway system.

THOMAS O'GORMAN AND ANITA PERICHON

Once a rogue always a rogue, and Thomas O'Gorman, or 'The Captain' as he preferred to be called, drifted in and out of debt and prison for the rest of his life. Soon realising Beresford and his soldiers would never be able to hold Buenos Aires against Linares's uprising without reenforcements from England, he hastily boarded a British Man-of-War before the fighting began and fled to Montevideo. Owing to his hurried exile, he would never see his wife and family again, probably much to Anita's relief, but his numerous creditors pursued her for the rest of her life.

In 1808, the Chilean Government jailed him for fraud when it was discovered that a cargo he had been shipping for a group of Chilean merchants had not, as he claimed, been jettisoned at sea in a Pacific storm but, on the contrary, secretly sold by him for a handsome profit. Unhappy with the accommodation and amenities of his Chilean jail, 'The Captain' wrote a long letter to Linares, now the Viceroy, brazenly asking him to transfer him to Argentina, and surroundings that were more comfortable. Diplomatically, he makes no mention in the letter of his wife Anita, now openly Linares's mistress, but his appeal was swiftly granted and, released from prison, he continued a criminal career that only ended in 1816 with his death in Spain.

In contrast, Anita's star continued to rise, but in the

summer of 1809 Buenos Aires society was startled to find she had vanished from the country, which caused a major sensation and gave birth to a mountain of rumours. The most popular of these was that, with the arrival of the new Viceroy Cisneros from Spain, Linares realised he could no longer defend her from the vengeance of Martin Alzaga and the *Cabildo*, and had therefore smuggled her out of the country. While another, more scurrilous, maintained that James Burke, a well-known English spy with a penchant for posing as a German scientist, had inadvertently revealed to the Viceroy that Anita was in fact in the pay of the English. Hearing this, Linares in a fit of rage expelled her from the country, especially as her relationship with Burke was hinted to be far from platonic.

Hurriedly fleeing to Brazil, Anita settled down in Rio where she found and entertained all the Independence party exiles, including Peña and Padilla, now receiving a pension from the British Government for helping General Beresford and Colonel Pack escape.

Rio was expanding rapidly. Palaces, Government offices, and barracks spread inland to house Regent Dom Joao and his wife Princess Carlotta, who had arrived a year earlier with the entire Royal Court from Lisbon. Owing to Napoleon holding her brother the Spanish King Fernando VII in captivity in France, Princess Carlotta at the time was claiming her right to the Spanish throne and with it the sovereignty of the Rio de la Plata. Court intrigue was rife and the stakes high, as the representatives of England, Portugal and Spain fought over the rights and wrongs of her claim. Entering headlong into this diplomatic game, Anita caught the roving eye of the British Ambassador, Lord Percy Clinton Sydney Smythe, 6th Viscount Strangford.

His Lordship had cut quite a dash with his flowing cravats,

well-tailored suits, and shiny buff topped boots on his arrival in Rio in July 1808, and these, combined with immaculate manners and romantic eyes, had made a distinct impression on the exiled court; among his many admirers was Princess Carlotta, whose claim he was heavily backing.

Despite all this activity and adulation, the Viscount was finding life in Rio distinctly boring, chiefly due to a lack of suitable female companionship. Writing to his friend Dom Domingos Sousa Continho, the Portuguese Ambassador in London, he rudely comments, 'The women in this country are awful!' It was therefore only natural that he and Anita should fall into each other's arms, and she soon became his mistress.

Owing to this steamy liaison, Anita quickly fell out of favour with Princess Carlotta, who also had designs on His Lordship's welfare not strictly of a diplomatic nature, and she curtly informed Madame Perichon that her presence at court was no longer welcome and ordered her to leave the country.

Banished from Brazil, Anita spent the following year on board His Majesty's frigate *Essex*, stationed in the River Plate, vainly seeking permission from the newly arrived Viceroy Cisneros to land at Buenos Aires. Her request was constantly denied and, frustrated by Cisneros's persistent refusal, she returned to Brazil at the end of a year, only to be banished again by the jealous Princess.

Returning to Buenos Aires, this time aboard HMS *Mistletoe*, she once again attempted to get permission to land but, despite the ceaseless efforts of the ship's Captain, Lt Ramsey, who had obviously fallen under her spell, the authorities refused to relent. However, on gaining power in 1810 the *Junta* granted her request, on condition she went straight to her *estancia* in Corrientes and stayed there. Agreeing to their terms, Anita kept her side of the bargain, and died there on 2 December 1847 at the ripe old age of seventy-two.

DESERTERS

After peace had been declared many of the British prisoners of war refused to be repatriated, but the exact figure is difficult to establish. It is, however, recorded that out of the 32 officers and 883 men of the 71st Regiment who left the Cape of Good Hope in 1806, 170, or almost a fifth of the Regiment, refused to leave Argentina.

Food was abundant. wine flowed; the people friendly, and the women pretty, so it was hardly surprising that the prisoner of war reckoned a future in this land of plenty infinitely preferable to returning home in a stinking troopship to face death on a foreign field for a tot of rum and five miserly pence a day.

Some of the officers made good marriages, like David Reid the medical officer of the 71st who had attended the dying Colonel Kington in Anita Perichon's house, who on 21 November 1806 married Maria Angela Gonzalez Rivadavia in the Convent of Santo Domingo. She was the widow of Don Urdaneta, Director of the Real Renta de Tabacco, and therefore, one suspects, very rich.

Other deserters, whom Major Gillespie calls the dregs of society or the black sheep of their regiments, were not so scrupulous. Encountering a dozen of these ruffians on a visit to the Retiro after his return from captivity in Cordoba, the Major indignantly writes,

'Instead of offering us congratulations, which would have been generous and manly in this moment of exultant, they poured on us abuse and ribaldry in which even the Spaniards themselves scorned to join in. I subsequently learnt that some of these dastardly traitors to their King and revolters from their columns in the hour of danger, tired of that service and under bitter remorse from their perfidious conduct had abandoned that cause. Finding their way back to their native country, they covered their disgraceful history so artfully as to receive their unclaimed shares in the capture of Buenos Aires and Montevideo'.

W. S. Robertson in his book *Letters on South America*, published in 1839, gives a first-hand description of one of these British deserters whom over the following years he would grow to know well. Arriving in Argentina only a year after peace had been declared, William and his brother bought a farm in Paraguay, then a part of the province of the Rio de la Plata. All went well to begin with, but when Paraguay refused Belgrano's offer to unite with Argentina in 1811, it fell under the rule of the mad dictator Dr Francia, who in one of his many maniacal purges expelled all foreigners from the country.

Hastily packing up their belongings, the Robertson brothers crossed the Paraná River into Argentina, where they purchased an *estancia* just outside Corrientes, not far from the Falls of Iguazu, and it was here that William Robertson encountered one of these deserters. Describing their meeting, he writes:

'Sitting one evening on my veranda peacefully reading a book, my attention was diverted by the sound of approaching horses and looking up I saw riding towards me a tall, raw boned, ferocious looking man in gaucho attire. Two cavalry pistols were stuck in his girdle, and from a besmeared belt of halftanned leather hung a sabre in a rusty steel scabbard. He had red whiskers, and mustachios with hair uncombed of the same colour matted with perspiration and powdered with dust. His face was not only burnt almost to blackness by the sun but blistered to the eyes, while large pieces of shrivelled skin stood ready to fall from his parched lips. He wore a pair of plain earrings, a forage cap; a large knife in a leathern sheath; a pair of potro (horse leather) boots with rusty iron spurs, and rowels an inch and a half in diameter. Close behind him followed his page who was an exact counterpart of his master except for the colour of his hair, which was jet black.'

Fearing them to be an advance party of the Uruguayan Caudillo Artigas's marauding bandits, Robertson nervously offered the strangers a seat and was about to go in search of porter, spirits, and a bribe, when the red-haired gaucho, respectfully doffing his cap, performed an awkward bow, and in bad Spanish with an accent that showed he was no Creole said, '*No se aflije, Señor Robertson, estamos bien aqui.*' (Don't put yourself out, Mr Robertson; we are happy as we are.)

Robertson continues: 'The Hibernian brogue; the mangled Spanish; the countenance when closely scanned; the carroty locks and bright grey eyes, all revealed to me a son of the Emerald Isle transformed into a more fearful looking gaucho than any native I had ever beheld. I politely asked him to whom I had the honour of addressing.

"Por Dios, don't'cha ya know Peter Cambell" he replied laying a strong accent on the last syllable. "Paythro Cambèll as the Gauchers calls me? Troth now, an ye never heerd of that name then you're the only chentleman in the who'al country as has not." This fierce apparition, late of His Majesty King George III's gallant little Army, turned out to be a deserter from General Beresford's invasion.'

Born in Ireland and a tanner by profession, Peter Campbell

was a Roman Catholic who the Spanish priests had successfully kept hidden until Whitelocke and his Army had left the country. Working his way north to Corrientes, the young Irishman obtained a job in a tanning factory belonging to Don Angel Blanco, and for the next few years lived a relatively quiet and sober life. This changed with the onslaught of the gaucho armies from Uruguay, who sweeping across the province robbed and killed everything in their path, leaving behind them a trail of dead cattle and smouldering farmhouses.

Driven by the fighting blood of the Irish coursing through his veins, Peter Campbell happily joined these murderous bandits and soon gained the reputation of being a fine horseman and fearless fighter. With a dagger in one hand and a poncho wrapped around the other, the Irishman soon became a fearsome opponent and few *boliches* (bars) existed in the province of Entre Rios that, at some time or another, had not witnessed the mangled remains of a drunken gaucho carried out of their doors having misguidedly challenged Don Pedro to a duel. These useful attributes soon gained him the respect of the gauchos, and more importantly the friendship of Artigas the Uruguayan Caudillo.

Peter Campbell, however, was no fool and he quickly realised that ravaging the land was a short-sighted policy, so instead he started up a first-class protection business. This proved an infinitely more profitable investment and many farmers like the Robertson brothers were only too happy to pay £250 a year to ensure their cattle and hides safely reached the riverboats to be transported unmolested and intact to Buenos Aires. Even the Governor of the province, Colonel Mendez, with only ninety soldiers at his disposal was content to enlist Don Pedro's help in controlling the bands of plundering gauchos.

The business quickly flourished and the Irishman soon became an important member of the community, and ended his career as an Admiral in command of a small flotilla of gunboats raised to protect the Argentine traffic on the Paraná River from Dr Francia's persistent marauders.

Fate plays strange tricks, for without Popham's mad venture and a revolution in this faraway land, Peter Campbell, a penniless Irish apprentice, would never have ended his life a rich landowner and respected member of the community. Not all the deserters were quite such flamboyant characters but, through hard work and acumen, many became *estancieros* or prosperous businessmen with British surnames often curiously spelt, and even more strangely pronounced. Many translated their names into Spanish, like Sergeant Armstrong of the 71st, a member of the Mendoza Regiment raised by the British prisoners of war to fight with General San Martin in the War of Independence, who changed his name to '*Brazofuerte*,' a direct translation of his Scottish surname. Many of their descendants still live in Argentina and, owing to the large number of Beresford and Whitelocke's soldiers marrying Argentine girls, even the most illustrious families in the country have hidden somewhere in their lineage British, Irish, or Scottish stock.

THIRTY-EIGHT

BUENOS AIRES TODAY

Two hundred years have passed since Beresford and his little Army marched proudly down the Calle Defensa into the Plaza Mayor, and little remains of the city that he, or Whitelocke, would recognise. Buenos Aires and its suburbs today cover an area of over 30 square miles, and important features like the Punta Galvez, the Riachuelo and Quilmes lie long buried under a sea of housing estates, and shopping malls. The city's main railway station now occupies the centre of the Retiro and, in 1857, President Urquiza demolished the Fort around which the great battles were fought and replaced it with the Casa Rosada, specially designed for him by the English architect Edward Taylor.

The churches remain and the battle-scarred colours of the 71st still hang in the Convent of Santo Domingo where Santiago Linares placed them two hundred years ago. Wooden replicas of cannon balls adorn the side of the Convent's tower facing the Casa Rosada, often wrongly attributed to the English invaders, when in fact they came from Colonel Saavedra's cannons mounted in front of the Fort attempting to dislodge Craufurd's riflemen.

The British regiments greatly appreciated the way the Bethlehemite friars had cared for their wounded soldiers after the battle and, in 1809, the 71st presented them with a handsome long case clock in gratitude for the help, and costing £45 (then a considerable sum of money). It is now on display in the Church of San Pedro Gonzalez in San Telmo.

Evidence of the invasion can be seen in the street names such as *Reconquista*, *Defensa*, and *Linares*. English visitors strolling down these bustling thoroughfares today should spare a moment's thought for the dead British soldiers' blood that once lay beneath their feet, spilt two hundred years ago due to the greed of one man, Commodore Sir Home Riggs Popham.

Unrecognised in their own country, their sacrifice is acknowledged in Argentina for, due to the confidence gained by their defeat, the citizens started a fight for independence that ended over three hundred years of Spanish domination and gave birth to the Argentine nation.

Printed in Great Britain
by Amazon